Cultural Memory
in
the
Present

Mieke Bal and Hent de Vries, Editors

THE ENDS OF MOURNING

THE ENDS OF MOURNING

Psychoanalysis, Literature, Film

Alessia Ricciardi

STANFORD UNIVERSITY PRESS

STANFORD, CALIFORNIA 2003

Stanford University Press
Stanford, California

The Northwestern University Research Grants Committee has
provided partial support for the publication of this book.
We gratefully acknowledge this assistance.

Printed in the United States of America
on acid-free, archival-quality paper.

Library of Congress Cataloging-in-Publication Data

Ricciardi, Alessia.
The ends of mourning : psychoanalysis, literature, film / Alessia
    Ricciardi.
        p. cm. — (Cultural memory in the present)
    Includes bibliographical references and index.
    ISBN 0-8047-4776-8 (cloth : alk. paper) —
    ISBN 0-8047-4777-6 (pbk. : alk. paper)
1. Death in literature.   2. Literature, Modern—History and
criticism.   3. Death in motion pictures.   4. Death—
Psychological aspects.   5. Bereavement—Psychological aspects.
I. Title.   II. Series.
PN56.D4R53   2003
809'.933548—DC21
                                                2003002089

Original Printing 2003
Last figure below indicates year of this printing:
12   11   10   09   08   07   06   05   04   03

Typeset by Tim Roberts in 11/13.5 Garamond.

Contents

Acknowledgments

There are many friends, teachers, and colleagues to thank for their assistance. I wish first of all to recognize Peter Brooks and Hélène Cixous for their vital encouragement and inspiration during the composition of this book. Paolo Valesio provided valuable guidance on my dissertation at Yale, which was the basis of the present work. Lynn Enterline, Richard Halpern, Geoffrey Hartman, and Michael Holquist all offered helpful responses at different stages. Jean Laplanche's classes in psychoanalysis in Paris and Aldo G. Gargani's courses in philosophy in Pisa were definitive experiences. I am grateful to Paola Marrati, who remains a delightful friend and an intellectual role model. Jared Stark and Armando Solis's affection, Tom Pepper's kindness, and Stephen Metcalf and Koethi Zan's enchanting company all have been sources of the greatest uplift. My colleagues in the Department of French and Italian at Northwestern University have been unwaveringly supportive. I wish to thank especially Michal Ginsburg and Scott Durham for providing strength and good counsel, as well as Mireille Rosello and Jane Winston, who have been enormously generous colleagues. My gratitude also goes to Hent de Vries for his interest in the project, to Helen Tartar for her highly perceptive and humane editorial work, to Norris Pope, Kim Lewis Brown, Tim Roberts, Karen Hellekson, and the rest of the Stanford University Press for their tireless professionalism, and to two anonymous Stanford University Press readers for their exceptional insightfulness and generosity. Special thanks to my family, in particular to my brother Alfonso.

A portion of Chapter 4 appeared, in a much different form, in *Modernism/Modernity* 8, no. 4 (November 2001). I thank the editors for permission to reprint the material.

A Center for the Humanities Fellowship at Northwestern University enabled me to finish writing this book. A visiting professorship at the Centre d'Études Feminines of the Université de Paris VIII was instrumental in the completion of much of the requisite research and preparation. An Elizabeth Hanscom Fellowship at Yale provided support during the final year of my doctoral studies. I acknowledge with great appreciation all of these sources of aid.

My love and deepest gratitude go to Chris Yu, to whom this book is dedicated. He has supported and helped me throughout this project; and thanks to him, to borrow James Merrill's phrase, my world has "put on a thin gold mask."

Introduction

Mourning: A Cultural Enigma

The Ends of Mourning chronicles the radical devaluation of the concept of mourning in the culture of the present day. In an age grown skeptical of traditional historical methods, contemporary thought, I maintain, has failed to develop an adequately critical approach to the past.[1] Why has the problem of loss been passed over by speculative discourse in the era of high and late capitalism, and what are the consequences of such an oversight? Without a sense of memory's ethical urgency, we have been left with the ability to relate to the past only as spectacle, as an image to be consumed in the virtual reality of mass culture. Modernity as a consequence has come to seem destitute, inauthentic, vulnerable to scorn for its empty cultural promises. How is such a predicament related to the seeming inability or reluctance of recent criticism to address in a committed way the problem of grief? Does the impression of superficiality conveyed by so-called postmodernity have to do with its refusal of a meaningful relation to the past? These will be my guiding questions as I explore the different facets of mourning that our current consumer society all too quickly has forgotten—psychological, spiritual, intellectual, and ethical facets that today seem radically intertwined and often enigmatic. To understand how we might begin to envision some answers, it is necessary to examine two distinct cultural moments.

My argument therefore pursues two paths of investigation. The first focuses on the origin of the problem in Freud and Proust's writings during the early decades of the twentieth century. The two authors reformulate the question of mourning as a central problem within the domains of psychoanalysis and literature. Yet as delivered by its two most influential proponents, the classic modernist account of mourning may be said to contain the seeds of its own disenchantment. For in the modern fascination with the casualties of history, the very experience of bereavement threatens to exhaust itself. Proust's relentless aestheticizing of the past in *In Search of Lost Time* is revealing on this score.

Lacan, however, takes the most radical step of all by denying any logical rationale for grief. Indeed, my first line of inquiry hinges on his establishment of a theoretical justification for the subject's ironic detachment toward the past. I argue that he abandons the Freudian notion of mourning as the working-through of a historically specific event of loss. What he proposes in its place is an idea of desire that celebrates the object's inherent absence. In so doing, he codifies the end of mourning, and hence of a certain spirit of modernity, by transforming disillusionment into a doctrine. In this sense, Lacan's work epitomizes the jaded, knowing spirit of what is now defined as postmodern culture, for lack of a better word.[2]

Of all the interpretive horizons abandoned by postmodernity, the outlook of mourning is one of the most crucial. Its demise perhaps carries the most far-ranging consequences, because such a failure implies the abandonment of any effort to provide a nuanced, ethical response to the claims of the past. With the ascendancy of populist commodity culture, fundamental projects of ethical and political emancipation have been discarded altogether, like so many theoretical frivolities to be pragmatically overcome. As a result, the abandonment of a hermeneutics of mourning both compromises our understanding of the past and sterilizes our vision of the future, as it deprives our culture not only of utopian inspirations and messianic inclinations, but also, finally, of the very notion of justice.

Having traced some of the parameters of the current devaluation of mourning in the book's first half, I turn in what follows to my second concern, namely to ask whether this devaluation in fact follows a genuine resolution of the dilemma. In particular, my interest is to determine whether, after the fading of a certain humanist conception of the arts within the emerging technocracy of mass media, a rediscovery of the ethical and political significance of loss is possible. Through the advancement of technology and mass consumerism, the spectacular character of the phenomenal world has increased to the point that it looks like no space exists for critical reflection or remembrance. For this reason, I set out in the last few chapters to examine the status of mourning in contemporary cinema as exemplified by the films of Pasolini and Godard. This course of reasoning responds to the peculiar flattening of the past in our present-day commodity culture. In order to clarify this context, I wish briefly to recall a somewhat different approach to the issue.

In his classic sociological study, *The Hour of Our Death*, Philippe Ariès proposed an influential interpretation of the recent decline of mourning.[3] In his view, the beginning of the twentieth century saw the fulfillment of a psychological impulse to remove the enigma of death from the domain of social exchange, thus invalidating public rituals and ceremonies and making commemoration of the dead a purely private act. The second milestone in the contemporary history of death was reached, according to Ariès, when not only life's terminal event, but the process of mourning and the language of grief also were barred or abolished from the public sphere.[4] The culprit in Ariès's opinion is the increasingly central role of technology in our society: "Technology erodes the domain of death until one has the illusion that death has been abolished. The area of invisible death is also the area of the greatest belief in the power of technology and its ability to transform man and nature."[5]

One reason why Ariès's sociological chronicle of the decline of mourning in modern society strikes me as less than completely satisfying is because he pays scant attention to the displacement of the question from the sphere of ritual or sacred activity to the larger context of society in general, which now primarily consists in mass culture. The reinscription of mourning in the new virtual space of the commercial media is signaled by the spread of the techniques of quotation and pastiche throughout all discourses and by the constant reemergence of spectrality and the phantasmatic in the very operations of technology. Technology is thus not only the cause of our mortality's dwindling significance, as Ariès contends, but paradoxically also the basis of its growing, if problematic, ubiquity as a signifier.

Since the heyday of modernism, we have witnessed a shift from an emphasis on the private, subjective, and psychic aspects of mourning to an emphasis on its public, intersubjective, and cultural aspects. Because of its preoccupation with questions of temporality and subjectivity, first-generation modernism by and large has succeeded in depicting the interiorization of loss. Freud and Proust, for example, certainly propound some of the most original and enduring figures of mourning in this sense. With the end of the modernist narrative and the decentralization of the arts in an ever-more consumerist culture, however, it has become increasingly urgent to discover the spectral or phantasmatic aspects of what Debord has called "the society of the spectacle."[6] In this sense, I wish to argue against Ariès that in contemporary society, we witness the perplexing dissemination and reinscription of mourning in entirely new modes and constellations, rather than its strict demise. To put it in a Freudian fashion, we might say that although Ariès is adept at exposing the various ways in which society seeks to deny the fact of death, he fails to recognize how culture might manifest the return of the repressed. It is through the investigation of such a return that we may yet recognize some occasion for the recovery of a public, ethical dimension of memory. I argue here that the question of mourning, despite being officially answered and resolved, reemerges, at times, in the contemporary imagination with the disquieting force of a cultural enigma.

Freud referred to mourning in some of his metapsychological essays as a riddle [*Rätsel*] in order to underscore the difficulty of accounting for the extravagantly painful demands of the work of mourning on the subject.[7] Ever the pragmatist, Freud regarded the subject's stubborn attachment to the lost object to be a mystery from a strictly analytic perspective. Complicating such a perspective, however, we might observe that what is enigmatic about the mourning process is surely not just the economic expenditure of psychic resources that it requires. As Jean Laplanche rightly has suggested, mourning is mysterious in a more radical way, because it confronts us with the ultimate enigma of the Other and thereby perpetuates questions that must be left forever unsettled. If, as Laplanche asserts, death always entails some form of the demand, "what would he/she have said?", we must challenge ourselves to remain mindful of the alterity of the departed addressee.[8] One important feature of Freud and Proust's respective handlings of the topic is that in different ways, both have sought to transform mourning from a drastically enigmatic constellation into a riddle or puzzle that, like all such distractions, implies a determinate resolution.

Our anguish at the shock of loss, I would contend, should not be viewed in such mechanical terms, but rather in terms of an ongoing, interpretive challenge without a prescribed end, without knowingness. Now, it is exactly this enigmatic and open-ended quality of mourning that is increasingly denied by contemporary culture's refusal of a genuinely critical relation to the past. The implication of such a refusal is that instead of being understood as an ethical question, mourning comes to be rephrased as an aesthetic device or posture (not a process of careful self-interrogation, but a kitschy display of nostalgia). The failure of the twentieth century to develop a hermeneutics of loss in this sense results in a problematic philosophical and ethical condition that I define as being beyond mourning. Yet

I wish to suggest two different ways of reading this phrase. The first follows a Nietzschean train of thought. Just as Nietzsche signaled his intent to explode the conventional terms of moral reasoning through his use of the preposition in the title of his treatise, *Beyond Good and Evil* (1886), consumerist pop culture might be understood to present itself as operating beyond the necessity of mourning and thus to transcend the ethical language of responsibility and regret for the past.[9]

The second follows a more complex itinerary. Having noted the triumphalism of the dominant contemporary culture, I hope to identify a "minor" or marginalized postmodernity that views the end of mourning as the critical horizon of a return of the repressed à la Freud. On this view, the possibility of a critical postmodernity emerges "beyond" mourning in the complicated and ambivalent sense in which Freud redefines the territory of the psyche in the title of his essay *Beyond the Pleasure Principle* (1920). Here the preposition "beyond" [*jenseits*] presents itself as a paradox, ultimately signaling the impossibility of simply getting over or past first principles. As Derrida says of Freud's speculative undertaking in *Beyond the Pleasure Principle*, a certain critical postmodernity, in its relationship to mourning, "does not go beyond but comes back within."[10] It is in this sense that Pasolini and Godard repudiate a nostalgic conception of culture and resolutely embrace new visual modes of expression in their films. By projecting back to us the figures and events of western civilization in a mood of bereavement, the two directors envision "the beyond" as a space in which the mournful imagination may be resituated and reinvigorated. The relevance of their undertakings consists not in the answers they give to the question of mourning, but in their renewals of its enigmatic force.

Mourning and Modernity: Freud and Proust

"Narratives of Mourning," the first section of this book, traces the vicissitudes of the modernist conceptions of mourning in psychoanalysis and literature through investigation of Freud's notion of a work of mourning and Proust's search for involuntary memories. How do these two concepts punctuate the modern history of mourning? In what sense may we say that these ideas provide paradigms of memory that remain influential in the postmodern epoch? What are the limits, boundaries, and demarcations impressed through their influence on a contemporary politics of memory? While drawing on different conceptual and cultural sources, both accounts contribute to a modernist conviction in the hermeneutic specificity and integrity of loss, even as they anticipate the dissolution of such a conviction due to an advancing postmodern incredulity toward unifying metacritical horizons.

Freud provides the twentieth century with the notion of mourning as a psychological work, classically articulated in his 1917 essay *Mourning and Melancholia*. For Freud, mourning is not simply an emotion but the performance of a *Trauerarbeit*, or "sorrow work": mourning, like interpretation, is an activity. By placing a high emphasis on the reality principle and on the idea of forgetting as a process that advances bit by bit at a soberingly slow rate, he frees modernity from a stereotypically romanticized or sentimentalized view of grief. In so doing, Freud's account of the working-through of loss adopts a pseudopragmatic tone that presupposes a certain indifference to the value of a past that the reality principle eventually must declare nonexistent.[11]

However, after the introduction of the death drive, Freud increasingly insists on a skeptical questioning of the idea of a successful work of mourning, retreating from the initial binary distinction between mourning and melancholia. The Freud of "Analysis Terminable and Interminable" ultimately seems to dissolve the distinction by suggesting that not only does mourning necessitate work, but that every work, particularly that of analysis, presupposes mourning, a suggestion that sets in motion the complex logic of the interminable. Freud, however, avoids the cynical nihilism that we will find prevails in Lacan. The logic of the interminable does not coincide with a critical overcoming of mourning, but with a resolute confrontation of the enigma of loss.

In outlining the contemporary configuration of mourning, I regard Lacan's revision of Freud's system as a particularly important turning point. Lacan's claim to have revived the original, Freudian spirit of psychoanalysis is well known. Lacan is obsessed by the example of Freud, to whom he incessantly professes to pay tribute. The significance of his reworking of Freud's theory in the end hinges on his radicalizing of the Freudian notion of the death drive. Such is Lacan's attachment to this concept that he makes it the inescapable truth of subjectivity, the origin of the stylized, unrelenting knowingness that for him defines the psyche. One of the most important lessons taught by Freud, according to Lacan, is that the subject's quest for the object always reveals it to be lost by definition.[12] So defined, however, loss in the Lacanian system looks like a transcendental principle of emptiness or absence rather than a historical event. Yet if desire is sustained by lack, if desire originates in castration, then psychoanalysis for Lacan can only affirm the *vanitas* of mourning. We might say that for the French analyst, mourning does not represent an enigma, but rather the a priori solution to the question of desire. In this picture, the "work" of mourning is devalued to the status of a social formality, the impossible but obligatory work performed at the level of the symbolic order to fill the hole in the Real elicited by the fact of death. Lacan, that is, does not truly believe in mourning. His "overcoming" of mourning, I wish to propose, in the end consorts with the ahistoricism of consumerist postmodernity. Mourning for Lacan intervenes at the level of a desire that is sustained by the inherent lack of an object, and hence by the erasure or flattening of history from the point of view of the subject. In this respect, I consider to be particularly meaningful Lacan's seminar on *Hamlet* and his interpretation of the Holocaust at the end of his *Séminaire XI*.[13]

A question that remains to be asked is whether Lacan's disenchantment of mental life, his postmodern delight in virtual loss, may be said to facilitate the waning of the cultural relevance of psychoanalysis.[14] By refusing the enigma of mourning, Lacanian psychoanalysis risks aligning itself with the dominant culture to the point of becoming a symptom, rather than a mode of criticism and reinterpretation. Indeed, it strikes me this conclusion is affirmed by the example of Julia Kristeva, whose belated attempt to reinvest the psyche via a persistent refocusing of attention on the melancholic imagination gains urgency from its implicit contrast and resistance to the Lacanian precedent.[15]

At roughly the same moment as Freud articulates the notion of the *Trauerarbeit*, Proust puts into practice a fictive experiment of involuntary memory. This concept shares with Freud's notion of mourning the attempt to redefine a more vital relationship to temporality and memory as opposed to the objectified historicism of the previous century. Involuntary memory in Proust's masterpiece, *In Search of Lost Time*, represents the decisive metamorphosis of historical time into a structure of feeling, thus perhaps suggesting the obsolescence of a public, political discourse of memory and tradition. In the context of the novel's disregard for ritualized forms of bereavement and relentless reaffirmation of the "law of oblivion," we may question the legitimacy of the prevalent view of Proust as a nostalgic writer. In accordance with Deleuze's provocative theory that *In Search of Lost Time* is not driven by the "work" of memory, I examine the contradictions and compromises of Proust's theory of involuntary memory as it is expounded in the last volume, *Time Regained.*

A similar view gradually emerges in the body of commentary on Proust's magnum opus by Walter Benjamin, who establishes himself as the most discerning critic of culture at a moment when art seems on the verge of metamorphosis into sheer experience, while nevertheless still reflecting the appeal of the auratic. We might say that, confronting its possible eradication, *In Search of Lost Time* produces or manufactures the auratic through imaginative strategies that will be assimilated in modern and postmodern culture to the all-pervasive fetishism of advertising. Is an aesthetic connoisseurship of the style of lost time an ethically appropriate answer to the enigma of mourning? This is the problem Proust ultimately leaves us to ponder. Proust, then, remains our contemporary in so far as the predicaments he imagined and the language he invented to describe them have grown ever more crucial to our culture since his time.

Reenchanting Mourning: Pasolini and Godard

A genuinely critical discussion of mourning in contemporary culture ought to avoid a nostalgic view of culture itself. From the recognition of mourning's devaluation under the regime of postmodern detachment, it follows that a certain denial or dismissal of loss facilitates the advancing transformation of culture by mass consumption and production. The centrality once granted the arts as registers of the past has given way to a more diffuse aesthetic landscape in which art and technology increasingly conspire to reflect the relentless spectacle of the present. Any consideration of the traditional forms must focus on their remaining dialectical force. Ultimately, however, it is more important from a critical perspective to identify what resources for mourning may be embedded within the operation of mass culture. In order to take into account the reality of our changed attitude toward the past, we must search for a new ground on which mourning may be redefined and thus allowed to retain its imaginative urgency. The reinvigoration of mourning in the domain of cinema is of particular interest, I argue, because film poses a potential challenge to the assumption that the image is the commodified medium par excellence of contemporary mass culture.

"Frames of Mourning," the second section of this book, takes Derrida's philosophical meditation on "spectrality" in *Specters of Marx* as the point of departure from which to explore the mise-en-scène of the concept itself in Pasolini and Godard's films.[16] Although the notion of a "spectropoetics" partly derives from Derrida's attempted revival of the spirit of Marxism in *Specters of Marx*, I wish to apply the term more broadly to the phantasmatic content repressed or marginalized by consumerist postmodernity and the critical reanimation of such content in the works of a wide range of cultural interlocutors.

Spectropoetics might also be regarded as a response to the contemporary search for a collective mode of memory, a mode that relinquishes the solipsistic ingenuity of certain strains of modernism. The term in this sense also designates the space in which art allows the enigma of mourning to resonate. As I elaborate it in the last two chapters, the spectral delimits a process of negotiation between individual and collective horizons of loss, at a time when technology and mass media make all the more elusive the demarcation between private and public dimensions of grief. Such negotiation questions the linear itinerary of forgetting posited by Freud in *Mourning and Melancholia*, an itinerary aimed at the replacement of an old by a new object. The poetics of spectrality neither upholds any myth of progress through forgetting, nor affirms a unique genealogical path back to the past through nostalgia. It insists instead on openness to different levels and components of loss.

In contrast to the stylistic fetishism of the past and celebration of the retro typical of commercial motion pictures, spectral cinema relentlessly rephrases the question of mourning not as an exercise in nostalgia, but as a call to reinterpretation and thus to change. To the historical glibness of the "nostalgia film" that Fredric Jameson rightly identifies with late-capitalist postmodernity, I oppose a new visual strategy of mourning that could be called the "spectral film." This strategy defines the emerging horizon of a critical postmodernity. Unlike nostalgia films, spectral films investigate the past in order to raise questions regarding the future. Both Pasolini's *Teorema* and Godard's *Histoire(s) du cinéma* conceive of mourning—of the departed houseguest in Pasolini's film and of the celluloid medium itself in Godard's—as an enigma. They thus refuse to neglect the burden of the future.

In the chapter on Pasolini, I assert that behind the author's embrace of cinematic language should be seen the effort to renew the scope and strength of his earlier elegiac poetic works. The chapter ends with a sustained reading of *Teorema*, a hybrid work consisting of a movie released in 1968 and a novel written simultaneously but not published until 1978. *Teo-*

rema recounts the story of a mysterious visitor who disappears after converting the individual members of a well-to-do Milanese household from bourgeois domesticity to agonized self-scrutiny. The film is structured by means of repeated, intermittent flashforwards to the empty vista of the desert, a mythical utopia that provides the setting for the film's narrative denouement and ethical resolution. As an updating of the Nietzschean myth of the death of God, *Teorema* confronts us allegorically with the enigma of mourning, offering in the end only the weak messianism of a mysterious and ambivalent resolution.

Godard's *Histoire(s) du cinéma* is a collagelike, four-and-a-half-hour compendium of film clips that seeks to reconstruct the history of the twentieth century by tracing the development of the motion picture. This study of the medium foresees a future in which the cinematic image might discover a renewed purpose, when, as the director puts it, "the image will come at the time of resurrection."[17] In *Teorema* and *Histoire(s)*, spectrality is not an aesthetic motif, as is nostalgia in kitsch films, but an ethical and political effort to resist the so-called rationalism of the mass market. Spectrality thus understood seeks not to deny or disguise the strangeness of the past, but in fact to visualize it critically and thus to greet it with ethical attention. Pasolini and Godard's specters are not the *unheimlich* ghosts of the romantic and modernist tradition, but morally demanding apparitions, visual guides on the path toward a new openness or vulnerability of memory. Pasolini's originality consists in redescribing the ghosts of western culture—from Medea to Oedipus, St. Matthew, and the messianic guest of *Teorema*—as ambivalent political emissaries whose cryptic presence resists easy consumption or idealization.

In his dazzling amalgamation of visualized text, voice-over commentary, and film fragments, Godard accomplishes the difficult task of mediating between personal and collective memory through the interplay of film traces. *Histoire(s) du cinéma* encourages a sort of visual equivocation with respect to the past, implying that cinema not only consumes our anteriority, but also projects it back to us. Instead of an avant-garde indifference to memory and the canon, he adopts a posture of "caring" for the past in a Heideggerian sense. He opens a place in his *Histoire(s)*, that is, for a cultural convalescence to be achieved through the performance of mourning.

The necessity of such a place seems all the greater now that the turn toward digital technology has deprived the image of its historical and ontological referentiality. In this light, Godard may be seen to resist the dissolution of the Roman concept of imago, which, unlike the Greek notion of *eikon*, was firmly premised on the principle of resemblance. In Roman culture, the imago originally referred to the portrait of the dead used during the funeral service, a pictorial work that oscillated between the functions of commemoration and representation.[18] The inherent spectrality of the imago, if once the hallmark of the film medium, has been superseded by a digital technology that threatens to abolish the spectral from the domain of the moving image altogether. In its attempt to redefine the endangered space of the imago through the mourning of cinema, Godard's *Histoire(s)* sets the stage for the ultimate confrontation between the spectral and the spectacular, a clash that finds its ideal territory in the celluloid moving image. As I argue in Section 2, works such as Pasolini's *Teorema* or Godard's *Histoire(s) du cinéma* exemplify mourning not as the narration or thematizing of an achieved experience of loss, but as the projection and spectral diffusion of an open-ended cultural enigma that is both subjective and objective.[19]

The Critic as Mourner: Benjamin and Derrida

Given my topic, I should not fail to remember the intellectual figures I consider crucial to the reexamination of mourning in contemporary culture. Indeed, I will invoke thinkers and philosophers who, rather than anatomizing the exhilarated forgetfulness of mass society in the manner of many contemporary commentators, have mapped a more complex and anguished territory of remembrance. On this score, I find invaluable Walter Benjamin's investigations of the obsolescence of aura in modernity and the separation between the magical, irrational imperative to mourn and the scientific, material reality of the living.[20] Benjamin consistently views the understanding of the past and the task of mourning as cultural mysteries that cannot be quickly dismissed. In his never fully completed magnum opus, *The Arcades Project*, he envisions modernity as something like a phantasmagoric *Trauerspiel* (i.e., a tragedy or "sorrow play") in which ghostly objects such as the "souvenir," a sort of dead memory, and iconic personae such as the gambler, the *flâneur*, or the prostitute are welcomed onto the dramatic stage of the imagination rather than expelled from it. Without denying that the authority of tradition and the past had been compromised by his time, he uncovers all of the new, original ways in which the modern present invokes or reinterprets the past, whether by citation, epic dramatization, historical materialism, or other means. In his work, he provides an example of a phantasmagorical criticism in which the ghosts and phantoms of culture are to be entertained rather than exorcised, because they manifest usually suppressed sociological and ethical concerns.[21] Such an understanding, if incompatible with a classical transparency or intelligibility of memory, does not altogether rule out the possibility of memory's spectral reanimation. Embracing not only the past, but also the future, Benjamin promotes an aesthetic and ethical spectrality compatible with the possibility of messianic redemption.

In addition to Benjamin, my mapping of contemporary modes of cultural mourning will invoke the crucial example of Jacques Derrida, whose philosophically self-conscious revision of the Heideggerian project of the mourning of metaphysics is crucial. Heidegger famously characterized metaphysics as the forgetting of Being and identified the mourning of the metaphysical tradition as the only way of overcoming such obliviousness.[22] Yet his notion of mourning clearly is limited by his inability to imagine it in any terms other than the ontological. Derrida, like Benjamin, manages by contrast to envision a horizon of history and political life that is reenergized rather than paralyzed by mourning. In its detachment from any historical or political considerations, Heidegger's retrospective posture of "dwelling" on the past, his claim to recover the truth of Being by taking a "step back" [*Schritt zürück*] from philosophy, comes to look like the decisive gesture of surrender to metaphysical nostalgia.[23] Without giving credence, as Heidegger does, to "a lost country of thought" or to a maternal language of Being, Derrida performs deconstruction as an aporetic work of mourning that, so to speak, succeeds most when it fails, which is to say when it cannot be resolved.[24] Rereading the Freudian notion of *Trauerarbeit* to accommodate the more nuanced, modulated figure of "semimourning," Derrida's exegesis has tried consistently to avoid the binarism of triumph over the past and nostalgia. If the French philosopher's early emphasis on the trace, *différance*, and dissemination gives to deconstruction a spectral character from the outset, the vocabulary he develops in later writings, from *The Post Card* to *Specters of Marx* and *Échographies*, suggests that his exploration of spectrality ought to be understood as revolving around two central questions: politics and technology. With regard to politics, spectrality entails our allowing ourselves to be haunted by the Marxist promise of emancipation without denying the collapse of certain "realized" experiments in Marxist ideology. When it comes to technology,

Derrida argues that despite its positivist drive toward mastery of the empirically knowable, the technoscientific realm paradoxically has enabled the emergence of a new poetics of spectrality in the manner of a return of the repressed. Photography, cinema, and television confront us with human referents whose mortality has been technologically suspended or annulled through the visual production of the perpetual simulacra of life.

Consideration of Benjamin and Derrida's works, it seems to me, is necessary to identify the territory of a critical postmodernity. Such an effort may appear from a certain perspective to struggle against the current of contemporary scholarship, to accept an untimely or peripheral condition. I wish to respond by advancing further queries. Is it possible to conceive of a "minor postmodernism" analogous to what Deleuze and Guattari have defined as a minor literature?[25] Does a postmodernism at the margins exist? The issues at stake in the definition of a critical postmodernity are ethical and political rather than merely stylistic. Finally, what hangs in the balance is the renewal of concern for a project of emancipation that has been too successfully mourned. The possibility of a critical postmodernism depends on our ability to imagine new forms of mourning that permit negotiation between the subjective and intersubjective spheres of memory. For the most significant artworks of contemporary culture are not works of mourning in the Freudian sense. They do not enforce the gradual detachment of libido or desire from the object. Instead, they function as resonant texts, textures, instances of an incipient spectropoetics, complicated webs of temporality in which memory is not only taken in, introjected, or accrued, but reworked, projected, and given back.

PART ONE

NARRATIVES OF MOURNING

1

The Twilight of Mourning

From Loss to Lack

It may be said that Freudian psychoanalysis constitutes a modernist discipline, not only because the establishment and initial development of the discourse coincide historically with the emergence of the culture of high modernism, but more importantly because the operations of psychoanalysis insist on such crucial modernist principles as the hermeneutics of fragmentation and the interiority or encoded "depth" of the psyche.[1] Above all, the status of Freudian psychoanalysis as a modernist discipline depends on its epistemological originality, its far-reaching ability to "make it new," opening to interpretation not only the territory of neurosis, but the neglected phenomenology of the everyday from dreams to verbal lapses. In Freud's conception, we find, intermingled with the experimental and optimistic postures of early psychoanalytic theory that were most enthusiastically adopted by the avant-garde and surrealism, expressions of melancholy and nostalgic regret that correspond to the dialectical counterturn of high modernism and punctuate in particular the last fifteen years of Freud's career from *Beyond the Pleasure Principle* to *Civilization and Its Discontents* and "Analysis Terminable and Interminable." In this sense, Kristeva's description of Freud as a revolutionary in search of lost time aptly captures the fundamental modernist ambivalence of the psychoanalytic enterprise.[2]

Keeping in mind Freud's ambivalence with respect to history, I intend in the first half of this chapter to explore how he positions his conception of mourning, categorically articulated in his metapsychological essay *Mourning and Melancholia* (1917), not only at the intersection of private and public temporalities, which is to say at the junction of the individual and society, but also at the meeting point of the two foundational stages of psychoanalytic thought: the first and second Freudian topics. First, I wish to establish Freud's notion of a "successful" or resolved mourning under the first topic as the basis of his view of the subject as made up of its history of lost object-relations and hence as a "modernist machine" perpetually working to replace its objects. Second, I will examine the transition from the first topic (the pleasure principle) to the second topic (the death drive) in order to point out Freud's increasing doubt in his later essays toward the idea of a successful mourning. Third, I contend that by promulgating the idea of interminable mourning in the form of the death drive, Freud paves the way for Lacan's insistence that the inaccessibility of the object, and hence of history, represents the *conditio sine qua non* of desire. This insistence, which provides the subject of the second half of this chapter, situates Lacan in a postmodern sphere beyond the very problematic of mourning. Fourth, I hope to suggest the limits of this postmodernist, Lacanian position by reference both to Jacques Derrida's alternate reading of the Freudian theory of the death drive and to Lacan's own hyperbolic denial of the peculiar historical urgency that mourning attains in the twentieth century.

Although devoid of a systematic or coherent account of the psyche, Lacan's thought doubtless provides contemporary culture with a vivid critical vocabulary, a powerfully skeptical approach to certain problems within psychoanalysis, and a compelling style of argument. Yet his theory suffers from important ethical and political limitations that I wish to highlight by raising specific questions. Is the ethics of psychoanalysis, which Lacan formulates as an ethics of desire, the only and ultimate moral position we should care about? Because such an ethics suppresses or displaces the problem of mourning, what are the consequences of adopting his outlook for our relationship to the past, to history, and to the Other? By comparing the French analyst's views to those of Freud, I hope to underline the radical, provocative, but also risky nature of the Lacanian project.

In Freud's theory, the very temporality of subjectivity is unequivocally retrospective, because the past is the source of the hermeneutic redemption promised by psychoanalysis.[3] The gravitational center of analysis always coincides with the subject's history and not with his or her phantasmatic relationship to the world in "real time." In fact, as late as in the *New Introductory Lectures* of 1933, Freud asserts that should analysis account strictly for the patient's present motives and expectations, the practice would lose its raison d'être and degenerate into a "school of wisdom" (21:143). For Freud, then, analysis will always be an act of mourning, a work that is successful during the discipline's first, optimistic phase in accordance with the triumphalism of the pleasure principle, but pathological and interminable during the second phase in accordance with the death instinct. Yet as we shall see, the temporal logic enforced by Freud's thinking will arrive within the course of his career at a cul-de-sac or impasse.

That the temporal orientation privileged by psychoanalysis might be particularly at odds with that of postmodern culture is suggested by the advancing obsolescence of Freud's theory and practice in recent times. By maintaining the necessity of mourning and history to the definition of the human and the composition of human values, analysis resists the characteristic ahistoricism of contemporary culture. Thus, to reflect on the question of mourning within the terms of analytic theory necessitates some consideration of the larger question of the fate of psychoanalysis as a discipline.

To trace exactly the vicissitudes of the concept of mourning will allow us to assess not only the modernist project of Freudian theory, but also its postmodern rewriting in Lacan's work. Of course, the word *postmodern* has a notoriously weak referentiality.[4] Although the very term *postmodern* appears to bespeak a memorializing or nostalgic consciousness, the designation appears at the same time to hint at the possibility of a condition beyond bereavement. Lyotard, for example, has famously related postmodernity to the successful mourning of the various narratives of emancipation of a subject who otherwise would be condemned to sink into "incurable melancholy" for his or her lost object.[5]

In what follows, my aim will be to ascertain to what extent postmodern culture thrives on a "consumerism of loss," an attitude that can imply either the jaded, pseudocynical knowingness of thinkers such as Lyotard or Lacan or the "artificial," impotent nostalgia promoted by the most populist strain of postmodernism. Freud's modernist methodology was predicated on an "overcoming" of loss in accordance with the "bit-by-bit" tempo that regulates the machinery of mourning he describes in *Mourning and Melancholia*. The question of loss he posed was framed as inherently subjective and linked to a unique, historically definite object. After the introduction of the death instinct, however, the focus of his inquiry began to shift from contingent, historical loss to transcendental lack. In the last fifteen years of his career, Freud abides in the space between loss and lack, terminable grief and interminable sorrow, propounding a sort of "fort-da" of mourning that refuses to settle the question.

With Lacan, who breaks with Freud's insistence on the integrity of the object and the centrality of loss to the history of the subject, the question of loss is reframed in intersubjective terms. He freezes the Freudian oscillation between loss and lack at the latter end of the spectrum, denying to the lost object the depth and weight of historical specificity. Radically enlarging the Freudian postulate of the death drive, the Lacanian law of desire presumes an acceptance of symbolic castration in a psychological landscape in which lack constitutes the core of the psyche. This belief generates the knowing, skeptical tone of the French theorist's system, a doctrine in which there is no room for the pathos of working through specific, historical losses.

Exploring the movement from Freudian to Lacanian psychoanalysis will help us to understand better not only the respective hermeneutics of history at play in their theories, but also the discrepancy between the different modes of cultural production those theories represent. Lacan's revision of Freud entails a substantial shift of focus, a shift that becomes particularly evident in light of the terms by which he assesses the importance of mourning and memory. Jameson associates the end of modernism with the effacement of inner time and the dissolution of subjectivity, which, he argues, facilitate the emergence of an idea of the past that is closer in character to a fashionable "alternative world" than an "imperfect primitive stage" of the present.[6] The passage from Freud to Lacan marks a shift from the paradigm of an elegiac and relatively integral subject to that of the ideological simulacra of intersubjectivity. Lacan pictures this symbolic consciousness as predominantly organized around the fundamental lack or inaccessibility of the object, whereas Freud defines the subject as constituted by its history of object relations.

In a culture in which time, as Jameson puts it, has become a function of speed, it is hardly surprising that the difficult, slow, human temporality of mourning has become effectively obsolete.[7] In 1917, Freud provides us with the crucial and pervasive notion of mourning as a psychological work or *Trauerarbeit* and with a phenomenology of the process that encompasses pathological mourning and melancholia. By placing an emphasis on the reality principle and by depicting forgetting as a mechanism that operates at a sobering, gradual, bit-by-bit pace, he frees modernity from a stereotypically romanticized view of grief.

Mourning is not simply an emotion for Freud, but the performance of a work that, like interpretation, is a psychically transformative activity. As he describes it, the working-through of mourning bears more than a passing resemblance to the procedure of analysis itself. Therapy and mourning correspond to one another insofar as both analytically dissolve pathogenic memories at a gradual rate, bit by bit, and insofar as both are supposed to reach an end after a finite amount of time. The untimely character of analytic therapy might even be understood to derive, after all, from its very proximity to mourning. With Lacan's ascendancy, the identification between mourning and analysis no longer appears plausible because the cohesion and temporality of the subject are thrown into such radical doubt that a prolonged, step-by-step process of forgetting cannot be sustained. Consequently, the basic aims and meaning of therapy undergo a radical change, as analysis abandons the humanist insistence on the unhurried temporality of mourning to fully embrace an inhuman, sublime ethics of desire, the uncanny opacity of the "Real."

If death for Freud has no symbolic representation in the unconscious because of its abstract quality (19:58), for Lacan, the death of "the thing" constitutes the primary step toward its becoming part of the symbolic order, eternalizing the subject's desire (E 104, F 319).[8] In other words, we might say that the use value of the object is completely forsaken in favor of its exchange value because what ultimately matters in Lacan's theory is the relation of the thing to other things. In this paradoxical emotional landscape that is dominated by a consumerism of loss, but within which loss acquires no romantic cultural authority, his thought defines a territory beyond the possibility of mourning and thus beyond history. If his thinking is very much in line with the postmodern outlook as a result of his predisposition to a certain ironic knowingness, Lacan places primary stress on modes of knowledge that enact or elaborate the phenomenology of lack and that, we might add, only the most enlightened forms of postmodern culture propound. At the same time that Lacanian analysis perpetuates the antihistoricist impulses of postmodernism, then, the theory makes claims to represent an enlightened and affirmative form of postmodern culture.

Freud's *Trauerarbeit*

According to Philippe Ariès, the beginning of the twentieth century saw the completion of the process of removing death from the social sphere, precluding the public ceremonialization of death and turning it into a private act.[9] Ariès argues that a crucial milestone in the contemporary history of death has been reached through the suppression and eradication of mourning. *Mourning and Melancholia* is written at a critical transitional moment in western culture: the moment when those practices that permit the sentimental representation of mortality have been exhausted. In this sense, we can surmise that the very fortune of the concept of *Trauerarbeit* depends on its offering a vicarious, theoretical mourning ritual, and thus confirms a crucial cultural role for psychoanalysis.[10]

In 1917, Freud published most of his writings that deal directly or indirectly with mourning, surely responding to the influence of World War I, among other things.[11] With *Mourning and Melancholia*, psychoanalytic theory contributes an original philosophy of time to the modernist tradition, encroaching in some sense on the territory of both philosophy and phenomenology. From a psychoanalytic perspective, mourning operates as a strategy of temporalization specific to the individual subject. On this score, Jean Laplanche's commentary is helpful. Laplanche distinguishes three levels or experiences of temporality: cosmological time or the temporality of the world, the time of perception that is common to humans and animals and is referred to immediate consciousness, and the temporality of memory and speculative projection that defines "human time."[12] The value of the temporality of mourning inheres in adding ethical weight and historical specificity to the economics of human time. As we have noted, Freud understands this strategy to represent a kind of mental labor more than an emotional attitude, a "sorrow work" that implies, however obliquely, a productive end or value. On this score, he undoubtedly inherits the humanist and romantic traditions in his depiction of the activity of mourning and of the melancholic affect.[13] As Ariès has noted, the psychoanalytic conception of mourning has been heavily influenced by the "beautiful death" of romanticism and the privileged relationship to the death of the Other.[14]

However, Freud's essay *Mourning and Melancholia* imparts to this tradition an ambivalent modernist spin by identifying the goal of the work of mourning in the replacement of the object.[15] Freud imagines at least one perfect scenario in which a successful mourning is guaranteed, no matter how great the object's importance to the subject. This scenario is organized dialectically around the homeopathic reexperiencing of loss conducive to an effective "overcoming." The limitations of this method are then ascribed to the pathological category of melancholia, a category that it may be argued reveals the obverse side of modernism, an age in which the break with the past is imagined as absolute and irrevocable. According to Freud, the goal of the work of mourning is the substitution of a new object for its lost predecessor; we might reformulate this point by stating that the work of mourning is successful and comes to an end only when it finds or produces a new libidinal object. For Freud, there are no objects that are not, or should not be, replaceable; yet the attachment to the lost object is only abandoned after great fatigue and expense of time, a fatigue that Freud finds infinitely puzzling from an "economic" point of view. Why the compromise by which the commands of reality are carried out piecemeal should be so extraordinarily painful is not at all easy to explain in economic terms (14:245).

Freud's reasoning becomes clearer if we recognize that in the essay, melancholia arises in response to an ideal loss, not to an actual death. In his rather vague, sparse clinical material on melancholia, he never confronts us with a case of irrevocable loss—say, a brother, as in *Antigone*, or a parent—and his initial choice of the history of a "betrothed girl who has been jilted" directs our attention to an instance of suffering for an eminently replaceable object (14:245). In this strange division of labor, the work of mourning deals with actual loss, melancholia with its ideal or abstract occurrence, making it difficult to envision melancholia as a "natural response" to death.

The virtual shortcoming of the process of mourning will be attributed a priori to pathological melancholia, the obverse not only of the Freudian theory but of modernism itself.[16] Insofar as modernism implies a new consciousness of time while dialectically occasioning the mournful expression of regret for the past, the Freudian essay evinces modernism's unmistakably melancholic ambivalence. By introducing the concept of *Trauerarbeit*, Freud dynamically reinterprets the process of remembering and forgetting as work, but voices at the same time the contradictions and aporias that have come to characterize the modernist reaction to loss. He, like Walter Benjamin, understands the twentieth-century break with the past as unique, absolute, irreconcilable to tradition.[17] In the work of both thinkers, we encounter the alternation of feelings of exhilaration and melancholy toward their respective modernities. In both their writings, we witness the attempt, however temporarily and imperfectly, to overcome the auratic value of the past. However, both thinkers, far from achieving this goal of overcoming, consign themselves to an agonizing and tragic process of self-revision that results in an increasingly melancholic view of history. Both figures, if qualitatively different in the economies of their respective works, set out to establish in their later writings a hermeneutics of history that, according to Freud in *Civilization and Its Discontents* (1930) and Benjamin in "Theses on the Philosophy of History" (1950), affirms the mourning or commemoration of the loss of the past.

Freud broaches the topic of mourning for the first time in *Studies on Hysteria* (1895), discussing the case of Elisabeth von R., a young woman whose physical pain, according to his account, was triggered not by actual and immediate impressions, but by their recollection in memory.[18] In his treatment of the case, he suggests the possibility of a day-to-day correspondence between her past experiences and her recollection of them, an elaborate rehearsal that culminates in an annual "festival of remembrance" (2:163). From the outset, he presents mourning as a privileged moment of psychological work and as a structured activity that operates bit by bit.

Twenty years later, we find the same ideas fully developed on metapsychological ground in *Mourning and Melancholia*. Freud's intention is to classify the field of the melancholic disorder according to a three-tiered hierarchy of complexity: mourning, pathological mourning, and melancholy. As I have already suggested, this hierarchy crucially provides an analytic or dialectical framework within which the success or completion of mourning becomes a logical necessity. The tripartite classification that Freud justifies here on clinical grounds, however, will lose its raison d'être after the introduction of the death drive later on in his career. It is precisely this erasure of the possibility of success under the second topic that argues for the paramount importance of mourning over melancholia in Freud's thinking. Consequently, I will focus in what follows on his concept of *Trauerarbeit*.

He observes that mourning can last only for a limited span of time, during which the mourner loses any interest in those aspects of the outside world unrelated to the dead. During this time, it becomes difficult to replace the lost object with a new one. Nevertheless, after a period of inhibition and after having performed the laborious work of "reality-testing," the

subject eventually regains his or her ability to love and enters into other ob-
ject-cathexes:

> I do not think there is anything far-fetched in presenting it in the following way.
> Reality-testing, has shown that the loved object no longer exists, and it proceeds
> to demand that all the libido shall be withdrawn from its attachments to that ob-
> ject. . . . Normally, respect for reality gains the day. Nevertheless, its orders cannot
> be obeyed at once. They are carried out bit by bit, at great expense of time. . . .
> Each single one of the memories and expectations in which the libido is bound to
> the object is brought up and hyper-cathected, and the detachment [*Lösung*] of the
> libido is accomplished in respect of it. (14:244–45)[19]

Here Freud clearly implies that mourning functions as a form of analysis
when it dissolves bit by bit [*im einzelnen*] the attachment to the lost object.
His notion of the *Trauerarbeit* takes as its ultimate goal the replacement of
the lost object and thereby honors the modernist imperative to "make it
new." Yet it should be noticed that the tempo he assigns to the mourning
process coincides with the pensive meticulousness of analysis rather than
the transformative speed of modernity. His ambivalence in this regard becomes even clearer if we consider his essay "On Transience," where he
voices an almost hostile sense of perplexity at what he calls here in *Mourning and Melancholia* the "great expense of time" [*großen Aufwand von Zeit*]
necessary for the completion of the sorrow work, an expense he views as
enigmatic from an economic point of view (14:306). In light of this sense
of perplexity, Freud seems ready to deny the analytic methods of the work
of mourning and to embrace a utopian faith in the resilience and self-suf-
ficiency of the psyche, in its ability to work as quickly and efficiently as a
modern machine.[20]

As difficult as it is, the successful work of mourning finally achieves
the detachment of libido from the "lost" object. Success is contingent on a
form of repetition—the reinvestment and hypercathexis of each bit of
memory—that, unlike the repetition-compulsion of the death drive, is benign and opens up the possibility of a renewal of the object.[21] The *Arbeit*
(labor) of mourning produces a shock that, however fleetingly, reinforces
and amplifies the significance of the object. In the economy of hegemonic
postmodern culture, by contrast, there is a sort of erasure or flattening of
the object. The psychoanalytic paradigm of this effect is Lacan's reduction
of the object to the category of the *objet a*, the interchangeable token of a
loss that can only be intuited as lack, as an a priori absence. The repetition
of libidinal activity that structures the Freudian *Trauerarbeit* performs the

function of reality-testing [*Realitätsprüfung*], a function Freud generally presents as answering a need to differentiate between perception and hallucination in the name of a sort of psychological pragmatism that satisfies and reassures the ego.[22]

The first Freudian topic, in which the concept of the death instinct plays no part, is devoted to the action of desire and the ego's anarchic mobility; within this theoretical context, both the attachment to a lost object and the difficult *Arbeit* of its mourning are highly enigmatic processes. In this respect, we can say that mourning functions along the lines of a sort of reality principle for the psyche, which Freud otherwise regards as driven by "unattached" desire. It is noteworthy that Freud does not include in his exploration of *Trauerarbeit* the function of dreams, instead preferring to enforce the idea of a voluntary, dynamic work of forgetting. In *The Interpretation of Dreams*, by contrast, Freud had dedicated ample space to dreams of mourning such as, crucially, his own following his father's death and the famous dream in which a grief-stricken father ascribes to his dead child the traumatic demand, "Father, don't you see I am burning?"[23] The absence of dreams in *Mourning and Melancholia* might be better explained if we observe Freud's determination to link the *Trauerarbeit* to the reality principle, even at the cost of neglecting one of the most important phenomenological manifestations of the work of mourning. Unlike the *Traumarbeit*, which draws on the unconscious procedures of displacement and condensation, the work of mourning for Freud categorically belongs to the pure, yet aporetic reign of "reality." The other reason we might surmise for Freud's neglect of dreams in his metapsychological work on mourning is his refusal to conflate the linear, bit-by-bit tempo of forgetting with the problematic temporality of trauma. In the father's dream of his dead child, mourning is inscribed within a traumatic repetition, a possibility that Freud reserves in *Mourning and Melancholia* exclusively to the pathological, melancholic reaction to loss. The implication that the reality principle might thrive on loss constitutes one of the most important ideological tenets of Freud's first topic, the pleasure principle.[24] The momentousness of Freud's discussion of the work of mourning resides in the proposition that analysis operates in analogical relation to mourning. In this sense, the *Trauerarbeit* represents the most important cultural capital of psychoanalysis itself. As if through a sustained exercise of self-discipline, the dissolution of libidinal links to the object is effected bit by bit with each scrap of memory. The work of mourning mimics the labor of analysis in the following sense: the very rhythms of the subject's withdrawal from the object and of the analysand's uncovering of repressed material are similarly defined by a *pars destruens* that resolves otherwise obscure psychic compounds into their discrete elements and that represents the necessary condition of any further reshaping of the psyche. In this light, it is no surprise that Freud identifies the work of mourning with the testing of reality, which is the very essence of analytic therapy.

Lacan will significantly revise the Freudian notion of *Trauerarbeit*, which he considers overly vague; instead of discharging the task of reality-testing, mourning in the French analyst's reckoning unveils the very limits of such an undertaking. The triadic Lacanian order of the Symbolic, the Imaginary, and the Real complicates, and to a large degree calls into question, the objective of "realism" in the work of mourning. As we will see, Lacan discovers in the symbolic the proper ground of mourning at that moment when the subject confronts its own lack in the shape of a "hole" in the Real. The passage from a Freudian vision of loss as a contingent, historical event to the Lacanian view of lack as an a priori, ontological condition of psychic life marks a decisive shift in the way that psychoanalysis as a discipline conceptualizes the relationship between subject and object.

The obsolescence of mourning as a model for the psychoanalytic process reveals one of the most disturbing tendencies of contemporary theory—namely, its incapacity, as Dominick LaCapra has argued, to distinguish between absence and loss, structural and historical trauma, mourning and melancholia. LaCapra observes that although losses may entail absences, the converse is not the case. Absence is situated at the transhistorical level, whereas loss retains a contingent, specific, historical value: "I think it is misguided to situate loss on an ontological or transhistorical level, something that happens when it is conflated with absence and conceived as constitutive of existence. . . . The conversion of absence into loss gives anxiety an identifiable object—the lost object—and generates the hopes that anxiety may be eliminated or overcome. By contrast, the anxiety attendant on absence may never be entirely eliminated or overcome but must be lived with in various ways."[25] High modernism by and large abides by an interpretation of loss compatible with a historicized view of the subject in which strategies of overcoming, like the Freudian notion of mourning, regulate the "healthy" negotiation of the past.

Already implicit in the work of mourning, of course, is the threat of degenerating into a manic triumph over the past, an attitude that may be said to characterize the avant-garde and that according to Antoine Compagnon deforms the initially more balanced stance of early modernism.[26] The hegemonic or dominant strain of postmodernism may be said to have taken the triumphalism of the avant-garde as the point of departure for its own posture of indifference toward the past, a distancing that operates in complicity with what Jameson has called "the logic of late capitalism." Nevertheless, it is possible in the peripheries of postmodern culture to detect impulses toward a critical reflection on history and tradition, impulses often directed specifically toward the revival of a certain modernist spirit as a means to the reaffirmation of a hermeneutics of the past. In the second half of this book, I will investigate these impulses in Pasolini and Godard's variegated, multidiscursive oeuvres.

The mainstream trend of contemporary culture, however, clearly accommodates a consumerism of loss that de facto coincides with the surrender to absence and lack lamented by LaCapra. Although he is right to recognize a widespread fascination with categories of absence and with forms of "quasitranscendental" mourning, he neglects to point out that rather than taking the emotionally definite shape of interminable melancholy, these categories work to generate the "virtual," affectless psychic space of postmodernity. The problem, in other words, is that the postmodern fascination with absence that, according to LaCapra, defines psychoanalysis from Lacan to trauma studies cannot produce melancholia, but only the uniformly flattened experiences of a consumerism of loss.[27]

Transience

At the end of *Mourning and Melancholia*, when Freud concludes that unlike melancholia, mourning does not convert ultimately into mania, he formulates the hypothesis that "this work of severance is so slow and gradual that, by the time it has been finished, the expenditure of energy necessary for it is also dissipated" (14:255). Indeed, with typical modernist ambivalence, he sets out to construe the psyche as the libidinal "reproduction" of the object, while avoiding the "manic" destiny that such a depiction might entail.

However, Freud's characterization of the experience of mourning betrays a significant connection to mania in the essay "On Transience," written shortly after *Mourning and Melancholia*. The essay is important, because it represents the last time that Freud will resort to such an unabashedly "surrealist" vision of psychic life, a horizon in which promiscuous and changeable desires occupy center stage.[28] But the interest of "On Transience" is also in helping us to determine the theoretical contours of the object of mourning and to define the specific quality of a modernist Freudian aesthetics.[29] On this score, it ought to be observed that the Freudian approach to loss in *Mourning and Melancholia* finds its natural conclusion not in the ethical or "political" domain, but rather in that of "aesthetics," betraying a preoccupation with the time of the "beautiful object," as Pierre Fedida puts it.[30] Enlarging on Fedida's point, we might say that "On Transience" fulfills the cultural or aesthetic vocation implicit in its predecessor essay.

What is striking about "On Transience" is that the essay represents the moment at which Freud most fully articulates his own avant-garde agenda, imposing on subjective experience in general an uncompromising aesthetic of the new that counts speed as a principal ideal. "On Transience" should be read as the manifesto of a sort of avant-garde psychology, a hyperactive condition of the libido that consorts with the "manic" attitude of the era's experimental poetics from futurism to surrealism. Thus, it might be said that in the modernist *Zeitgeist* we encounter the proper ideological or cultural correlate of a psyche that is animated and defined by loss.

Freud's short essay recounts the anecdote of a pleasant summer walk through "a smiling countryside" in the company of an older, taciturn friend and a young, celebrated poet, probably Rilke.[31] Freud reflects on the poet's lamentation over the increasing proneness to decay of all beautiful things in response to winter's approach. Yet if the transience of everything beautiful (whether belonging to the realm of nature or of art) is inescapable, we should not, in Freud's opinion, indulge our melancholy; to do so would be tantamount to a request for immortality on the assumption that transience necessarily means a diminution of the value of existence: "On the contrary, an increase! Transience value is scarcity value in time. Limitation in the possibility of an enjoyment raises the value of the enjoyment. It was incomprehensible, I declared, that the thought of the transience of beauty should interfere with our joy in it" (14:305). By stressing the "increased" value of the lost object, Freud identifies in loss a surplus aesthetic and ethical value. Replacing the lost object entails a sustained shock to the subject that amplifies, albeit momentarily, the object's significance. "We only see that libido clings to its objects," writes Freud, "and will not renounce those that are lost even when a substitute lies ready to hand" (14:305–7).[32] The essay falls into two parts: the anecdote recounting the outing, and Freud's retrospective theoretical interpretation of the anecdote. The two halves of the essay not only reflect two very different narrative strategies, but also reflect two different dialectical and historical moments organized around a temporal lapse that inheres in the break between the anecdote and its interpretation; indeed, if the conversation takes place before the commencement of hostilities, then the "lapse" or division between the two sections may be said to mark the outbreak of the war itself, because Freud is writing in November 1915.

In the meantime, the war has exposed the ephemeral quality of things and robbed the world of much of its beauty. Yet at a significant moment, when Freud reworks the question raised by his friends, he will reaffirm that what has proven perishable is nonetheless beautiful, that mourning should not entail a permanent repudiation of beauty as a value. Freud's usual deference toward poets is superseded in the essay by the sustained assertion of his own authority with regard to the devices of the psyche. He refuses to consider the possibility that the experience of unresolved mourning might supply a privileged source of inspiration for poets. Ironically, if we credit the suggestion that the "celebrated poet" of the anecdote may have been Rilke, Freud suddenly comes to seem like one determined to challenge the relevance of romantic elegy and in favor of an almost avant-garde praise of the fugitive. Indeed, Freud's tone in the concluding paragraph turns abruptly optimistic, leaving the reader with an overall impression of tragicomic hyperbole: "When once mourning is over, we shall build up again all that war has destroyed, and perhaps on firmer ground and more lastingly than before" (14:307).

Although certainly cooler in tone, Freud's rhetoric differs in degree rather than in kind from Marinetti's praise of war as the world's only form of "hygiene." In Freud's rhetorical exaggeration, one might detect the impulse to perpetuate cathexes ad libitum, as if to enact in his own writing the triumphal phase of melancholia. The significance of the Freudian essay is to unveil the implicit "economic" assumptions and ideological beliefs of the first topic as aesthetic principles that are divorced from any ethical and political consideration.

In Mourning and Melancholia and in "On Transience," Freud mobilizes the concept of mourning, as well as its derivatives melancholia and mania, in order to unveil the "economic arrangements" and aesthetic horizons of modern, capitalist culture, a social formation within which the capital of libido must shift and be displaced according to an overriding consumerism of loss. It is no surprise in this sense that for Freud, "a particularly striking feature" of melancholia is the fear of poverty, a fear that occupies a "prominent position" in the clinical tableau (14:248, 252). That we touch the ideological core of the culture becomes evident if we notice how Freud in "On Transience" single-mindedly pursues his argument regarding the enigmatic "economic" conditions of mourning, how he doggedly characterizes mourning as a riddle. He can offer no justification for the pain of the libido's detachment from its former object, nor for the stubbornness of the ego's resistance to reabsorption; he adds that if mourning is a natural process for the analysand or layperson, this is not the case for the psychoanalyst: "To psychologists mourning is a great riddle, one of those phenomena which cannot themselves be explained but to which other obscurities can be traced back" (14:306). By opposing the belief of the layperson to that of the psychoanalyst, Freud highlights the analyst's commitment to an unsentimental historical pragmatism, to a conviction that the pleasure principle should rule the psychic life and that all loss can be overcome in due time.[33] Yet we well might regard Freud's assertion that mourning is not enigmatic to the layperson to be coy and disingenuous. Indeed, mourning is not just "economically" enigmatic, but drastically so. As Jean Laplanche has remarked, every occasion of mourning challenges us to respond to the radical and ultimate enigma of the dead Other and thereby raises questions that are destined to remain unanswered: "There is certainly no mourning without the question, what would he say?, what would he have said?, without the regret or remorse of not having been able to hold a sufficient dialogue, to understand what the other had to say."[34] By way of contrast, Freud seems to regard mourning in "On Transience" as a cognitive riddle or puzzle awaiting its due resolution, rather than as a genuinely problematic philosophical and ethical enigma. These two positions suggest the distinction between a solipsistic conception of mourning in which the enigma of the Other might be denied or kept at bay and an ethical conception in which such an enigma demands active critical engagement.

The kind of naiveté Freud attributes to psychologists reflects the modus operandi of capitalist culture at large, a culture that advances according to a mechanical rhythm of attachment and detachment, construing detachment in the process not as a tragic event, but as a prelude to the renewal of desire. His notion of mourning in this sense may be said to represent the blind spot of the ideology of modern capitalist culture, an ideology that functions by suppressing or keeping at bay the "enigmatic" existential and philosophical questions raised by loss. However, although "On Transience" may represent an elaborate act of ideological self-evasion when it comes to the Freudian analysis of grief, it would be wrong to liken its author's aesthetics of mourning to the later, more cynical notions of loss that belong to a postmodern perspective. Indeed, despite the radical implications of his espousal of what he calls "transience value," his theory of mourning still presupposes a whole and durable object, although the viability of such an object comes into question at least partially over the course of his career.[35] Thus, the essay should be considered as the ultimate argument for the ideal of successful mourning and not as an excursus into the more uncertain territory beyond mourning. As Bowie observes, the position eventually taken by Lacan stands in direct opposition to Freud's implicit assumptions in "On Transience," because, for the French theorist, "there is no point in daydreaming of a future cataclysm, in reminding the physical object or the psychological theory of its coming disintegration, for the disastrous separation of desire from its object has already occurred. Such is the price that human beings unwittingly pay for their admission to language and to culture."[36]

From the Riddle to the Enigma

Under the auspices of the first topic, Freud describes the work of mourning as a process that is regulated by a methodical, bit-by-bit meter and that gradually dissolves the riddle of loss. In his later work, however, we see that he increasingly comes to regard mourning as an enigma to which neither the layperson nor the psychoanalyst possesses a ready solution. The transition from this account to his later, more "sentimental" views becomes evident if we examine a letter to Ludwig Binswanger dated April 12, 1929. Written in response to the death of Binswanger's son, Freud reminds his friend that his own dead daughter would have been thirty-six years old that day:

Although we know that after such a loss the acute state of mourning will subside, we also know we shall remain inconsolable and will never find a substitute. No matter what may fill the gap, even if it be filled completely, it nevertheless remains something else. And actually this is how it should be. It is the only way of perpetuating that love which we do not want to relinquish.[37]

Contradicting his own claims as articulated in *Mourning and Melancholia* and "On Transience," Freud now acknowledges that the rupture occasioned by the death of a loved one may never be repaired, that the replacement of a cherished object may in fact be impossible, and with the optative pronouncement, "This is how it should be," reframes the question of mourning in ethical terms.

After the introduction of the death instinct and the articulation of his second model of the psyche (comprising ego, id, and superego), Freud's initial confidence in the work of mourning appears to waver. We increasingly come to find him expressing doubts regarding not only the possibility of a successful mourning without residue, but also the benefits of analytic therapy. When he comes in *The Ego and the Id* (1923) to regard the ego as a precipitate of lost attachments, he inaugurates a more problematic, less mechanistic way of conceiving of loss. Although in *Mourning and Melancholia* he posits the resolution of grief through the detachment of the libido from the object, in his investigation of the new topic of the structure of the psyche, he views mourning and melancholia as processes that instead deepen the relation to the object, allowing for the very formation of identification (19:28–29).[38]

After writing *The Ego and the Id*, Freud essentially abandons the concept of mourning as an independent topic of discussion and reabsorbs it into the larger category of the phenomenon of repetition. Already by the time of *Beyond the Pleasure Principle* (1920), he had come to consider nostalgia as a manifestation of the death instinct, as a symptom of the subject's natural drive toward regression and the recapitulation of an earlier emotional state.[39]

Freud's ostensible goal in the essay is to introduce the death drive, to establish that every organism strives to return to an inorganic state, that "the aim of all life is death" (18:38).[40] More than characterizing the response to the loss of an object, a state of mourning in *Beyond the Pleasure Principle* comes to characterize the very ontology of the psyche, thereby putting at risk the pragmatic economy that originally underlies the notion of *Trauerarbeit*. In the movement from the first to the second Freudian topic, we thus proceed from a view of loss as a contingent event to that of loss as a structural component of the very functioning of the psyche, a factor that enforces a traumatic tempo of "the perpetual recurrence of the same thing" (18:22). Indeed, the theoretical postulate of a drive per se comes to be defined in this context as "an urge inherent in organic life to restore an earlier state of things" (18:36).

The essay is crucial to determining the role played by the concept of mourning in the progression from Freud to Lacan. If the hypothesis of the death drive is accepted at face value, as it is in Lacan's theory, it is clear that the importance of mourning as a psychic activity is diminished or downplayed by way of contrast to the predominant task of accepting the death drive as an ontological reality. On the other hand, the introduction of the death drive might also be considered not as the psychoanalytic equivalent of a Heideggerian "event," but as an ambivalent and paradoxical gesture that, as Derrida has suggested, exemplifies the only adequate response to the "spectral," mournful nature of analysis.[41] As I will show in what follows, Derrida assumes an antithetical relation to Lacan by reconciling the death drive to the concept of mourning. Rather than aim at a rhetoric "beyond" bereavement, he maps a terrain of "hauntology" that represents an ethically and politically energized space of unresolvable "midmourning," a domain of remembrance in which the subject is perpetually reexposed to history rather than removed from it.

According to Derrida, the procedures and the stakes of Freud's gambit in *Beyond the Pleasure Principle* are far from simple and come into play in the staging of an elaborate scene of writing. The French philosopher's brilliant analysis of Freud's language demonstrates the self-negating, nonpositional structure of the essay by tracing the appearance and disappearance of the elusive death drive throughout the text. The reluctance of Freud to reach any decisive conclusion with respect to the existence of the death drive is enacted by the guileful rhetorical procedures of an argument that mimes walking without advancing, repeatedly pretending to move a step forward without gaining an inch of ground (as Derrida notes, Freud uses the expression "one step further" ten times in the essay). The very title of Derrida's essay, "Legs de Freud," propagates a punning confusion of terms (legs, legacy) as a means of burlesquing Freud's repeated claim to proceed another step forward, a claim that inaugurates each of the essay's seven paragraphs.

The most cogent elucidation of Freud's rhetoric focuses on the psychoanalyst's celebrated anecdote relating his grandson's habit of playing the fort-da game, in which the child symbolically acts out the disappearance and reappearance of his mother by casting away and retrieving a toy. Having recounted his grandson's actions, Freud concludes: "No certain decision can be reached from the analysis of a single case like this" (18:16). Compulsively repeated, the game does not necessarily imply the intrusion of the death drive, as the analyst acknowledges, because it is possible to explain the economy of the game in terms of a desire for mastery [*Bemächtigungstrieb*]: "They [the games] give no evidence of the operation of tendencies beyond the pleasure principle, that is of tendencies more primitive than it and independent of it" (18:17). Derrida argues persuasively that Freud replicates the action of the fort-da game in the rhetoric of his own essay, painfully advancing his thesis, only to dismiss it soon after and start over from scratch. The anecdote, in other words, comprises a *mise en abîme* of the overall shape of the essay's argument. This interpretation of the essay is important not only because of its recognition of the logic of *différance* behind Freud's claims about the relation of the death drive to the pleasure principle, but also because it makes available a new angle of reflection on the question of mourning.

In a footnote to *Beyond the Pleasure Principle*, Freud obliquely alludes to the death of his daughter Sophia: "When this child was five and three quarter, his mother died. Now that she was really gone (O-O-O), the little boy showed no sign of grief. It is true that in the interval a second child had been born and had roused him to a violent jealousy" (18:16). Derrida dismisses the clumsy attempts of some psychobiographers to demonstrate a causal link between the death of Sophia Freud in 1920 and the publication of the essay in the same year.[42] Adopting a more speculative manner, he will draw on the biographical background of the fort-da story in the course of reinterpreting the repetitive activity of the game as the work of "midmourning," a concept that for the French philosopher "forms an original and irreducible category" and that should be considered as "introjection and/or incorporation, mid-mourning here being represented by the bar between and/or, which for structural reasons seems to me as necessary as it is necessarily impure."[43] Implicit in the movement of the fort-da is the endlessly deferred possibility of the restoration of the lost object, a suspended outcome that betokens an insuperable ethical indecision, contravening the more mechanical, bit-by-bit economy of the *Trauerarbeit*. The fort-da story, Derrida ventures, perhaps offers Freud a means of recalling Sophie, Ernst's mother, in a manner that allows the grandfather to usurp the psychic position of his grandson: "Freud can have the desire to recall [her] and to undertake all the necessary work of her mourning. In order to speak of this one could mobilize the entire analysis of *Mourning and Melancholia* . . . and the entire descendance of this essay. I will not do so here."[44]

The reason why Derrida refrains from discussing this "descendance," I suspect, is his awareness that his description of the fort-da as an interminably repetitive process of midmourning in which all object-relations conform to a logic of the *"revenant"* does not belong to the economy of Freud's metapsychological project in *Mourning and Melancholia*. Mourning, pathological mourning, and melancholia adhere in this essay to a strictly categorized taxonomy, a dialectic in which failure and success in the overcoming of loss are sharply contrasted. If it is true that the horizon beyond this dialectic, which is first glimpsed in *Beyond the Pleasure Principle*, elicits a softer but more compelling gesture of mourning, such a horizon is made available only by a fundamental break with the conceptual scheme of *Mourning and Melancholia*. Between the metapsychological aim of *Mourning and Melancholia* and the more speculative undertaking of *Beyond the Pleasure Principle*, Freud himself recognized a clear divide, as he confesses in his *Selbstdarstellung*: "The attempt [at metapsychology] remained no more than a torso; after writing two or three papers—*Instincts and Their Vicissitudes, Repression, The Unconscious, Mourning and Melancholia*, etc.— I broke off, wisely perhaps, since the time for theoretical predications of this kind had not yet come" (20:59). Although Freud is keen in his essay to point out that speculation does not entail an abandonment of clinical observation or a surrender to the consolation of philosophy, he is adamant that the regime of psychoanalysis is now significantly different from that of a "theoretical predication." Midmourning, the crucial economy of the fort-da, is not a "theoretical predication" like the concept of *Trauerarbeit*, but an intransitive and quasiontological concept.

Derrida regards the speculative logic of "the beyond," of the step forward that goes nowhere, of the step that always comes back as a *revenant*, as raising a possibility for psychoanalysis to articulate a politics and ethics of midmourning.[45] Unlike the *Arbeit* of mourning, midmourning does not pretend to achieve a successful "dismissal" of the lost object, but instead adopts an inconclusive psychic rhythm of oscillation between introjection and incorporation. Although in his essays Freud can seem less than precise on the distinction between introjection and incorporation, often presenting the terms as synonyms, Nicolas Abraham and Maria Torok have insisted on the necessity of recognizing incorporation, rather than introjection, as defining all the possible pathological forms and variations of mourning.[46] Incorporation in this sense should be viewed as the first stage of introjection because the first means of introjection is through oral incorporation. As opposed to incorporation, introjection does not signal a magical, instantaneous recuperation of the object, but follows instead a gradual course. To amplify the distinction, Abraham and Torok liken incorporation to a photograph and introjection to a metaphor. By educing the concept of midmourning and thus demarcating a zone between introjection and incorporation, Derrida highlights the interchangeability in Freud's perspective of the two categories differentiated by Abraham and Torok. His point is that the game of lost and found is never resolved (through introjection) or permanently jeopardized (though rigid incorporation), but simply repeated ad infinitum.

The consequences of Derrida's reading of *Beyond the Pleasure Principle* are much more than rhetorical, however. The oscillation between introjection and incorporation that he outlines in "Legs de Freud" corresponds to an ethical standpoint, a subject position that refuses to completely assimilate and "cannibalize" the object. The impossibility of successfully mourning the Other clears a space for what Derrida defines as the "hauntology": a domain inhabited by the *revenants* and *arrivants* of memory.[47] As we have noted already, the French philosopher clearly resists granting too much credit to the thesis of the death instinct at the core of *Beyond the Pleasure Principle*: "There are those who have taken [Freud's argument] 'seriously,' and have constructed an entire discourse about the seriousness of the Beyond. . . . In this respect, the most interesting and spectacular case, I believe, is that of Lacan."[48] Unlike Lacan, Freud never completely abandons the idea of a subjectivity achieved through the interiorization of memory.

Of all his writings, Freud's last essay, "Analysis Terminable and Interminable," ought to be deemed the most informed by not only theoretical but also ethical concerns, precisely on account of its emphasis on an endless, irresolvable hermeneutic effort. Freud comes to conceive of his contribution as no more than the romantic frettings of a melancholic thinker, a brooder whose proposal of the clash between the death and life instincts as the blueprint of psychic life is hardly original; he even describes himself as a sufferer of "cryptomnesia" for having appropriated the very idea of strife as a structural aspect from Empedocles (23:245).

At the conclusion of "Analysis Terminable and Interminable," Freud declares that the two topics posing the greatest difficulty to the analyst are both related to castration. Penis envy in the female psyche and emasculated resentment in the male together constitute the "bedrock" of analytic therapy, the ultimate form of lack beyond which it is impossible for criticism to penetrate (23:252). Freud's assertion of the universality of castration will be reformulated by Lacan as the a priori condition of psychic life, according to an ethic of human finitude that performs the function of a psychological imperative.[49] Lacan will take Freud's last words as the first principle of his own theory and practice, diverging from his predecessor's example, however, to make of necessity a virtue by teaching not merely a stoic acceptance of loss, but a cynically rapid acquiescence to lack. Through the "*séance courte*," a method he increasingly favors over the course of his career, he achieves a gradual transformation of Freudian melancholy into the rhythm and character of contemporary life, where the logic of castration and that of speed are congruent.

At this point, it might be useful to dwell at greater length on the different responses of Derrida and Lacan to the Freudian theory of mourning. Psychoanalysis, like cinema, is for Derrida essentially a "*science du fantôme*," a spectral discourse that resonates closely with the phantasmatic effects enforced by contemporary technoscience.[50] However, his resorting to the language of the supernatural does not so much foreclose the question of mourning as it reframes the problematic with a gain in traumatic intensity at every step. As his reading of *Beyond the Pleasure Principle* demonstrates, his primary objective is to bring to light, both within the terms of psychoanalytic inquiry and of the general culture at large, the concept of midmourning as a means of continually renegotiating or rephrasing the question of loss, and hence as a means of combating its reification as absence. Derrida is more than aware of the urgent need for psychoanalysis to find a way to respond to this question. In his most recent philosophical assessment of the state of the discipline, he observes that whereas one historical condition in the crisis of psychoanalysis may be the cultural obsolescence of Europe, which has been hastened by the emergence of an increasingly American "global" capitalism, another factor that must be acknowledged is the "autoimmune disorder" of the discipline itself, the refusal of psychoanalysis to mourn its own past identity (that is, as a critique of traditional views of the family or the law), a denial that is "equally responsible for [the discipline's] actual crisis."[51]

In fact, I would argue that Lacan's "liquidation" of the question of mourning does not consort with Derrida's more complicated stance. The disparate readings of *Beyond the Pleasure Principle* propounded by Derrida and Lacan sponsor two radically dissimilar perspectives on the proper role of mourning in contemporary culture. According to the Derridean view, the practices of mourning, introjection, and incorporation structure the cultural space of deconstruction, a space that appears qualitatively different from that of postmodernity and redolent of modernist pathos. As Lyotard observes, the modern aesthetic indulges nostalgia, whereas the postmodern thrives in presenting the "unpresentable."[52] Derrida's thought ought to be understood as a synthesis of nostalgia and sublime epistemological pride in the territory of what I define in the second half of this book as a critical postmodernity. Unlike Lacan, Derrida still seems to believe in the ethical potential of a subjective, poetic, phantasmatic history. According to the Lacanian view, the ontological conditions of the death instinct and castration ground the skeptical knowingness of a posthistorical epoch. For LaCapra, Lacan is at fault for proposing a conception of desire that is determined more by "absence" [*manque à être*] than by loss.[53] And yet, paradoxically, by taking the death drive "seriously," Lacan, unlike Derrida, pretends to have reached an "enlightened position" of wisdom immune to melancholia. It is this attitude that defines the way in which the hegemonic cultural ideology has reconfigured the psychic life of loss for postmodern times.

The Future of the Past: Lacan's Return to Freud

The investigation of the activities of reminiscence and mourning remains a centerpiece of Freud's project throughout his career, ultimately resulting in the enlargement of the notion of remembrance to include the phenomena of repetition and transference. In a sense, it might be said that he never advances his conception of the subject beyond the last paragraph of *The Interpretation of Dreams*, which establishes the basic grammatical tense of all psychic expressions, including dreams, as the past rather than the present or the future: "By picturing our wishes as fulfilled, dreams are of course leading us into the future. But this future, which the dreamer takes as the present, has been moulded by his indestructible wish into the perfect likeness of the past" (5:621). That his theory of subject formation is inflected toward the past, and hence essentially historical, is confirmed by Freud's final, melancholic view of the fate of analytic therapy. In contrast, by privileging the explication of desire, Lacan's theory appears to take the future as the basic horizon of psychoanalytic interpretation. As he affirms in his celebrated lecture "Function and Field of Speech and Language in

Psychoanalysis," delivered in Rome in 1953: "Analysis can have for its goal only the advent of a true speech and the realization by the subject of his history in his relation to a future" (E 88, F 302).

In "Function and Field of Speech and Language in Psychoanalysis," Lacan praises the Freudian values of anamnesis, remembrance, and the historicity of the subject and opposes them to the techniques that transform therapy into an affair of the *hic et nunc* and thereby hasten the behaviorist degradation of the true spirit of psychoanalytic inquiry (E 40–48, F 247–56). At first glance, Lacan's espousal not only of memory but of Freud's specific terminology appears to situate the French theorist decisively within the bounds of the modernist ethos of mourning. However, Lacan's return to Freud and reading of the past are far from simple or self-evident positions. Through a reinterpretation of Freudian theory and a reorientation of psychoanalysis around the locus of language and the Symbolic, Lacan explores a territory that looks more like an attitude of jaded knowingness toward the past than anguished mournfulness. We might note as well that in his explication of the death drive, Lacan, unlike Freud, is never interested in defining the drive as the inherent instinct of organic life to resume an earlier state of things. To the contrary, at the end of his seminar on the ego, Lacan comes to perceive the death drive as the mask of the symbolic order in as much as the symbol stands for the absent object in a potentially infinite Symbolic that "has never been realized."[54] Unlike Freud, who keeps a more literal interest in questions of life and death, Lacan mainly seems concerned to achieve the decentering and deconstruction of the subject beyond the imaginary boundaries of the ego, according to an antihumanist agenda that more than once has been defined as postmodern.[55] Such a definition might apply on account not only of the jaded knowingness that seems to pervade both the French analyst's stance and certain strains of contemporary culture, but also of a fundamental, shared indifference toward questions of the past, of history, and of justice. For Lacan, mourning no longer represents a riddle, as it did for Freud, but rather an a priori solution to the question of loss.

In what follows, I will argue that Lacan's treatment of the past and of the question of mourning not only differs from the classic precedent of Freud, but in a number of crucial aspects also exemplifies the "stylistic" and economic principles of postmodernity. Here it would be worthwhile to consider the role of the notion of the "future anterior" in the larger context of Lacanian theory. Lacan characterizes the achievement of a formal, psychoanalytic theory of language in "Function and Field of Speech and Language in Psychoanalysis" as dependent on an understanding of the process by which the patient "brings back into present time the origins of his own person":

> He does this in a language that allows his discourse to be understood by his contemporaries, and which furthermore presupposes their present discourse. Thus it happens that the *recitation of the epos* may include a discourse of earlier days in its own archaic, even foreign language, or may even pursue its course in present time with all the *animation of the actor*, but it is like an indirect discourse isolated in *quotation marks* within the thread of narration, and, if the discourse is played out, it is on a stage implying the presence not only of the chorus but also of *spectators*. (E 47, F 255)

As Kaja Silverman has pointed out, Lacan in fact proposes a very different treatment of the past and of the function of mourning.[56] The true psychoanalytic act, Silverman remarks, is interpreted by Lacan as the advent of a full or mature mode of speech, a manner of language usage by means of which the patient does not subjugate the past but rather claims it, cites it "through the signifier."[57] If, according to Freud, reliving and repeating the past is the way to overcome it, adopting a poetics of animated quotation, according to Lacan, permits the subject to relive his or her own past through performance, thus evincing the deliberate artificiality of a postmodern politics of memory.[58] The task Lacan assigns to the patient is the knowing, deliberate "recitation" of his or her past, not its repetition. The "full speech" of analysis depends ultimately on the analysand's responsiveness to the necessity of addressing a spectator rather than of incorporating a tragic chorus, and hence on the subject's capacity to allow the emergence of a simulacrum of the past, not its replica.

The temporality of analysis for Lacan thus ideally ought to be aligned not toward the past, but toward the future anterior, that domain where the subject can make sense of his or her history in the course of a shifting relation to experience: "What is realized in my history is not the past definite of what was, since it is no more, or even the present perfect of what has been in what I am, but the future anterior of what I shall have been for what I am in the process of becoming" (E 86, F 300). Lacan's insistence on the future past might be explained by considering the retroactive achievement of meaning that language performs, for only at the end of a sentence, only a posteriori, does the logic of the contingent elements of a symbolic structure begin to appear.[59] To be sure, Lacan betrays some ambivalence between the future of the psyche and the influence of the past, as his iden-tification of the tense of desire with the future anterior demonstrates. It must be noticed, however, that the retrospective dimension of the human temporality of desire, as he explains it, cannot be interpreted as mournful. The Lacanian dialectic between the anticipatory and retrospective axes of desire plays a logical function rather than a truly temporal one, for the style of knowledge he prefers revolves around an interminable experience of lack, rather than a historical event of loss. Although the sort of knowing-ness permitted by the future anterior seems to provide logical and philo-sophical comfort, we might ask what are the ethical implications of a strictly logical understanding of temporality? In the French analyst's culti-vation of the idea of the future anterior, we should recognize the strategic intent not to succumb, as Freud did, to cultural nostalgia. Samuel Weber has called attention to the fact that by supplanting Freud's perfect tense with the future anterior, Lacan throws into question the very definition of subjectivity in terms of the internalization of memory. The "past," after all, can never be entirely remembered if it is regarded as never having fully taken place.[60] The paradoxical logic of the future anterior, then, undoes the very notion of subjectivity, replacing the conventional idea of the subject with what Lyotard calls the "unpresentable" of presentation itself (the *ob-jet a, Das Ding*, etc.) and which he identifies as the fundamental temporal experience of postmodernity, thus as a refusal of history.[61] Although La-can's undoing of the traditional notion of subjectivity might be considered one of his more important accomplishments, it is puzzling how he rarely seems to address the ethical consequences of his positions.

The Lost Object of Psychoanalysis

Lacan's central endeavor, Malcolm Bowie suggests, should be identi-fied with his recuperation of a notion of human mind that is compatible with radical transience.[62] For Freud, however he may have hedged his po-sition with caveats and pessimistic qualifications, at least one perfect, psy-chological "object" in which transience could be written off was imagina-ble. Lacan instead constructs a scenario according to which the psyche must work precisely to overcome the Freudian ideal of the object as an in-tegral, historically unique entity that requires mourning when lost. Recog-nition of the pervasive presence of death in the structural organization of all human production is for Lacan the *conditio sine qua non* of access to language and culture. In place of the "great expense of time" that Freud claims is necessary to complete the bit-by-bit recapitulation of the past and thus the overcoming of loss, Lacan will substitute the interminable, monotonous tempo of lack, a rhythm that flattens the singularity of the object and renders its historical circumstances irrelevant. Whereas Freud envisions the process of mourning as structured by an orderly, step-by-step advance in the direction of forgetfulness, Lacan may be said to focus ultimately on the psychoanalytic domain that lies beyond mourning. By taking such a decisive step, however, and embracing the rhetoric of "the beyond," his theory runs the risk of depriving analysis of the very concept of mourning that constitutes an important part of its cultural capital.[63]

It would be wrong to regard the Lacanian turn as fundamentally tragic in tone, particularly if we consider the last phase in the development of his thinking. In light of this concluding phase, as Bowie observes, Lacan's outlook, for all its emphasis on death and transience, finally aligns the tragedy of mourning in continuity with the human comedy of desire. The French analyst's ultimate accomplishment, then, might be seen as an acute spectacularization of the tragicomic vanity of human motives.[64] Given his frequent insistence that psychoanalysis is not a psychology, because in his view our "emotions" are staged in advance by an external, symbolic machine, the difficulty of identifying mourning with a specific affect or psychical work in Lacan should come as no surprise. As he puts the point in *Séminaire VII*, the most personal feelings, such as the anguish of mourning, can be delegated to the tragic chorus of others with no loss of sincerity, a theater or domain of intersubjectivity that provides emotional expression and reflection for the subject: "Therefore, you don't have to worry; even if you don't feel anything, the Chorus will feel in your stead."[65]

If, on the one hand, Lacan wants to demonstrate how we may fulfill certain psychic obligations through the intervention of the Other, his observations, on the other hand, betray a cynical acceptance of emotional simulacra. As Žižek puts it, while our surrogates performs for us the work of mourning, "we can spend time on more profitable exploits."[66] Commenting on the French analyst's choice of metaphor, Žižek arrestingly has proposed an analogy between the canned laughter of contemporary television and the "canned" grief exhibited by Lacan's tragic chorus.[67] In this sense, we can say that his promotion of the intersubjective dimensions of psychological experience consorts for Lacan with a downplaying of affect, of emotional engagement. Indeed, his theory hinges on the mobilization of simulacra of feelings that are radical in kind, which is to say not simulacra of an original, authentic psychical experience, but simulacra of no unique, determinate source.

Not only does the tragic Freudian drama of the lost object acquire a radical new meaning under Lacan's rethinking, but also, more importantly, the impression that Freud conveys of analysis as an act of cultural mourning for a certain romantic conception of nostalgia is undermined by the French theorist's persistent recourse to the knowing rhetoric of the Enlightenment. If this rhetoric sounds more contemporary than Freud's, we might ask whether such currency is a virtue or a liability. In a sense, Lacan's psychoanalysis might be viewed as "too timely" for its own good. Lacan, as Žižek argues, ought to be considered a postmodernist by virtue of his rejection of the modernist myth of a historically authentic, if catastrophic, relation between subject and object in favor of the nonchalant acceptance of irredeemable alienation: "It is only with Lacan that the postmodernist break occurs, insofar as he thematizes a certain real, traumatic kernel whose status remains deeply ambiguous: the Real resists symbolization, but it is at the same time its own retroactive product."[68]

To understand Lacan's "resolution" of the question of mourning, it will help to determine his account of the object and its relationship to desire. On this score, it is important to note that his thinking differs significantly from the thesis Freud first began to develop in *Three Essays*. Freud's proposal that the subject is comprised of a legible narrative or history of object-loss becomes in Lacan's revision the parodic image of a subject premised on the prior absence of the lost object, the principle of *objet a*. Of course, the status of the object changes according to the different phases of Lacan's theory. Yet we can say that throughout his work, he never arrives at an equivalent of the Freudian narrative of object-loss. For Lacan, as Weber points out, the idea of the "loss" of an object is misleading, because the *objet a* is constituted precisely by the presumption of its loss: "Anxiety, therefore, arises not from the loss of an object, but rather from the loss of this loss or as Lacan puts it, 'When the lack comes to be lacking' [*quand le manque vient à manquer*]. . . . The 'loss' that triggers anxiety, then, is not that of an object that once was possessed, but rather the effacement, through objectification, of what Lacan refers to as the 'lack.'"[69] Anxiety is occasioned not by loss, in other words, but by the proximity of the incestuous object.[70] Moreover, Lacan comes to regard as paradoxical the very Freudian notion of a "lost object," because the object is, properly speaking, always "found again" [*wiedergefunden*]: "The object is by nature a refound object. That it was lost is a consequence of that—but after the fact."[71] Assigning a merely retroactive value to the loss of the *objet a*, Lacan radically reduces the scope and importance initially given by Freud (and subsequently by other prominent theorists such as Melanie Klein) to the concept of mourning.

We may recognize two main periods of Lacan's thought regarding the object. The first, which runs through the end of the 1950s, provides a structuralist assessment of the unconscious in terms of language, in terms of the synchronic horizon of a symbolic order governed by the death drive. The human being is "mortified" and caught in the web of the signifier.[72] In this phase, Lacan places little importance on the object, a notion he defines simply as a point of imaginary fixation on which a psychic drive may satisfy itself.[73] The point is not to credit the process of mourning a lost, intact, psychically resonant object, which by definition belongs to the fraudulent territory of the imaginary, but to accept the absence that organizes the symbolic domain. Lacan instead wishes to promote the virtue of "symbolic recognition" [*la reconnaissance symbolique*] at the expense of "imaginary reminiscence" [*la réminiscence imaginaire*] or, in other words, the understanding and performance of symbolic laws rather than the sentimental recovery of psychic content.[74]

The second period of Lacan's thought, which runs from the 1960s onward, no longer construes the symbolic around the locus of the death drive, but around the complex negotiations of the pleasure principle. During this stage the most prominent organizing principle in Lacan's theory is that of "the Real," the traumatic kernel of the psyche that resists symbolization. Lacan will reorient his theory around a different rhetoric, no longer "representing" loss and lack, but "incarnating" it. In this context, the concept of mourning becomes increasingly superfluous. In *Séminaire XI*, for example, he will refine the idea of a tantalizing, original absence with the introduction of the *objet a*, a term that at once designates the cause of desire as well as the embodiment of lack. The *objet a* cannot be understood as a cognitive object, as it bears the mark of irreducible heterogeneity, being a sort of transcendental category for the "framing" of desire and the staging of its drama.[75] Concepts such as *objet a, la chose,* or *le phallus* that Lacan typically substitutes for the object do not so much revolve around emptiness as materialize it through a sort of inert presence.[76] The originality of the notion of an "incarnated loss" becomes more apparent when we turn our attention to the role of the phallus in Lacanian theory. We might agree with Žižek that unlike prephallic objects such as the breast or excrement, the phallus is not merely a lost object, but an object that gives a positive status to loss.[77] Insofar as Lacan conceives the symbolic order as organized by castration, the phallus becomes the most important "object" of his theory of mourning, which ultimately undertakes to describe, and thus in some sense to effect, the decline of the Oedipus complex.

When we think of desire in this light, we should not imagine it as an appetite or instinct. In a sense, there is no real difference between the desire for life or death in Lacan's theory, on account of his definition of the concept in terms of language, the medium in which the "death" of the object and the "life" of the symbolic order are one and the same. A fundamental negativity of desire pervades the subconscious, according to which the most radical of desires is the desire of death, the desire to submit as a subject to the destructive automatism of the symbolic order.[78] The Freudian poles of Eros and Thanatos as established in *Beyond the Pleasure Principle* are not to be found in Lacan's theory, and the *coincidentia oppositorum* that inflects his thought cannot but influence his approach to mourning as well. As we shall see, Lacan finds the only adequate interpretation of mourning in "structural" terms, as mourning of the phallus. The concept in his theory plays a specific role in the phenomenology of desire but again seems to correspond to the satisfaction of the a priori conditions of desire, not the psychological work necessitated by loss. The consequence of such a position is that mourning is denied any historical significance as a response to the loss of a temporally situated object, raising the possibility of an aporetic interpretation of history. Lacan, as we will see, pushes this line of argument to its extreme logical limit, finally reading the Holocaust as a figure of the very structural trauma that informs life.

Lacan does not profess a model of desire grounded in romantic nostalgia for the lost object, but rather in an enlightened acceptance of loss as the condition of psychic functioning.[79] There is indeed no place for romantic nostalgia in this model, but rather only for a continuous "performance" of loss that is practiced at the synchronic level of the signifying chain, in the absence of any imaginary consolation, and that supplies the basis of a postmodern politics of transience and detachment. The Lacanian subject knows that the different, "historical" objects of desire are only simulacra.

What remains to be seen is whether such a jaded, detached consciousness will be revealed as the ultimate fate of analysis. Many critics, including Bowie and Julia Kristeva, have criticized Lacan for unduly simplifying the question of loss and suffering, dispensing with the problematic through "word magic" and "matheme magic."[80] According to Kristeva, Lacan's insistence on lack as the basis of *parlêtre* is so inflexible and unconditional that it runs the risk of necessitating an acting out of distress, when a phantasmatic expression of loss would have been sufficient.[81] Preempting the possibility of analytic therapy to question the vicissitudes of castration and mourning, processes endowed by Lacan with a magical performative value, he threatens to undermine the raison d'être of psychoanalytic therapy.

Postmodern Hamlet

In recent years some of the most original interpreters of *Hamlet*, among whom we ought to count Lacan and Derrida, have stressed not so much the prince's proverbial inability to act, but the role of mourning in his drama. In *Specters of Marx*, for example, Derrida commences his exploration of the themes of haunting, spectrality, and mourning with a rereading of the Shakespearean tragedy. Of course, his ultimate aim in this important book is a political and philosophical meditation on the destiny of Marxism, but his explication of the play, to which I will briefly turn later, presents interesting points of comparison with the Lacanian interpretation. Whereas Derrida's reading of the play consistently affirms a view of mourning as an endless, enigmatic task, Lacan's interpretation of *Hamlet*, albeit ostensibly revolving around the problematic of mourning, effectively dissolves the specificity and ethical urgency of loss and its psychical acknowledgment, as we shall see.

The seminar, "Desire and Its Interpretation," in which Lacan devotes seven lectures to *Hamlet*, is the only text in which Lacan overtly tackles the issue of mourning. Although they propound different approaches to the tragedy, both Lacan and Derrida affirm the centrality of the problematic that the latter defines as the "spectral anteriority of the crime," a problematic that frames the crime of the Other, in contrast to the essential dilemma of self-identification in *Oedipus Rex*.[82] For Lacan, this means not only that the primary guilt and criminality delimited by the narrative belong to Claudius (and Hamlet's father, whose sins have not been redeemed in time), but also that the libidinal economy of the drama is properly focused not around Hamlet's desire, but rather around Gertrude's desire as incorporated by Hamlet. In Lacan's interpretation of the play, desire becomes a condition painfully "achieved," rather than instinctively found. For the French analyst, Hamlet's predicament brings to light the involvement of the *Bildung* of desire with the question of symbolic castration, and mourning becomes just an occasion for the definition of desire. According to Freud's classic reading, Hamlet suffers from an Oedipus complex that remains unresolved through the end of the narrative and accounts for his inability to act. Lacan, on the contrary, credits Hamlet with overcoming his Oedipus complex through acceptance of his symbolic castration, a method first posited by Freud in his essay, "The Dissolution of the Oedipus Complex" (1924) (19:171–79).[83]

Hamlet is the tragedy around which mourning is theorized in psychoanalysis, but it is also itself an object of cultural mourning. Freud, in his reading of the drama, decides to mourn or memorialize the original enigma of psychoanalysis, the Oedipus complex. Lacan, however, will react to the institutionalization of the Freudian reading not with nostalgia, but rather with disenchanted skepticism. If, for Freud, Hamlet is the prototype of the melancholic, for Lacan, the prince instead exemplifies the condition of the subject finding his own desire.[84] Lacan regards the main dramatic cruxes of the tragedy as manifesting the very mise-en-scène of desire, according to the graph "Che Vuoi."[85] The French psychoanalyst's suggestive rereading of the tragedy is exemplary of his overall approach in the following sense: it can be said that his seminars mark the transition from a Freudian focus on the object "of" desire to a new focus on the object "in" desire.[86] From this perspective, the most telling moment in the play for Lacan is the encounter between Hamlet and Gertrude in her bedroom after the performance of *The Mousetrap*, during which the prince initially tries to convince her to renounce her desire for Claudius, only to waver on confronting the reality of that desire, eventually relenting and taking his leave. Shakespeare's characters allegorically represent different positions in the process of the articulation of desire but are not to be considered as motivated by some sort of hidden psychology.

Most critical for Lacan in the process of mourning is the constitution of the object of desire, which he does not consider as a preexisting entity. This concern for object-formation takes the place of the problem of the introjection of the lost object in the Freudian theory of mourning. As we will see, the "object" in Lacan's system is formulated as a substitute for whatever the subject has been symbolically deprived of, a deprivation that calls for mourning. In this context, mourning represents not the gradual, pragmatic affirmation of the reality principle, but rather the a priori solution to the riddle of desire, a solution he associates with the acceptance of castration. Lacan's reduction of the ethics of mourning to that of desire represents a decisive step in the postmodern search for a concept of mourning compatible with the ideal of self-gratification.

Knowingness, or, The Mousetrap of Desire

According to the canonical, Freudian standpoint set forth in the *Interpretation of Dreams*, the transition from *Oedipus* to *Hamlet* registers what he calls the "secular" triumph of repression over the emotional life of mankind (4:264). This hypothesis anticipates the full-blown account of western history articulated in *Civilization and Its Discontents*. By contrast, Freud identifies the fascination of *Oedipus Rex* with the possibility of establishing an analogical relation between the cathartic resolution of tragedy and the revelatory outcome of psychoanalysis: "The action of the play consists in nothing other than the process of revealing, with cunning delays and ever mounting excitement—a process that can be likened to the work of psychoanalysis—that Oedipus himself is the murderer of Laius, but further that he is the son of the murdered man and of Jocasta" (4:262). Given that in *Mourning and Melancholia* Freud names Hamlet as the epitome of the melancholic mechanism of self-reproach, the Shakespearean drama can hardly be said to exemplify such an analogy (14:246).[87]

For Lacan, the most important aspect of Hamlet's character is not his melancholia, but a verbal wit and impulse to equivocation that make him an archetypal example of what psychoanalytic "style" or language should look like. If for Freud repression turns out to be the chief psychological condition of the drama, for Lacan, knowledge or knowingness is the principal mode of the tragedy and what distinguishes it from the classical paradigm. Hamlet knows about a crime, the denunciation of which provides the dramatic conflict as it does not in *Oedipus Rex*. In this sense, Hamlet might be said to embody allegorically the situation of consciousness after the advent of psychoanalysis, within which situation being knowledgeable about a crime does not ensure any resolution, because what matters for the subject is the "performance," rather than the cognition, of desire.[88]

What happens after Freud's epochal disclosure? How can we offer a new interpretation of *Hamlet* in the age of awareness? Lacan's approach to the drama may be seen as a direct response to this difficult problem. On the one hand, he seems intent on denying that there is something to add to his predecessor's already classic explanation: "It is to this approach so right and so balanced, to the bright impetus in Freud's intuition that we'll have to refer all that will be later imposed on us as detours and embroideries."[89] On the other hand, the French analyst frames the comparison between Oedipus and Hamlet around knowledge in such a manner as to overturn the spirit of the Freudian hermeneutic, which he suspects of enacting a decadent impulse. It is clear that through his interpretation of the Shakespearean tragedy, Lacan wants to position himself not only beyond his Viennese predecessor, but also beyond a certain reading of modernity as decadence.[90]

Could we be satisfied by Freud's remark that *Hamlet* as a modern fiction features people that in comparison with the ancients should be considered as poor degenerates? We would embrace in so doing the style of the nineteenth century. . . . We will never know, even if it is likely, if Freud at the time knew Nietzsche's work. Should Freud's reference to the moderns be enough for us? Why should modern people be more neurotic than the ancient? It is a *petitio principi*; let us venture further.[91]

Whereas Freud wants to make Hamlet into a drama of the development of subjectivity that also indicates the cultural history of the subject, Lacan wants to deny both arguments. If Freud imagines Hamlet to be modern, decadent, and repressed, Lacan pictures the prince as ironic, self-aware, and playful. He thus refuses to mourn the ritualized but unconscious world of Oedipus.[92]

Lacan's lack of interest in the issue of decadence ought to be seen as evidence of the radical incompatibility of his thinking with any historical metanarrative of the development of the subject, and hence with any exercise in cultural nostalgia.[93] The ethical quandary of the modern hero who confronts the insoluble hermeneutic circle of his or her own knowledge, according to Lacan, compels a response of feigned madness, of deliberate parody, of *faire le fou*:

This is the sense in which Hamlet's drama has the precise metaphysical resonance of the question of the modern hero. Indeed, something has changed since classical antiquity in the relationship of the hero to his fate. As I have said, the thing that distinguishes Hamlet from Oedipus is that Hamlet knows. This characteristic explains, for example, Hamlet's madness. In the tragedies of antiquity there are mad heroes, but, to the best of my knowledge, there are no heroes . . . who feign madness. Hamlet, however, does.[94]

If Freud, by insisting on a narrative of decadence, is cast in the theoretical role of an unwitting Oedipus, Lacan implies in the essay his own identification with Hamlet, whose task, like the French analyst's, is to produce puns, calembours, double entendres, and other forms of equivocation.[95] "Why," writes Lacan, "on the threshold of the modern period would Hamlet bear witness to the special weakness of future man as far as action is concerned? I am not so gloomy, and nothing apart from a cliché of decadent thought requires that we should be, although it is a cliché Freud himself falls into when he compares the different attitudes of Hamlet and Oedipus toward desire."[96]

The importance of *Hamlet* to Lacan has to do with the grounding of the play in an intersubjective dialectic of desire that discloses the centrality of the performative and "spectacularized" measures of the psyche's operation. In *Hamlet*, unlike the Oedipus cycle, there are no doubts about the spectral anteriority of the crime of the Other; the prince thus embodies a kind of consciousness that is less solipsistic than that of Oedipus reflecting on his original guilt at Colonus.[97] Elsinore may also be considered the symbolic locus of analysis because Hamlet seems, on the evidence of his virtuosic rhetorical mannerisms, much more conscious than Oedipus of his own actions as constituting a performance for an audience. There is in *Hamlet* an interpretive horizon beyond that of a chorus in the implied perspective of the spectators to whom the prince addresses his knowing theatrical and verbal displays. Defining the characteristics of a therapeutically "full" speech in "Function and Field of Speech and Language in Psychoanalysis," Lacan stresses the importance not only of the dramatic participants, but also of the spectators in the recitation of the psychoanalytic epos.[98] According to the postmodern tenets of his argument, the symbolic order is not, in fact, best or exclusively incarnated by the chorus, but by the emergent society of spectacle in which the performative aspect of every speech act must be interpreted as unveiling not only the effective nature of language, but also the contingent succession of "recitations" in which we are captured. It might be said that Freud aims, through his interpretation of *Hamlet*, to show that there is no getting beyond the Oedipal myth, that analysis recapitulates and thus elucidates the "fall" from myth into history. Lacan, however, contends that *Hamlet* performatively advances us beyond the Oedipal myth, but in the direction of the society of spectacle, rather than that of historical awareness.[99]

To better understand the parameters of Lacan's argument, it is helpful to compare his interpretation of *Hamlet* to Derrida's. Although both thinkers stress the importance of the prince's relation to others, thus refusing the solipsism of the Freudian account, Lacan's rhetoric, which is radically dissimilar from Derrida's, reflects a very different sense of the psychological terrain that lies beyond Colonus. For Derrida, Hamlet's situation within the social order of Denmark poses the infinite question of justice beyond both repression and restitution; for Lacan, the prince exemplifies an enlightened surrender to castration, effectively pointing the way to the postmodern rewriting of the ur-narrative of psychoanalysis. Derrida cogently argues that Hamlet should not be looked on as a latter-day Oedipus who has progressed further down the path of repression, but as a psyche who raises the possibility of thinking what lies beyond repression, of responding to the appeal of justice beyond vengeance and restitution.[100] Of course, such a messianic notion of justice presumes that a work of mourning can never be successful because it is the condition of being haunted by the Other that, according to Derrida, represents the ethical promise of justice. As we shall see, Lacan contends, on the other hand, that mourning in *Hamlet* achieves a drastic resolution that he equates with the acceptance of castration and thereby of the symbolic order. The problem with his instrumental interpretation of mourning as an acknowledgment of finitude, of the psyche's limitations, is the loss of historical perspective that results within his theory.

Lacan's reading of the tragedy privileges three scenes in particular: the prince's encounter with the ghost, the confrontation between Hamlet and Gertrude in her bedroom, and the graveyard scene. Of these three moments, the turning point when it comes to explaining Hamlet's overcoming of his inability to act is the scene of Ophelia's burial in the graveyard. His very focus on this dramatic crux bespeaks the discrepancy between Lacan's agenda and that of his Viennese predecessor. Indeed, he gives no credence to Freud's hypothesis that Hamlet's procrastination is motivated by the identification of his own incestuous desire with Claudius. In his opinion, Hamlet's problem is Gertrude, not Claudius,[101] for she functions not as an Oedipal object in the economy of the play but rather as the source of demand and of an excess of pleasure that paralyzes the dialectic of desire.[102] Lacan maintains that when Hamlet at last faces his mother directly, he cannot articulate his desire in accordance with the dialectic of lack. Only through Ophelia's death does Hamlet recognize the lack of an object of desire as the symbolic equivalent of castration. The object has to be made unavailable to be mourned and thus desired.

In Lacan's theory, tragic conflict is a matter of epistemology more than of pathos: the burden of the protagonist is first to recognize and acknowledge his dilemma. In *Hamlet*, the initial knowingness of the prince after being visited by the ghost is counteracted in the course of the play by the exposure of Gertrude's desire for Claudius, which the French analyst alleges is the principal source of Hamlet's procrastination.[103] Taken together, the dialogue between Hamlet and the ghost, the repudiation of Ophelia, and the confrontation with Gertrude may be said to delimit the process of procrastination in the drama. The play changes course, however, at the point of Ophelia's death and burial. Lacan observes that at the start of the action, Hamlet takes a cynical view of the mourning rites granted to his father: "Thrift, thrift, Horatio. The funeral bak'd meats / Did coldly furnish forth the marriage tables" (1.2.180–81).

The problem of mourning resurfaces dramatically during the graveyard scene, when, stung by jealousy of Laertes' demonstrations of grief, Hamlet appears to rediscover Ophelia as an object of desire. In Lacan's judgment, what this occurrence makes clear is that the tragedy's resolution depends not on the sentimental mourning of Ophelia, but on the very birth of desire for her, an event made possible by Hamlet's symbolic castration. Lacan's originality in this case is to have linked the search for the place of the object of desire to the paradigmatic work of mourning, the mourning of the phallus; ultimately, he positions this work in relation to the *Untergang* of the Oedipus complex described by Freud in his 1924 essay: "We may be able to shed some light on the decline of the Oedipus complex as mourning for the phallus if we refer to what Freud's writings tell us about the mechanism of mourning. There is a synthesis to be made here."[104] Ironically, the French theorist suggests that the "decadence" Freud decries with reference to the succession from classical to modern culture is, in fact, a necessary stage in the development of the subject and of the subject's capacity for desire.

According to Freud, the symbolic moment in which the subject overcomes the Oedipus complex is that in which he discerns the threat of castration. In the essay "The Dissolution of the Oedipus Complex," Freud presents the banishment of the complex as dependent on the frustration of desire, on painful disappointment (19:171–79). The threat of castration for the male child, which for the female finds its symbolic analog in the threat of loss of love, finally enforces the victory of narcissistic interests over libidinal cathexis. Freud declares that the process he labels *Untergang*, a word he uses to denote the "destruction" of the complex, marks the limit between normal and pathological repression (19:177). Through this word choice, which Ferenczi was moved to criticize as too extreme, Freud strongly suggests the overcoming of the Oedipal mentality.[105] However, the term also is suggestive of the overall course of Freud's theory. It indicates that after the introduction of the second topic, even the Oedipus complex must be reconsidered in a less privileged light, graduating from the weak mediation of repression to face the possibility of "abolition." What Freud defines as the *Untergang* of the Oedipus complex, then, leads to the genital stage, the apogee of the subject's sexual normalcy, a stage that, as Lacan drolly observes, presupposes a "weak mourning" [*deuil leger*] of the phallus. This development does not represent for Lacan an intermediary point on the way to consciousness so much as a foundational moment of consciousness as such, because it establishes the opportunity for the subject to find his place in the symbolic exchange by relinquishing an object—a "real thing" [*chose réelle*] that has not yet been symbolized—in favor of a signifier.[106] The difficulty for the subject is that with respect to mourning the phallus is not merely one more object among others: "Here as everywhere else, it has a place of its own, a place apart."[107] The only possible answer to such radical loss seems to be of a hyperbolically imaginary, psychotic nature.[108] Precisely because the subject is deprived of a fundamental signifier (the phallus) can a particular object come to occupy the position of the object of desire.[109] At the graveyard, Hamlet can finally recognize his desire for Ophelia, thus installing her at the phantasmatic level in the place of what he as a subject has been deprived: the phallus.

In this sense, Lacan educes a fundamental relationship between mourning of the phallus and desire, a relationship he places at the very core of the tragedy: "From one end of *Hamlet* to the other, all anyone talks about is mourning."[110] However, to assimilate the concept of mourning to the acceptance of castration means de facto to undermine its Freudian meaning and theoretical function. In *Mourning and Melancholia*, the object, prior to being lost, is whole and present to the subject, so that the work of mourning prepares the subject for the replacement of the object. In Lacan's theory, the mourning process enables the subject to achieve a new, creative relation to the object. Indeed, the French analyst overtly chastises his predecessor for failing to pursue his own line of reasoning to its logical conclusion: "What is the incorporation of the lost object? What does the work of mourning consist in? We are left up in the air, which explains the surcease of all speculation along the path that Freud nevertheless opened up in *Mourning and Melancholia.* The question hasn't been posed properly."[111] Lacan's topology of desire represents the translation of key Freudian concepts into a vivid, new vocabulary, although such reinterpretation also shifts their original meaning and purpose. The intolerable loss of the object in Freud's system becomes, in Lacan's terms, "a hole in the Real," a disruption in the overall economy of the psyche that provokes the mobilization of the entire battery of signifiers. The hole in the Real reverses for Lacan the logic of the *Verwerfung,* the process of rejecting a signifier at the symbolic level which results in its emergence in the Real because the hole provides a space on which to project that missing signifier so essential to the structure of the Other—that is, "the veiled phallus": "It is there that this signifier finds its place. Yet at the same time it cannot find it, for it can be articulated only at the level of the Other."[112] The phenomenon of the ghost in *Hamlet* is therefore the direct consequence of the prince's inability to "fill" the lack of the signifier by any means other than phantasmal images, all the more so if the proper mourning rites have not been administered, as is the case for Hamlet's father.

According to Lacan, the work of mourning entails the paradoxical performance of the entire symbolic game in order to cope with the hole in the Real, a hole that can be filled only by the totality of signifiers at the level of logos: "The work of mourning is accomplished at the level of the *logos.* I say *logos* rather than group or community, although group and community, being organized culturally, are its mainstays. The work of mourning is first of all performed to satisfy the disorder that is produced by the inadequacy of signifying elements to cope with the hole that has been created in existence, for it is the system of signifiers in their totality which is impeached by the least instance of mourning."[113] But by conceiving the work of mourning at the intersubjective level, Lacan voids the concept of the original structuring role for the psyche which it played in Freudian analysis. Lacan's treatment of mourning indeed seems intended to undermine parodically the Freudian notion of *Trauerarbeit.* Whereas Freud stresses the importance of a gradual analytic activity of bereavement, Lacan proposes a synthetic, global intervention of the signifying system, in effect revising Freud's "sorrow work" into its antithesis.

To conceive of "a hole in the Real" as the precondition of mourning is highly perplexing insofar as the Real by definition already represents a hole in discourse, and it is unclear from Lacan's explanation what it would mean to fill a hole in a hole. All indications he gives in fact make clear that any attempt by the subject to fill the hole in the Real is doomed to be ineffectual, all the more so in a culture that essentially has renounced mourning rites. Lacan does not concern himself with trying to resolve the question of mourning because what is decisive to his own understanding of desire is, in fact, an oxymoronic notion of the positive purity of loss. A hint of farce colors Lacan's reformulation of the mechanism of mourning into an intense exercise of forces, a mobilization of the entire battery of signifiers that inevitably proves unsuccessful. On a more urgent note, he insists on the paramount symbolic significance of castration, a condition that he depicts in "The Signification of the Phallus" as emblematic of the "power of pure loss."[114] For Lacan, the shadow of the phallus always falls on the subject, which is why the subject is "barred," bears the mark of his fundamental emptiness.[115] Although the defining task for the subject remains the work of mourning, such an activity represents in this case not a gradual overcoming of loss, but a traumatic renunciation of "what he has borne in sacrifice, in holocaust, to the function of the missing signifier."[116]

To summarize Lacan's position, we may draw a radical distinction between the classic, Freudian paradigm of *Trauerarbeit* and the Lacanian conception of mourning. Mourning on the latter view would be identified with the pathway of *Hilflösigkeit* on which the subject arrives at a recognition of the fundamental role played by the *coupure signifiante*, embracing its own psychic impoverishment through a recognition of the law of castration (and not only its own, but also the Other's, who for Lacan is always barred). Mourning thus loses its historicity, its capacity to register the pathos and contingency of loss, to become a sort of transcendental category of desire. The work of mourning is accomplished at the symbolic, intersubjective level in order to fill the hole in the Real. But because such a lack can never be wholly appeased, the very idea of a psychological work reveals in the end its own dispensability, its decorative status. Bearing in mind this conclusion, we may say that Lacan draws for readers the ultimate "moral" of his explication of Shakespeare's play in *Séminare VII*, published a year after his work on *Hamlet*.[117]

In his interpretation of Sophocles's *Antigone*, Lacan identifies the true problematic of the play as the "space between two deaths," rather than its overt theme of mourning.[118] He imagines this space as spanning the interval between a symbolic death—that is, castration—and an actual, biological death. Similarly, Ophelia's death in *Hamlet* represents the first presentiment of Hamlet's own impending doom, a foreboding that is recapitulated at the moment of his symbolic mortal wounding during the duel with Laertes, which itself looks ahead to the prince's literal, physical expiration. In the space between his symbolic and actual deaths, Hamlet will finally summon the resolve to kill Claudius.[119] The space between two deaths is the traumatic kernel around which the Symbolic develops; however, as Žižek notices, the concept seems to suggest the possibility of the complete erasure of historical tradition.[120] For Lacan, *Hamlet* and *Antigone* are tragedies of desire, not mourning. Lacan increasingly comes to equate this desire with the sublimity of the death instinct as such.[121] He promotes an ethics of desire, rather than of mourning, an ethics that in its insistent search for sublimity, as he makes clear in *Séminare VII*, is not interested in the value of "goodness."[122] Indeed, it is an ethics that by his own admission looks more like an aesthetic phenomenon of "shining radiance" [*rayonnement éclatant*] than a variegated moral spectrum.[123]

In this light, the end of analysis is not the accomplishment of a more or less successful mourning, or the reassertion of the integrity of the symbolic web, sustained by an identification with, or an incorporation of, the analyst. Lacan fears that the only outcome of such a process would be the irreducible nostalgia for being or having the phallus, which according to Freud dooms analysis to the condition of an interminable, ungratifying process.[124] The endless analysis conceived by Freud is replaced by a more abbreviated paradigm, according to which the impulse to melancholia is interrupted by the forceful evocation of the horizon of castration and the resulting emergence of the territory of the sublime.[125] Lacan thus envisions the end of analysis as belonging to the zone of transition from life to death, not to the domain of mourning.[126] The end of the analytic process comes to look like an encounter with a virtual simulation of death in a space in which the subject undergoes a radical loss of significance. Analysis ought to be perceived along these lines as a relentless inscribing of the horizon of transience around the life of the subject, a gradual unveiling of the tragic structure of experience: "At the end of a training analysis, the subject should reach and should know the domain and the level of the experience of absolute disarray."[127] However, this ultimate confrontation with the tragic nature of life, simulated by the end of analysis, always contains a parodic element in Lacan's theory. It is a tragedy without pathos, already informed by full knowledge of its resolution, even if such knowledge consists in the skeptical conclusion that there is no resolution. In this light, the knowingness and resignation of the Lacanian subject seem closer to the perspective of a comedian performing a slapstick routine, such as slipping on a banana peel, than to that of a tragic protagonist suffering a mysterious and sublime fate.

Lacan's reading of *Hamlet* shows the intrinsic, logical inadequacy of the mourning process, thus thematizing a real traumatic kernel that is impossible to avoid. In this sense, Lacan exhibits none of the interest shown by Freud in the integral and mythical world of Oedipus, in the Eldorado of a society that is engaged in the fullness of its ritual processes. Whereas in the Freudian model the task of recovering past experience equips the analyst to resist mass society's inclination to amnesia, in the Lacanian model, the analyst can claim no significant role as a cultural therapist. At the core of the French theorist's methodology, we find the belief that our civilization revolves around a traumatic kernel, a bit of the Real that, evoking Žižek, we might define as the obscene object of postmodernity.[128] For Lacan not only is the subject "barred" or rendered inaccessible, but the symbolic order itself is crossed out and organized around a central lack.[129] If psychoanalysis in this context has any particular value relative to the other "human sciences," it is ultimately through the rejection of any ideal of redemption, through its demystifying insistence on its own impossibility.[130] Debunking the romantic myth of plenitude, psychoanalysis in Lacan's account engages in the stoic attempt to unveil the *vanitas* of human desire and of historical phenomenology in obedience to the "anti-ideological" imperative of reality.[131] Although we can recognize the advantages of his position, we ought to scrutinize with critical rigor his denial of the task of redemption and insistence on regarding desire as a tragicomedy. We might observe in this connection that when rehearsing the history of desire, he is quick to dismiss the issues of justice and ethics as preposterous.[132]

Through his radical interpretation of the Freudian death drive, Lacan de facto abandons the belief in a hermeneutics of history. History for him comes to mean the history of desire, in the context of which Freud's introduction of the death drive represents the epochal turning point. Yet although Lacan certainly assigns to his predecessor a strategic role, it would be wrong to interpret his seminars as rites of mourning for Freud's thought or for a particular inheritance within western culture.[133] More than rituals of cultural mourning, Lacan's seminars ought to be considered as instances of sublime aesthetic shocks. In this light, it is particularly telling that at the institutional level Lacan has never felt comfortable with the kind of ritual uses to which, at different points, his *Séminaires* and *écoles* threatened to be put, more than once abolishing such institutions.[134] His aim is not to promote a particular theoretical explanation of mourning, which would be the equivalent of an ideological chimera, but through his seminars to keep alive the "grief of existing" [*la douleur d'exister*] and thus to renew the shock of the Real.[135] Writing and teaching for the French theorist thus ought to work in a fashion far from that of well-executed ritual performances. Indeed, he aims in his seminars to enforce a paradoxical pedagogical style, to teach in such a way as "to incarnate" lack by refusing, as Žižek puts it, to obliterate the distance between the Real and the Symbolic.[136]

The proper outcome of a successful Lacanian analysis might ultimately be defined as incredulity toward the metanarratives of desire, an outlook that in other words anticipates Lyotard's description of postmodernity.[137] For Lyotard, as for Lacan, historical synthesis already has become impossible: the process of mourning for the "whole" and the "one" has been completed, and the urge to melancholia is thus simply inappropriate.[138] On this view, a more appropriate response is to affirm the decidedly antimelancholic aesthetic of the sublime. The sublime attitude captures for both Lacan and Lyotard precisely what is historically extraneous or unmetabolizable about the present moment. When the imagination fails to present an object that might match the concept, the sublime brings to light the inhumanity of consciousness or the power to conceive.[139] We find, in other words, that the sublime facilitates access to a postmodern regimen of sense. According to Lyotard, if the modernist sensibility still betrays a certain nostalgia, it does so because it insists on setting forth the unpresentable as missing content with the consolation of good forms. The postmodernist mentality instead exposes the unpresentable in the presentation itself, thus avoiding any nostalgic glamorizing of the unattainable. In Lacan's theory, we experience the exhilaration of confronting the "sublime" object of psychoanalysis, of witnessing the presentation of the unpresentable, across a metamorphic spectrum of incarnations proceeding from the Real, to the phallus, to the thing, to the *objet a*. If he thus successfully avoids the enigma of mourning and the pathos of nostalgia, however, the question remains: what price must the subject in his theory pay in order to achieve such a rarefied state of sublime enlightenment?

The Holocaust According to Lacan

The cultural consequences of Lacan's idealization of the ur-narrative of castration are large insofar as his theoretical stance forecloses the possibility for psychoanalysis to accommodate any view of the unconscious as a product of historical contingency. Whereas for Freud cultural history is important to psychoanalysis, for Lacan, it is psychoanalysis that is important to cultural history. During a conference at Yale University in 1975, Lacan stressed the necessity of psychoanalysis in world-historical terms: "Psychoanalysis has a weight in history. If there are certain things belonging to history, they are things of a psychoanalytic order."[140] Like science, history for Lacan must be in tune with the logical universality of the unconscious.

It is not surprising that Lacan's deconstruction of subjectivity is accompanied by a fading of belief in history construed as the self-identical subject of self-consciousness, as Weber puts it.[141] The French analyst's adherence to the synchronic axis of language, his aversion to any organic, developmental view of the subject, and his insistence on the importance of the future past are all elements of a theory that makes it virtually impossible to invoke history as the ground of subjectivity.[142] In this sense, it can be said that a central task for Lacan is to mourn successfully the lost fullness or comprehensiveness of historical explanation. Although Lacan identifies the objective of therapy in the *Écrits* as the assumption by the subject of his own history, what he means by this remark needs to be given further consideration (E 48, F 257). What notion of history is at stake for Lacan? Do personal and collective levels of history intersect in the context of his theory? Reading the *Séminaire* on *Hamlet* reinforces the impression given by Lacan in the *Écrits* that the "facts of history" that structure the unconscious persist at an intersubjective level, such that their very articulation undermines any possibility of a historicization of culture apart from that of the individual subject (E 52, F 261). By identifying castration as the absolute precondition of the enunciation of desire, Lacan lays claim to the discovery of something of fundamental importance, something "that has never been said" [*qui n'a jamais eté dit*].[143] Whereas the subject's desire in Freud's thinking precedes castration, the fact that in Lacan's theory castration precedes desire entails a logical and chronological upheaval.

Lacan's system seems to oscillate between a "logical" conception, according to which history incarnates the articulations of desire, and a kind of parodic conception, according to which Freud must be read, as Heidegger reads the pre-Socratic philosophers, in order to achieve a gradual unveiling of truth itself.[144] On the latter view, Freud's introduction of the death drive represents the revelation or epochal disclosure of the history of desire.[145] However, where Heidegger conceives of logic as a function of time, Lacan aspires to transform history into a sort of logic.[146] Lacan's theory thus establishes a posthistorical horizon within which the vicissitudes of desire unfold beyond the question of mourning and thus beyond history. By maintaining not only the symbolic centrality of castration, but also a conception of the object (or *objet a*, to adopt one of his several terms) as being, like Yorick's skull, essentially a memento mori, he rewrites the history of desire from the point of view of its impossibilities.[147]

For the French theorist, there is no question of revealing this truth in the manner of a pessimist or an existentialist, two modes of thinking he finds as ludicrous as a historicist belief in decadence.[148] Lacan's radical resistance to a reading of contemporary culture in historical terms is finally evinced in its most extreme form through his references to the Holocaust. The definitive crisis of subjectivity arrives, as we have seen, at the moment of the subject's symbolic sacrifice of "what he has borne in sacrifice, in holocaust, to the function of the missing signifier."[149]

It is no accident of rhetoric that Lacan evokes the Holocaust and Hitler in his reading of *Hamlet* because the murder of the Jewish people constitutes the historical event par excellence that cannot be mourned, the Real of the twentieth century. The French analyst shockingly compares Hamlet's position before Claudius to that of western modernity before Hitler: "We were troubled at the time by the question of why, after all, no one assassinated Hitler. . . . Doesn't this lead back to what we are discussing here?"[150] As Lacan will make clear in his *Séminare XI*, he refuses to look at the Holocaust as a singular historical event. He even ventures to speak of the need to cast a "courageous look" at history, to recognize in the web of circumstances a testimony to our obscure and mysterious acts of sacrifice: "I would hold that no meaning given to history, based on Hegeliano-Marxist premises, is capable of accounting for this resurgence—which only goes to show that the offering to obscure gods of an object of sacrifice is something to which few subjects can resist succumbing, as if under some monstrous spell."[151] As Guyomard has observed with regard to this stage of Lacan's theory, the very attempt to establish an ethics of desire, of pure desire, seems coincident paradoxically with the monstrosity of Nazism, because desire on Lacan's view is murderous and demands sacrifices.[152] Recalling Hannah Arendt, we could say in a sense that for Lacan desire functions through the acceptance of a certain "banality of evil."[153] His reading of the Holocaust as a decisive historical rupture that provides an important figure of castration or constitutes the necessary structural trauma at the heart of civilization ought to be viewed as both a compelling and perilous strategy. It is compelling because the Holocaust indeed appears to function in contemporary culture as the obverse or end limit of comprehensible experience. Yet it is perilous because such an explanation provides a libidinal rationale for an event that from an ethical and political perspective should not be treated as somehow unavoidable. Moreover, once we grant the Holocaust a structural role in the economy of desire, we oblige ourselves to dismiss as a logical impossibility any argument for the mourning of its victims.

The implications of Lacan's positions on history and ethics have been explored and elaborated recently by readers with such different approaches as Dominick LaCapra and Slavoj Žižek, the first of whom bemoans his identification of history with structural trauma whereas the second celebrates it as a form of enlightened postmodernism.[154] LaCapra faults Lacan (as well as the Freud of *Civilizations and Its Discontents*) for having conflated absence and loss, opening up a structural but transhistorical horizon for analysis. To LaCapra's mind, such a conflation results in the dubious idea of a "melancholic configuration" that promotes paralysis or manic agitation but suppresses any possibility of mourning, and hence of any coming to terms with specific historical losses: "Indeed, specific phantoms or ghosts that possess the self or the community can be laid to rest through mourning only when they are specified and named as historically lost others."[155] However, *pace* LaCapra, I would argue on the evidence of Lacan's analysis of *Hamlet* that the French analyst does not replace mourning with a Derridean "hauntaulogie" or a "traumatic" reading of history, but with an impulse toward resolution that, however cynically presented, cannot be assimilated to the melancholic aesthetics and ethics of so-called trauma studies. Lacan considers the teleological illusion of mourning to be dangerous, preferring a feeling of exhilarated awareness to what LaCapra defines as a melancholic configuration.

It seems to me that Žižek is more convincing than LaCapra when speaking of the authentic "postmodern mood" of Lacanian psychoanalysis. He indeed draws the dividing line between modernism and postmodernism in strikingly Lacanian terms: "The lesson of modernism is that structure, the intersubjective machine, works as well if the Thing is lacking, if the machine revolves around emptiness; the postmodernist reversal shows the Thing itself as the incarnated, materialized emptiness."[156] Lacan, then, is not postmodern for Žižek because he upholds a relativist cultural credo, but because of his willingness to investigate the death drive, the void, and the domain beyond truth: "If there is an ethico-political lesson of psychoanalysis, it consists in the insight into how the great calamities of our century (from the Holocaust to the Stalinist *désastre*) are not the result of our succumbing to the morbid attraction of this Beyond but, on the contrary, the result of our endeavour to avoid confronting it and to impose the direct rule of truth and/or goodness."[157] In this light, the French theorist is not a postmodern melancholic who believes in the impossibility of an encounter with the Thing, for if he argues that the void can never be filled by an adequate object of desire, he nevertheless envisions a place for the "surplus" libidinal object that has been banished from the symbolic structure, assigning such an object to the "out of joint" domain of the Real.[158]

However, Žižek unduly radicalizes the spirit of Lacanian theory when, in the course of rebuking the "overrapid" historicization of subsequent psychoanalytic theory, he simply equates the horror of the concentration camp with a "kernel" of the Real that returns throughout history across different moments and societies. According to Žižek, the point is brought to light by the vain attempts of critics to affix the phenomenon of the concentration camp, "the perverse" obverse of twentieth-century civilization, to a specific political system: "All the different attempts to attach this phenomenon to a concrete image ('Holocaust,' 'Gulag'), to reduce it to a product of a concrete social order (Fascism, Stalinism . . .)—what are they, if not so many attempts to elude the fact that we are dealing with the Real of our civilization which returns as the same traumatic kernel in all social systems?"[159] LaCapra in his response rightly criticizes this passage as a "dubious theoreticist gesture."[160] We can say that Lacan's position finally ends in an impasse, in ethical quandaries. By pretending to achieve a psychoanalytic decoding of history, Lacan, and often the institution of psychoanalysis itself, has avoided recognition of the singular, contingent, incommensurable political events of which history is made. In the French theorist's facile answer to the agonizing question of the Holocaust, we might recognize much the same tone of knowingness that he adopts in his discussion of mourning. Transcending the imperative to mourn, analysis runs the risk of impertinence when it pretends to explain the perplexing confluence of historical and political circumstances behind the Holocaust or the Gulag by simply providing these dire predicaments with a name, that is, the Real. Yet should we not ask whether giving a name to such crises is the same thing as critically coming to terms with them?

"Here Mourning is at Fault": The Style of Analysis

Lacan insists on psychoanalysis as a strategy of demystification that from the outset proposes itself as an exercise in style, a style, however, that seems voided of either epistemological or therapeutic value, representing instead what might be regarded, following Derrida, as an "art of the evasion."[161] It is specifically in the project of affirming psychoanalysis as the paradoxical doctrine of a nihilistic knowingness beyond loss and mourning that Lacanian style takes its measure and obtains its purpose. Not accidentally, the French analyst's emphasis on style throughout his career is involved in the question of his so-called return to Freud.

After 1957, Lacan maintains that any return to Freud must be a matter of style: "Every return to Freud which might produce a lesson worthy of the name is going to occur only on the course by which the most hidden truth manifests itself in the revolutions of culture. . . . It is called: style."[162] The Lacanian idea of mourning is transformed here into a labor of style in the sense that it becomes a process through which analysis must examine the very conditions of its own enunciation. Lacan's "return" to his predecessor therefore should be looked on neither as a nostalgic act of surrender to the words of the master, nor as a redemptive mourning of culture, but as an ironic attempt to spectacularize the function of analysis. As Bowie notes, to be a follower of Freud ultimately means for Lacan to provoke the exasperation of the defenders of decorum, to reproduce the force of the original, alienating shock of psychoanalysis.[163] If Freud's thought represents the first occurrence of the traumatic event of analysis, Lacan's work represents its second more decisive iteration. Lacan, we might say, secures the destiny of psychoanalysis as a type of cultural trauma beyond melancholia.[164]

Toward the end of his career, the antimelancholic stance of Lacan's theory is expanded into a strategy that increasingly relies on the gesture of "style." Style in Lacan's theory has always meant an emphasis on the conditions of telling and of enunciation, but his insistence in the end on a mathesis and topology of the psyche seems to serve an increasingly "ornamental" purpose. Indeed, after having explored the sadism of desire and the paradoxes of *jouissance* in *Encore*, Lacan abandons altogether the vain attempt to establish an "ethics of desire" and espouses instead what he defines in *Television* (1973) as the "ethic of the Well-Spoken" [*ethique du bien dire*], which is to say an ethics of style.[165] Lacan deemphasizes the importance of affect in this essay, particularly as regards feelings of sadness and depression, two conditions that he now describes as "moral" rather than psychological problems and that consequently must be discussed in relation to the ethic of the Well-Spoken: "For example, we qualify sadness as depression, because we give it soul for support, or the psychological tension of Pierre Janet, the philosopher. But it isn't a state of the soul, it is simply a moral failing, as Dante, and even Spinoza, said: a sin, which means a moral weakness, which is ultimately located only in relation to thought, that is, in the duty to be Well-Spoken, to find one's way in dealing with the unconscious, with the structure."[166] Sadness or melancholia thus function for Lacan as unforgivable moral failings that trouble the structural consistency of the Well-Spoken domain of analysis. By denying that a feeling such as sadness might qualify as a "state of the soul" or *état d'âme*, Lacan adopts a pristinely theoretical position in order to defend the ultimate priority of those concerns he associates here with "the structure." He thus seeks to stifle any suggestion that the ethical quest for justice often depends on the ability to turn certain constellations of emotional revolt, such as melancholia, to productive ends.[167]

The paradox, Guyomard has pointed out, is that Lacan, the successful mourner of the "whole" and the "one," seems never to have achieved a complete, successful mourning of the power of language and theory as such.[168] To the mourning of that power, Julia Kristeva and Jacques Derrida have devoted important works. Although accepting the linguistic turn of psychoanalysis, Kristeva's thinking refuses the affectless detachment of Lacanian theory. In her eyes, the reenchantment of analysis and of culture at large must proceed through a reinvestigation of mourning and melancholia. Kristeva's lengthy study of melancholia, *Black Sun*, defines the allegorical procedures of the imagination as inherently melancholic and ends with a brisk paragraph about what she calls the "postmodern challenge" to melancholia: "The postmodern is closer to the human comedy than to abyssal discontent. . . . The desire for comedy shows up today to conceal—without for that matter being unaware of it—the concern for such a truth without tragedy, melancholia without purgatory."[169] The hint of regret betrayed by such a remark is amplified and given an increasingly keen ethical and political edge in her more recent work.

In these subsequent writings, she observes that the very notion of a subjective imagination runs the risk of obliteration by the hegemony of the "intersubjective" domain of the mass media.[170] Venturing somewhat further than the chiefly aesthetic concerns of her earlier investigation, she expresses concern in *La révolte intime* that in the "realized imaginary" and virtual space of the contemporary society of spectacle, there is no place for nothingness and transcendence.[171] As a corrective to this state of things, she lately has pursued a critical reenchantment of psychoanalysis by aligning the discourse with the culture of "revolt." And it is telling that she explicitly predicates her elaboration of this idea of revolt not on the example of Lacan's theory of lack, but on Freud's revolutionary definition of the impossible temporality of the unconscious (14:248).[172] Revolt, as Kristeva describes the impulse, ought to be understood in its etymological sense not as an advance, but as a return.[173] The revolutionary value of culture is promoted by psychoanalysis insofar as the discipline enacts an anamnesis, a "search for lost time" through the elaboration of narrative.[174] For the French semiotician, the "Freudian scandal" resides not only in Freud's reliance on a paradoxical notion of time, the lost time [*Zeitlos*] of the unconscious, but also in his meditation on death and mortality. As she suggestively puts it, with Freud, death "lives a human life."[175] Under the aegis of such an understanding, psychoanalysis raises the possibility of renovating and, to some extent, surmounting the symptomatology, not to say the pathology, currently attached to postmodernity. Psychoanalysis can give rise to a "revolt" only by assuming a Proustian air, by refusing to abandon memory as the horizon constitutive of human experience: "I repeat that I use the word 'revolt' in the etymological and Proustian sense of the term: return of sense to the drive and vice-versa for the awakening of memory and reinauguration of the subject."[176] Psychoanalysis in this sense would be the source for Kristeva not of a humanist moralism, but of a humanism endowed with gravitas.[177]

To relinquish, as Lacan effectively does, the hermeneutics of mourning and melancholia means to put aside the most sophisticated critical framework for the interpretation of subjectivity per se. If psychoanalysis can be said to teach us anything, it makes clear that the subject is nothing without its losses—that, as Freud points out in *The Ego and the Id*, the ego is in fact a precipitate of its lost attachments (19:28). The historicity of the ego in Freud's theory becomes irrelevant to Lacan's thinking, however, because loss is conceived as the "transcendental" condition of desire and the ego, more than a "precipitate," as an imaginary construction. If philosophically and aesthetically original, the French analyst's dissolution of the very notion of the subject, which it presents as barred and outmaneuvered by the symbolic order, also ought to be recognized as ethically and politically questionable.[178] In Freud's view, the lost object is a political and historical agent, not the spectacularized, aestheticized Other we find metabolized by the Lacanian notion of style. To renew reflection on postmodern culture and thus to identify the space of a critical postmodernity, it will be important to rework, as Kristeva proposes, the foundational temporal strategy of Freudian analysis. However, this project might be dismissed as merely regressive, as an exercise in melancholia, if not reinforced by an understanding of the need to mourn with critical vigilance the waning of psychoanalysis itself. Such a mourning cannot consist of a simple "overcoming." It cannot even be performed in a Lacanian way, as the inevitable, ritual mobilization of the psychoanalytic battery of signifiers. Kristeva's emphasis on the melancholic imagination, for example, threatens to accommodate a ritualistic understanding of psychoanalysis, for she stops short of any more overtly political revolt against the contemporary parameters of the discipline. To be sure, the response to the absence of mourning ought not to be the "aesthetic" evocation of a generalized, cultural, melancholic pathos.

Whereas Kristeva's work on mourning over the course of time has moved away from a largely aesthetic conception of melancholia (as in *Black Sun*) to a more engaged notion of mourning, other thinkers such as Judith Butler and Jacques Derrida have insisted even more strongly on the need for a political and ethical reinterpretation of the task of mourning. To these two thinkers, it has become increasingly urgent to recuperate mourning and melancholia as means of ethical and political critique, thus redefining analysis itself. For Butler, psychoanalysis must mourn those traditional ideas of family and kinship that increasingly reveal their obsolescence and dangerousness when assumed to provide the imperturbable foundations of cultural intelligibility.[179] Derrida has recently raised the question whether the very fate of psychoanalysis does not coincide with a return to the question of mourning from an ethical and political point of view, a return that will test the "conditions of the soul" of the discipline.[180] If Lacan's career ends on a note of scorn for the *états d'âme*, Derrida rightly brings them back to the forefront of psychoanalytic discussion. He perceives in the refusal of psychoanalysis to mourn its own past the symptom of a sort of autoimmune disorder afflicting the discourse, a self-assault responsible for its current crisis.[181] If analytic theory does not work through the articulation of its own discipline with ethics, politics, and the law, its growing aloofness will render it irrelevant:

If psychoanalysis is not dead, nobody could doubt it, it is mortal and it knows it. . . . At any rate, it seems to carry a burden that it doesn't know whether or not it owns. What is the grievance or, otherwise put, the sorrow and grief, suffering and mourning about which psychoanalysis, after a century of existence, finds itself complaining? . . . What is it that psychoanalysts from the world over are mourning or refuse to mourn, to confess their work of mourning, their *grief* but also their *grievance*, their grief, their reaffirmation, their reclamation, their demand?[182]

Derrida's constant recourse in these sentences to the mournful language of loss, his litany of terms such as *deuil, douleur, grief, grievance,* and *souffrance,* encodes the very answer ostensibly begged by his questions in the first place. It is precisely the imperative to renew the means of articulating or dealing with loss that constitutes the "grievance" of psychoanalysis, an onus it represses but finally cannot escape.

As we have seen, Freud early on recognized loss as a specifically psychoanalytic question. Gradually, however, psychoanalysis itself reorients this question from the epistemological effort to discover the appropriate measure or rhythm of mourning—that is, the pace at which the reality-testing of the sorrow work can play itself out, to an ontological constancy of desire sustained by the object's absence, an acceptance of loss as an unresolvable trauma. This shift de facto marks the cultural obsolescence of the ethical significance of mourning. Yet even after the introduction of the second topic of the death drive, Freud's theory never entirely progresses beyond mourning. Under the aegis of the second topic, the emotional life described by Freud grows ever more spectralized but does not culminate in the detachment and knowingness that typify Lacan's approach to loss and mourning. Perhaps one of the most important challenges that lies ahead of psychoanalysis is to find a way to give voice to a mournful ethical and political imagination that transcends the aesthetics of nostalgia. If it can do so, psychoanalysis will take a significant step to avoid encouraging or abetting the forces of reification and depersonalization with which, throughout its history, it has too often cooperated in the interest of establishing and protecting its own authority. And, as a consequence, it may help to indicate how the phenomenology of posteriority that is the postmodern, by reflecting with greater openness and care on the singularity of the past, may begin at last to conceive of a future.

Cool Memories

Proust's Mannerism of Memory

Marcel Proust elaborates a poetics of memory in *In Search of Lost Time* [*A la recherche du temps perdu*] that comprises two decisive stages, each of which affirms its own distinct model of mourning. The first stage is associated with the emotional experiences of loss that Proust labels the "intermittencies of the heart" [*les intermittences du coeur*] and that, as Antoine Compagnon points out, belong to the earlier episodes of the novel.[1] The paradigm case of such intermittencies of the heart, which I will explore later in this chapter, is the narrator's grief-stricken reencountering of "my real grandmother" [*ma grand-mère véritable*] in an accidental epiphany of memory while traveling one year after her death (2:783; JYT 3:153). The second stage is coincident with a "cool" or ironic sense of alienation from the past that Proust establishes when he unveils his full-blown theory of involuntary memory [*la mémoire involontaire*] at the conclusion of the *Recherche*. The emblematic instances of involuntary memory that Marcel, the narrator, catalogs in the final volume are, as I will eventually contend, trivial or quotidian sense-data—the action of tripping over uneven cobblestones, the clatter of a spoon, the stiffness of a starched napkin—that appear to function in such a way as to free the narrator from the emotional and ethical burden of the intermittencies.

The novel, then, requires us to keep in mind two views of Marcel's relation to "lost time." According to the first view, the narrator looks like an inconsolable mourner of the past, the distraught author of the motto, "The only paradises are those we have lost" [*le seul paradis sont ceux qu'on a perdu*]. According to the second, he looks like a jaded semiotician, a disenchanted ironist with a taste for what Richard Rorty calls "contingency."[2] What Rorty means by this characterization is complex but in essence may be thought of as a radical suspicion of historical metanarratives—of anything, as he puts it, that smacks of "a method, a platform, or a rationale."[3] In Rorty's opinion, such distrust reconciles us to the accidental or arbitrary condition of the past that we inherit, a past that might easily be replaced by another:

Proust temporalized and finitized the authority figures he had met by seeing them as creatures of contingent circumstance. . . . He finitized authority figures not by detecting what they "really" were but by watching them become different than they had been. . . . The result of all this finitization was to make Proust unashamed of his own finitude. He mastered contingency by recognizing it, and thus freed himself from the fear that the contingencies he had encountered were more than contingencies.[4]

To be free of such fears, however, is to be free of any real regret for the uniqueness of our objects and their irrecoverability upon being lost.

As Malcolm Bowie points out, Proust's ordering of the two stages of the *Recherche*, which gives the final word to the doctrine of *la mémoire involontaire*, indeed removes or liberates the narrator from an anxious interlocutory role in which he is often cast as the instrument of textual discontinuities and intermittencies, thus rewarding the masterful, cool, psychologizing, philosophizing persona of the final volume. Bowie observes furthermore that such a position is antithetical to the reasoning of another preeminent modern theorist of mourning; in his opinion, Freud and Proust follow exactly opposite paths.[5] Whereas Freud's thinking on the topic of mourning progresses from the first principle of the sorrow work in an increasingly pessimistic direction over time, Proust depicts Marcel's life in the novel as preparation for the climactic recognition of his literary vocation and hence as a finally comic or optimistic teleology. The movement from intermittency to the involuntary opens a point of access to the unconscious that results in a state of aestheticizing bliss utterly unlike Freud's conception of a costly or painful *Arbeit*.

The novel in other words presents the author's life as illustrating a kind of dialectical logic. Marcel's "search" represents a drama of the overcoming of a tragic conception of memory as an agonistic confrontation of loss by a seriocomic conception that regards remembrance as an assertion of aesthetic detachment or distance. The implications of Proust's narrative argument are profound for an understanding of the subject's relationship to history; Bowie, it seems to me, has intuited something crucial about the novelist's achievement when he contrasts Proust's outlook to Freud's, whose theory of mourning I associate in the previous chapter with modernism. Indeed, if in the domain of literature the project of high modernism might be defined as the epic expression of longing for a native point of origin or *nostos* from a position of exile, Proust might be said to differ insofar as his narrator never really leaves home.

It is interesting in this respect to observe that no less an authority than Gilles Deleuze emphatically rejects the nostalgic view of Proust, maintaining that the role of memory in the novel is "secondary."[6] As I will argue, readers such as Deleuze and Benjamin experience a certain critical discomfort on confronting the "machinery" of involuntary memory, a discomfort Deleuze attempts to relieve rhetorically by pleading that memory is not so important after all, not even in the definition of the artistic task.[7] Deleuze is right to observe that one must refrain from taking Proust's poetics of resonance at its face value as a phenomenological investigation because art would have nothing to add to a life in which resonance effects were the ultimate goal: "What is new in Proust . . . what constitutes the eternal success and eternal signification of the madeleine, is not the simple existence of these ecstasies or of those privileged moments, of which literature affords countless examples. Nor is it merely the original way in which Proust presents them and analyzes them in his own style. It is rather the fact that he produces them, and that these moments become the effect of a literary machine."[8] Like Lacan, Proust's final response to loss is one of style. The machine of Proustian literary style, which perpetually equivocates between the languages of phenomenology and of autobiography, results in a narrative system geared toward the continual production of simulacra. On this score, it becomes all the more important to examine the *coup de théâtre* of the final volume, *Time Regained* [*Le temps retrouvé*], and to interrogate the rhetoric of the novel's climactic revelation regarding art and memory, an epiphany that, if never actually experienced by the author in such a form, is nonetheless granted the authority of first-person narrative in the novel.[9] By resolving the narrator's search for the past through the happy ending of the discovery of his artistic mission, the novel fabricates the paradigmatic simulacrum of contemporary culture, namely the image of interior recollection totally externalized: the perfect, remainderless equivalence between written signs and their symbolic value.

As I have been describing them, the two stages of the novel's narrative dialectic may be aligned respectively with the archetypal modernist and postmodern attitudes toward history. The *Recherche* thus can be seen to reveal elements of both sensibilities at the same time. In what follows, I will categorize the first notion as more modernist in the sense that it reserves some space for the enigma of grief, a space in which the Otherness of the object is not irrelevant. Moreover, the idea of the intermittencies of the heart is never articulated as a systematic general theory, as is that of involuntary memory. It is my contention that through the novel's concluding exposition of *la mémoire involontaire* Proust provides a self-explanatory reading of the more elliptical narrative instances of *les intermittences du coeur* but, in so doing, dissolves historicist angst into ahistorical ecstasy, arduous work into instantaneous joy. In the passage from the intermittencies to the involuntary what has happened to the melancholic claim of the past? The same question might be asked of the transition from modernism to postmodernism.[10]

The evolution of the theme of memory within the *Recherche* from the intermittencies of the heart to the full-blown theory of the involuntary as delineated in the final volume thus marks the progressive movement of the novel away from an attitude not only of sentimentality and melancholia, but of historicity as well. Proust's tart skepticism with regard to modernity's crisis of consciousness is all the more striking if we think that by his own proclamation, his most important poetic influence was Baudelaire, the proponent par excellence of the tragic heroic conception of modernity. If, as Max Pensky suggests, the Baudelairean emphasis on alienation is most fully manifest in his notion of *spleen* and may be considered an implicit critique of early capitalism, the concept of *la mémoire involontaire* provides a perhaps overly schematic, dialectical "happy ending" to Baudelaire's melancholic project as well as an artificial refuge for subjectivity.[11]

At the moment when the narrator proposes an overtly philosophical explanation of involuntary memory, we can identify precisely in what sense he exemplifies a "cool" attitude. In claiming to have attained a kind of atemporal or extratemporal state via the involuntary, to have become "a fragment of time in the pure state" [*un peu de temps à l'état pur*], he de facto renounces any melancholic relationship to the past (3:905; JYT

4:451). Memory, in other words, comes to represent a territory beyond temporality and historicity from which a "weak" subject may confront its finitude with a certain nonchalance or coolness. Accordingly, I wish to stress the similarity between Proust's definition of *la mémoire involontaire* and Baudrillard's contemporary notion of cool memories, his disjunctive, fragmentary tableau of postmodern souvenirs.[12] Transience is radically embraced, historical sensitivity abandoned, and nostalgia manufactured according to the mechanism of involuntary memory, which transforms modernist shock into an aesthetic souvenir. The word "involuntary" thus evinces a spirit of coyness, affectation, and regressiveness as it insists on the happy ending of an art that forever disjoins aesthetics from ethics. To the extent that Proust espouses a redemptive use of artistic forms, it becomes necessary to investigate the ethical and political limits of an operation within the parameters of which, as Bersani suggests, the singularity of human experience and history can be eradicated by the universalizing nobility of art.[13] The *Recherche* affirms an aesthetic ideology that raises the possibility of art's delivery of the subject from historical circumstance.[14]

The ideology revolving around mourning and memory establishes an imaginary, phantasmatic relation to culture and history that is highly problematic—and not compatible with a view of Proust as a nostalgic writer.[15] In her most recent work on Proust, Anne Henry, like Deleuze, strongly opposes the received idea of Proust as a nostalgic mourner. She contends that genuine nostalgia presupposes a naive belief in a notion of self-identity that is incompatible with the flexibility and fragility of the Proustian subject.[16] However, we might add that the Proustian fluency of identity is fully compatible with the protocols of "artificial" nostalgia, defining that mentality as the transient, aesthetic attachment to an ever-changing lost object. One of the most important elements of postmodernity is the production of artificial nostalgia, a phantasmatic impulse that is manifest in the reification of tradition throughout all the various artistic domains from architecture to literature to film and that is the sign par excellence of an extreme fluidity of subjectivity. Indeed, the two issues are related, for it is only through the flexibility of the weak subject that the market can sustain its cycle of perpetual, hyperbolic consumption. On this score, Proust's work is one of the most important points of reference with regard to the establishment of a modernist genealogy of our contemporary notions of self and memory. A subject who is not an agent but the "involuntary" recipient of a random assortment of sense-data sets the stage for the spectacular consumerism of identities enforced by the cultural logic of postmodernism.

It is my belief that Proust's final aesthetics of remembrance, with its extreme deconstruction of the subject and full acceptance of a schism between private and public spheres that, contra Joyce or Eliot, may not be bridged by either myth or tradition, inaugurates an outlook we have come to regard as postmodern. Proust's *chef d'oeuvre*, which insists on the consolation of good forms, as Lyotard would put it, is often considered the epitome of a certain nostalgic modernism insofar as the novel's explicit ideology of memory is taken at face value. This ideology, however, is applied not as an organic process of mediation between the individual subject and collective memory, but as an artificial engine of glamorization aimed at the reenchantment of the subject in an increasingly opaque and commodified society. The distinction between voluntary and involuntary memory reinforces the discrepancy between public and private space; thus, the final triumph of the involuntary in the novel definitively marks the obsolescence of history and collective memory as viable points of reference. These reference points are replaced by a new zone that has been called "the publicity of the private," a frame of mind that Proust relentlessly glamorizes or romanticizes.[17] On this score, the *Recherche* might be said to anticipate the spurious rehabilitation of nostalgia in postmodernism in as much as the novel promises recuperation of "lost time" less as a political or historical act than as a stylistic gesture, the striking of a pose of receptivity or acquiescence to the past, an attitude well expressed by its association with the term *involontaire*.

That the logic of the involuntary might represent a form of false consciousness has been underscored by the recent transposing of Proust's masterpiece to the cinematic screen by Raoul Ruiz. The much-noted theatricality of Ruiz's adaptation (*Le Temps retrouvé*, 1998), more than being strictly a decision of cinematic style, corresponds to a real impulse within the *Recherche*, as Ruiz rightly contends.[18] One might think that the phenomenology of *la mémoire involontaire* ought to find in the moving image its ideal medium of expression; through the techniques of superimposition and montage, film offers the absolute coincidence of past and present toward which Proust's language can only gesture. It is hardly coincidental that Deleuze identifies the novelist as a fundamental source of inspiration for the concept of the "time-image."[19] Yet the depiction on screen of the involuntary exemplifies a troublingly stagey mannerism of memory that is sharply at odds with the impressionistic rhetoric of the book. Ruiz's visualization of the novel, which concentrates primarily on the final volume, has drawn criticism for its dramatic artifice, for its betrayal of the "simplicity" of the Proustian message.[20] The manner in which he envisions the scene of the narrator's tripping in the Guermantes courtyard, the moment at which the narrator is seized both by the memory of Venice and by the idea of the literary opus he has yet to write, is particularly stylized. For several seconds, the actor is frozen in a posture of imbalance like a puppet on invisible wires while the background scenery rotates around him, before he regains normal movement. Stéphane Bouquet describes the moment as one of "ironic fetishism": "The passage from the text to the image is effected through the detour, as we have said, of theater. Ruiz multiplies, across the entire duration of his *Time Regained*, the theatrical possibilities of the fake."[21] However, as Ruiz is quick to observe, what looks like a caricature, a gross exaggeration of the symbolic moment par excellence of the *Recherche*, faithfully replicates the theatricality of the original text: "It's in the book: people stop because the narrator stays for a long time in an absurd position" [C'est dans le livre: les gens s'arrêtent parce que le Narrateur reste longtemps dans une position absurde].[22] And indeed the director's observation evokes the dramaturgical interest of the original scene in the novel:

I continued, ignoring the evident amusement of the great crowd of chauffeurs, to stagger as I had staggered a few seconds ago, with one foot on a higher paving stone and the other on the lower. Every time that I merely repeated this physical movement, I achieved nothing; but if I succeeded, forgetting the Guermantes party, in recapturing what I had felt when I first placed my feet on the ground in this way, again the dazzling and indistinct vision fluttered near me, as if to say: "Seize me as I pass if you can, and try to solve the riddle of happiness which I set you."[23] (3:899)

The narrator's emphasis on the "amusement" of his observers and his effort to stage the revelation anew by resuming the exact posture he was in when the recollection of Venice first struck him underlines the performative artifice of this most crucial instance of involuntary memory and belies the narrator's idealist claim to a "dazzling and indistinct," impressionist perception.

To brand Proust's novel as an anticipation of postmodernism will seem odd only if we consider the dividing line between the modernist and the postmodernist to be synonymous with a hard division between "high" and "low" art, or if we accept the overly simplistic understanding of postmodernity as a blanket renunciation of modernity.[24] No doubt the

Recherche also exemplifies at various moments a typical modernist elitism and high-mindedness. However, not only does the reception history of the novel possess a too-rarely acknowledged populist aspect, which tends to embrace the narrator's fetishizing of the material traces of history (for example, the madeleine), but, as I will argue, the emphasis of Proust's theory of involuntary memory on the "general law of oblivion" consorts in various ways with the doxa of postmodernism.[25] By positioning Proust's work between two centuries, Compagnon begs the question of categorization, ultimately choosing to view the *Recherche* as a supposedly timeless classic.[26] Leaving aside for a moment such philologically and chronologically "correct" interpretations of Proust, however, we may conceive of a different approach that is more speculative in spirit. According to such a line of reasoning, what is significant in the novel is not its affirmation of a fin de siècle idea of beauty, but rather the epistemological upheaval that its narrative procedures enforce. Indeed, Compagnon himself seems momentarily to consider a related view when he asks, "Was not the Proustian sentence, with its twist and turns of hypothesis and torrents of conditionality, already postmodern?"[27] We might well add, was not the Proustian mise-en-scène of involuntary memory already postmodern? In what follows, I will explore the unresolved ambivalence suggested by Compagnon's phrasing of his point in the form of a question.

To pursue such a line of inquiry, however, ultimately means to confront Proust's crucial and idiosyncratic representation of mourning. The received popular view of Proust as the author of an epic of nostalgia generally gives no more than a partial or incomplete account of the conception of mourning developed in the novel. Far from providing the transcendental framework of speculation, this conception enforces a nihilism of memory that is quite the opposite of the poetics of nostalgia it is supposed by naive readers to uphold. Mourning in the *Recherche* does not provide any occasion for the establishment of a link between private grief and public commemoration, sorrow and ritual. Proust proceeds to undo systematically this traditional idea of mourning, replacing it with a set of improvisatory, private practices that find meaning only through their elaboration as works of art. From Mlle. Vinteuil's sadistic rituals to the narrator's involuntary poetic epiphanies, memory is emptied of its social meaning. As in baroque allegories, however, salvation is mysteriously promised through the redemptive aura of the work of art.[28] In the novel, the violent disavowal of mourning that comprises the narrative's *pars destruens* is commensurable in spirit with the ecstatic, aestheticized experience of involuntary memories that constitutes its *pars construens*. The narrative, before articulating its own ideological justification, progresses toward increasing degrees of complexity. This progression, I will argue, culminates in the chapter entitled "The Intermittencies of the Heart."

Against Mourning

Throughout the *Recherche*, the conception of mourning as a socially ritualized moment is discredited by Proust, who seems to suspect the very idea of devoting a prescribed lapse of time to the commemoration of a dead loved one. Loss in the *Recherche* initiates a process of fragmentation and metamorphosis of the self that each time reaffirms the validity of what Proust called "the general law of oblivion" [*la loi générale de l'oubli*] that comprises the first principle of the novel's overall economy (3:659; JYT 4:223). Unlike Freud's final theory of the ego, in which identity is established through identification with lost objects, Proust's theory of mourning entails letting each former self die away according to an increasingly destabilizing logic of self-annihilation in which art functions as a kind of "epistemological surreality."[29] The very fragmentation of the self and the world brought about by this logic makes mourning in some way the articulation of the necessity of oblivion in terms of a law. The narrator of the *Recherche* gives voice to a startlingly cynical point of view, according to which nothing and nobody, neither his grandmother nor Albertine, may be considered unforgettable. If Proust's *chef d'oeuvre* may still be considered a bildungsroman, this is much more by virtue of his depiction of the narrator's gradual coming to terms with "the general law of oblivion" than of his description of the narrator's artistic education. In fact, the latter narrative is a function of the former because only forgetfulness provide the epistemological condition for the chance encounters of involuntary memory, encounters that in the novel will define the narrator's vocation as a writer.

The narrator punctuates the *Recherche* with scenes in which an anticipated moment of mourning is either travestied or averted: from the flagrant desecration of Vinteuil at Montjouvain, to the scant attention Mme. de Guermantes pays to Swann's death, to the narrator's own involuntary mourning of his grandmother. Mourning for Proust is not a duty to perform; in order to achieve significance, the experience cannot be willed or "voluntary."

Early in the narrative, the "coolness" of Proust's conception of memory is evinced at the moment of Aunt Léonie's death. Much to the narrator's surprise, Aunt Léonie leaves him almost all of her fortune (1:489; JYT 1:445). Among the other possessions she leaves him are some items of furniture that he does not think twice about giving to the proprietress of a bordello (1:622; JYT 1:568) and a "magnifique" set of antique silverware that, over the objections of his parents, he sells in order to be able to send "more flowers to Mme. Swann" [*plus de fleurs à Mme Swann*] (1:622; JYT 1:568). Most remarkably, he gives to the whorehouse the couch on which, while experimenting with a girl cousin in his aunt's room at Combray, he lost his virginity. And then, belatedly, he suffers pangs of remorse:

> But as soon as I saw them again in the house where these women were putting them to their own uses, all the virtues that pervaded my aunt's room at Combray at once appeared to me, tortured by the cruel contact to which I had abandoned them in their defenselessness! Had I outraged the dead, I would not have suffered such remorse.[30] (1:622)

His ingratitude is all the more startling if we pause to consider the narrator's relationship to his aunt in light of his much celebrated reminiscence over the madeleine. For it was Léonie, of course, who would feed him madeleines when he was a child and to whom he owes the epiphanic memory of Combray that results from a taste of the same confection years later.

Proust's nihilism of memory manifests itself most fully in the two crucial reminiscences regarding M. Vinteuil and the narrator's grandmother. These two narrative strands play complementary roles in the novel's overall economy.[31] Their task is to expose the traumatic nature of mourning in the modern epoch, a shock value that achieves its narrative fulfillment with the establishment of the Proustian aesthetic ideology in *Le temps retrouvé*. However, in the movement from these first two moments of mourning to the apotheosis of involuntary memory in the last volume, we witness the dissolution of an oblique, modernist approach to grief into the pretense of a direct contact with the sources of truth. Both episodes stage an event (the lesbian scene witnessed by the narrator, his grandmother's death) that, according to Freud's theory of traumatic *Nacht-räglichkeit* set forth in *The Wolfman*, may be understood only at a later stage when the emotional repetition of the event (imagining Albertine as Mlle. Vinteuil, acknowledging the grandmother's death while at Balbec a year after the fact) will finally be treated in a "symbolic" way. A discrepancy looms, however, between Proust's conception of mourning as trauma and his consistent search for a happy ending to the process, a resolution that would bring about not only forgetfulness but the auratic redemption of the Real.

When the first volume of the *Recherche* was initially published, the public reception of the Vinteuil episode was more than a little scandalized. The importance of the episode to an understanding of the novel cannot be overstressed because Proust achieves in the Vinteuil subplot one of the great modern elaborations of the theme of sadism, a motif that sharply highlights Proust's cynicism toward the past and perverse exhilaration in debunking nostalgic impulses. Early in the novel, the narrator recounts his experience of a "primal scene." En route to Méséglise during a summer holiday, the narrator, while out for a walk, discovers Mlle. Vinteuil and her lesbian partner in the act of performing a blasphemous memorial rite. Spying through an open window, the narrator observes Mlle. Vinteuil in mourning, "*en grand deuil*," due to the recent death of her father, a composer.[32]

From his vantage point, the narrator watches Mlle. Vinteuil displace her father's picture from the fireplace to a small table near the sofa where she lies in a seductive posture. When her "*camerade*" arrives, she treats her with brusque familiarity, yet with a hint of bashful reticence reminiscent of her father's manner. Telling her friend that she is anxious of their being seen, Mlle. Vinteuil offers to close the window, thus threatening to deny to the narrator the "spectacle of the closet": "When I say 'see us,' I mean, of course, see us reading. It's so tiresome to think that whatever trivial little thing you do, someone may be overlooking you" (1:176).[33] To Mlle. Vinteuil's suggestion of closing the window, her friend replies with an air of reciting from a well-rehearsed script, "All the better that they should see us" (1:176), thus initiating the lovers' rites of desire.[34] The scene gives the impression of an almost liturgical sequence, in which every sentence responds to a prior signal according to a routine. Playing out her role, Mlle. Vinteuil tries to distance herself as much as possible from her customary good-natured timidity, to adopt instead an artificially sadistic pose. Calling her companion's attention to her father's photo, she feigns surprise and bewilderment at finding it on the nearby table: "Oh! There's my father's picture looking at us; I can't think who can have put it there; I'm sure I told them a dozen times that it isn't the proper place for it" (1:177).[35]

As the scene unfolds and the momentum of sexual excitement gathers, her friend does not disappoint her expectations, first proposing, and then participating in, the climactic act of spitting on the portrait. Proust appears to imply in this scene a conception of sadism as the original medium for mourning. It is hardly accidental, we might surmise, that this shocking display of cruelty is triggered by a photograph. As Barthes has pointed out, photography, whose *eidos* is death itself, corresponds to the withdrawal from our society of ritual and the establishment instead of an unsymbolic, literal death, an event marked by the photographer's click.[36] Barthes traces what Edgard Morin describes as the "crisis of death" back to the second half of the nineteenth century. Proust's depiction of sadism as the natural response to photography not only exemplifies the impossibility of faith in unoriginal or mechanical acts of mourning, but also the diffi-culty of finding any public meaning in such acts. The age of photography corresponds for Barthes to the explosion of the private into the public and the ascendancy of a new social value, "the publicity of the private," that the *Recherche* might well be said to uphold.[37]

The Vinteuil episode thus reveals the impulse on Proust's part toward the spectacularization of the personal, an inclination that achieves its fullest expression in the narrator's rehearsal of the theatrical mise-en-scène of involuntary memory at the end of the novel.[38] Explaining the distinc-tion between Mlle. Vinteuil's sadism and the "wholly wicked," the narrator declares that when it comes to "virtue, respect for the dead, filial affection," if Mlle. Vinteuil had been truly evil, "since she would never have practised the cult of these things, she would take no impious delight in profaning them" (1:179).[39] Her "impious delight" hints at both the early piety of her upbringing and her capacity to assert her individuality against that up-bringing. To attack "the cult" of convention, in effect, is to demonstrate one's singularity of imagination.

As is well known, the scene of profanation of M. Vinteuil's portrait will have a traumatic effect on the narrator and will be replayed and re-phrased many times in his mind when he confronts Albertine's possible lesbianism. Later in the narrative, however, the narrator will come to ap-preciate Mlle. Vinteuil and her lover's nonconformism insofar as they be-come symbolically responsible in the novel for introducing him to the epiphanic inspiration of art.[40] When the narrator discovers a new kind of joy, a "super-terrestrial joy," on listening to a performance of M. Vinteuil's chamber septet, he discloses that it was through the work of Mlle. Vin-teuil's lover that the father's musical manuscript had been deciphered: "Mlle Vinteuil's friend had disentangled, from papers more illegible than strips of papyrus dotted with a cuneiform script, the formula, eternally true and forever fertile, of this unknown joy, the mystic hope of the crimson Angel of the Dawn" (3:264).[41] Proust thus unveils the "work" of mourning as the production of joy or pleasure, establishing an equivalence that Freud's more sober view never suggests.

The novel's absolution of Mlle. Vinteuil and her lover implicitly affirms the narrator's own ethos of mourning, which prizes originality rather than tradition or ritual. Proust likens a successful or completed mourning to an act of adultery, a practice that reinsinuates the subject into a narrative that married life may have left behind as a "dead letter" [*la lettre . . . morte*] (3:264; JYT 3:766). At first glance, it would seem the meaning of the episode could not be clearer. What counts toward the fulfillment of mourning is not pious conventionality but artistic devotion to the original, a devotion revealed rather than obscured by the practice of translation. Yet this seemingly idealist position quickly complicates itself. In the interpretive coda revolving around the recuperation of M. Vinteuil's manuscript, Proust's allegorical message seems so unconditional, the transformation of cruelty into benevolence so magically complete, that the narrator's account exposes its basic operation as a form of ideology, begging the reader's skepticism and disbelief. Mlle. Vinteuil's sadistic mourning ritual thus finds its figural echo in the interpretive violence of Proust's hyperbolically lenient construction of her story and motives regarding her father. The overdetermination of the narrator's effort to find "aesthetic" justifications for Mlle. Vinteuil's radical irreverence toward the memory of her father unveils his "ideological" posture. Indeed, adopting a position reminiscent on an allegorical level of the mediating role played by Mlle. Vinteuil's friend, the narrator will define his task and find his vocation in the "deciphering" and "translating" of the riddle of the involuntary. By transforming Marcel from a spectator into an actor, the symbolic identification between the narrator and Mlle. Vinteuil and her lover conveniently supplies him with a tacit ethical justification or alibi for his own cruelties toward loved ones. The same identification, however, suggests the possibility of construing as a form of sadism the "general law of oblivion" that constitutes the first principle of the theory of involuntary memory.

In a move that strikingly reprises the narrator's own, Walter Benjamin finds evident relief in recognizing his own melancholic theory of allegory in Proust's narrative. In his "Moscow Diary," Walter Benjamin captures the iconoclastic thrill of the vandalization of M. Vinteuil's portrait by his daughter and her lesbian partner, eagerly recalling how he read the passage to his lover, Asja Lacis:

Then I read the lesbian scene from Proust. Asja grasped its savage nihilism: how Proust in a certain fashion ventures into the tidy private chamber within the petit bourgeois that bears the inscription *sadism* and then mercilessly smashes everything to pieces, so that nothing remains of the untarnished, clear-cut conception of wickedness, but instead within every fracture evil explicitly shows its true substance—"humanity," or even "kindness." And as I was explaining this to Asja, it became clear to me how closely this coincided with the thrust of my baroque book . . . it had become clear to me that Proust was here developing a conception that corresponds at every point to what I myself have tried to subsume under the concept of allegory.[42]

The development of the Vinteuil segment in the *Recherche* might be considered Proust's contribution to a modernist rewriting of the *Trauerspiel*, one in which interpretive violence is pushed to the limits of unreadability. Unlike Proust, however, Benjamin will extend his allegorical method to history itself, devising a theoretical constellation in which art can have a redemptive power, though not at the expense of historical or political judgment. In Proust's work, instead, art is supposed to redeem catastrophic experience single-handedly, according to an aesthetic ideology that will find in the poetics of the involuntary its most sophisticated form.

An Involuntary Mourning

After the Vinteuil segment, the most disconcertingly "unreadable" mourning in the novel is certainly that of the narrator's involuntary and belated remembrance of his grandmother. In *Time Regained*, we come to witness the reworking of the Ovidian myth of Orpheus into a happy, harmless recovery of experience, raising the possibility of a cool act of retrospection by means of the passive epiphanies of *la mémoire involontaire*. The illusory nature of Proust's production of happiness, however, becomes sharply apparent if we compare the concluding volume to "The Intermittencies of the Heart," a chapter in which the concept of the involuntary is represented as a radical enigma rather than as a redemptive solution. The artificiality of Proust's final theory of art, the staged quality of the narrator's epiphanies of memory, the ideological contrivance of the involuntary become all the clearer by way of contrast to the irreparable disruption of intermittency. In this light, we may comprehend Proust's decision not to retain the title, *Les intermittences du coeur*, for the novel as a whole because the section does not function as a synecdoche of the total enterprise, but rather as something more like its blind spot.[43] The section, in other words, comes to look like a sort of textual unconscious when compared to the highly conscious manipulations of the final sections of the *Recherche*. It should come as no surprise, then, that Beckett, a reader who was highly attuned to the complicating self-contrarieties of mental life, considered "The Intermittencies of the Heart" to be Proust's single greatest accomplishment.[44]

Before the narrator comes to formulate his overall theory of memory in terms of *la loi générale de l'oubli*, he experiences one decisive occasion of grief in his life: his grandmother's death. When she dies, he at first gives no hint of any feelings of sorrow and instead pursues his social life and deepening involvement with Albertine as though nothing had happened. After a period of latency that lasts for more than a year, however, the grandmother resurfaces once more in his thoughts, restructuring his imaginative life and readying him to proceed to a new stage in his emotional development. In the economy of the *Recherche*, the mourning of his grandmother represents an interpretive blind spot that marks the narrator's encounter with death as the ultimate mystery. Proust's way of circumnavigating such an obstacle is paradoxically to conflate mourning and involuntary memory. In this section of the *Recherche*, the narrator, rather than sustaining the performance or pretense of a fully mastered, analytic understanding of events, permits himself to indulge the impulses of a textual or poetic unconscious, unveiling the signs of his desires, his imaginings, and dreams. Such signs, as Deleuze observes, are superior to the sense-signifiers deployed by involuntary memory.[45] Despite the temporary shock of the loss, however, Marcel soon resumes his customary attitude of distance from the object of his grief and affection, a shift underscored in the narrative by his repeated, matter-of-fact avowals of having thoroughly forgotten his grandmother.

In "The Intermittencies of the Heart," we witness the narrator's resurrection not only of his grandmother, but also of the theme of involuntary memory, the enlargement of which he apparently had abandoned after his initial rapturous response on tasting the madeleine. In the case of his grandmother's return through the workings of memory, the powerful grip of the moment on the narrator's mind will lead him back through time to an unmediated revelation of the past and, most especially, to the paradox of an "involuntary mourning." Antoine Compagnon has pointed out that Proust's interest in the notion of intermittency, defined as the discontinuous temporality of subjectivity, developed at an earlier stage in the composition of the novel than did his investment in the idea of *la mémoire involontaire* and remarks furthermore that the passages in the novel on *les intermittences* are less dogmatic and more moving than the final section on the involuntary, in which Proust spells out his philosophy of memory as such.[46] Unlike the epiphanies of the involuntary, the intermittencies do not affirm any transcendental law and contribute nothing to a theory of the novel. The shift of focus in the novel from intermittency to the involuntary signals the movement toward an increasingly artificial, instrumental model of subjectivity in which memory and forgetfulness function as the ideological principles of an art that aspires to transcend the unhappiness of the enigmatic. Involuntary memory from this perspective may be seen as a paradigm of certain aspects of contemporary culture, in which we perceive a consumerist view of loss to coincide with emotional detachment and the artificiality of aesthetic solutions. By way of contrast, the intermittencies of the heart coincide with an obsessive temporality of repetition, rather than a nonchalant acceptance of the ephemerality of "pure time." More than that, insofar as such pangs of feeling represent the shocking reassertion of lapsed or forgotten attachments, they confront us with the unknowability of the object of mourning, the radical strangeness of the Other. An ethical understanding of mourning still remains possible, therefore, in "The Intermittencies of the Heart." We shall see that in the last volume, *Time Regained,* the narrator renounces the anguished hermeneutic burden of the intermittencies in favor of the exhilarating aesthetic puzzle of involuntary memory. We can think of the difference between these two ideals in relation to the distinction between a genuine enigma, which may have no answer, and a riddle or puzzle, which promises the satisfaction of an inevitable, predetermined solution.

It is interesting to note on this score that the episode of the novel to which Proust referred as "la perte après-coup de ma grand-mère" was at first envisioned as taking place during the narrator's trip to Italy, as we know from an earlier draft.[47] That Proust decided to substitute Balbec for Milan in the finished version underscores the importance he assigned to presenting intermittency as a mode of repetition. Hence, the narrator's memory of his dead grandmother returns on the occasion of his second trip to Balbec, indeed in the very same hotel room in which he stayed during his first trip. Caught as it is in the movement of repetition, this remembrance cannot be as aesthetically abstract and "fulfilling" as the sequence of involuntary memories in the last volume, whose arbitrary nature and resonance work to disclose "a fragment of time in the pure state" [*un peu de temps à l'état pur*] (3:905; JYT 4:451). Whereas the narrator's anguish "*après-coup*" over his grandmother in other words conforms to the rhythm of a traumatic event, marked by a lack of understanding (hence the delay in the work of mourning), repetition, and the sublimation of anxiety by means of dreams, the involuntary memories at the end of the *Recherche* will grow increasingly distant from the experience of shock and closer to a simulacrum of experience. As we will see, however, even in the most sentimental section of the novel, Proust does not refrain from a healthy dose of skepticism and ambivalence with respect to memory. Not accidentally, we find the death of the grandmother and the narrator's desire for Albertine juxtaposed in the narrative, and the emotional counterpoint of the second theme to the first suggests a cynical or pessimistic critique of the possibility of pure, intact, and lasting memories. The pathos of the intermittencies of the heart is quickly superseded by the narrator's attachment to Albertine as "the general law of oblivion" reasserts its primacy with a vengefulness that moves the narrator to strike a cruelly fatalistic note: "Do we not see, in the very room in which they have lost a child, its parents soon come together again to give the little angel a baby brother?" (2:811).[48] Even the narrator's grief for his grandmother is informed by an acid skepticism regarding the endurance of memory. As he will repeat in *Time Regained,* both his grandmother and Albertine are beings whom he is fully capable of forgetting; it is doubtful, in other words, that art will be enough to rescue the past from what we might call its essential "forgottenness."

In "The Intermittencies of the Heart," the narrator adamantly insists he is not traveling to Balbec in the same poetic spirit of his first visit because "there is always less egoism in pure imagination than in recollection" [il y a toujours moins d'égoïsme dans l'imagination pure que dans le souvenir] (2:781–82; JYT 3:151). On the contrary, he seems more than vaguely aware that there he is likely to meet "*les belles inconnues.*" What he actually meets with is all the more surprising, then; when he retires on the first night to his room (the same one he occupied during his first visit), he is struck, on bending to remove his boots, by what he feels to be a divine presence, an influence that irresistibly moves him to tears.

I had just perceived, in my memory, stooping over my fatigue, the tender, preoccupied, disappointed face of my grandmother, as she had been on that first

evening of our arrival, the face not of that grandmother whom I had been aston-
ished and remorseful at having so little missed, and who had nothing in common
with her save her name, but of my real grandmother, of whom, for the first time
since the afternoon of her stroke in the Champs-Elysées, I now recaptured the living reality in a complete and involuntary recollection.[49] (2:783)

A year after the burial of his grandmother, the narrator experiences an
overwhelming desire to embrace her, to throw himself into her arms, and
it is only then that he realizes for the first time the full reality of her death.
According to him, the "*troubles de la mémoire*" he presently endures must
be ascribed to his egoistic wish first to deny her sickness and then her loss.
Yet to discover her in his memory, to recall the proper nature of her person in his mind, and therefore to recover his own past self, means to realize first and foremost that he has been cut off from her forever. As if acting
out a latter-day version of the myth of Orpheus, the narrator loses his
beloved grandmother for good precisely when he indulges his desire to
gaze on her face once more. His involuntary memory and his dream's further expansion on that memory, therefore, outline a heroic descent into
the underworld.

The circuit of associations surrounding this first recollection of the
grandmother gradually swells to touch all the salient episodes of their life
together, especially the most painful and regrettable moments: "Gradually
[*peu à peu*] I began to remember all the occasions that I had seized, by letting her see my sufferings and exaggerating them if necessary, to cause her
a grief which I imagined as being obliterated immediately by my kisses"
(2:785–86).[50] The narrator's description of memory advancing "*peu à peu*"
might be taken as a sign of his entrance into a mourning period shaped to
a rhythm of classically Freudian, "bit-by-bit" measure. Why, then, has the
mourning period been delayed by one year? Why does Proust locate the
meaning and truth of mourning in its paradoxically involuntary condition?
The only, timid explanation offered by the narrator is that his oblivion was
a simple "negation," a "wakening" of a faculty of thought incapable of
recreating the full reality of a moment in time and thus resorting instead
to representation of the past via conventional images (2:787; JYT 3:156–57).

From a critical perspective, the answer might be that in order for the
narrator to be able to articulate his ideology of *la mémoire involontaire* as
such, to mobilize the totalizing sign system of theoretical discourse, he
must confront what can only be described in Lacanian terms as a hole in
the Real, the anxious knowledge of a death that cannot be processed by

means of the customary rites of mourning. Unlike other instances of involuntary memory in the *Recherche*, the resurrection of his grandmother in the narrator's mind clearly functions as a traumatic event, particularly insofar as the recurrence of her image does not coincide with any enlightening insight on his part. Far from being a revelatory moment, his mental recuperation of her presents him with the enigma of the unendurable synthesis "of survival and annihilation" [*de la survivance et du néant*] (2:787; JYT 3:157). Yet what the narrator construes as a metaphysical paradox, we might reinterpret more pointedly in an ethical sense, in terms of his grandmother's wishes and desires and of her inexplicable, ongoing importance to him. As we have seen, Proust from the very start of the novel refuses to grant the value of a mourning conventionalized or authorized by society. Benjamin reminds us that there are no festivals or rituals in the *Recherche*; what remains to be noted is how strange it is that there are not even any funerals.[51] According to the German critic's sociological explanation, as long as experience itself has not been exhausted, the possibility still exists of joining the content of the individual's past to the material of the collective past, but that possibility is on the wane. Ideally, an effective ceremony or ritual ought to mingle the two varieties of memory, providing an occasion to bring to light what otherwise would remain no more than a phenomenon of private recollection. Proust's distrust of voluntary memory, however, entails his sure disdain of any such event. Sincere and dignified grief is not to be sullied by the banality of social custom, by the rigidity of devoting a prescribed period to commemoration. Time, the artist, must always have the last word.

As in the case of traumatic injuries when, according to Freud, the subject is doomed to relive in his dream the moment of traumatic danger over and over again, the narrator's thoughts as he falls asleep begin to revolve obsessively around his grandmother. His anxiety and guilt in his dream are signaled by his sudden panic at the realization that "for weeks on end I had forgotten to write to my grandmother" [depuis de longues semaines j'avais oublié d'écrire à ma grand-mère] (2:788; JYT 3:157). His father promptly reassures him that

You needn't worry. Her nurse is well trained. We send her a little money from time to time, so that she can get your grandmother anything she may need. She sometimes asks what's become of you. She was told you were going to write a book. She seemed pleased. She wiped away a tear.[52] (2:788)

Here the narrator makes plain in what sense we can say that mourning always brings to light the enigma of the Other. On this score, it is telling that he identifies his grandmother's ultimate wish in his dream as a desire to know more about him. The dream itself seems to function as a sort of compromise between a traumatic repetition and a wish fulfillment, enabling the narrator to imagine his father's consolatory words as a remedy to the grandmother's distress, which itself suggests a projection of the narrator's own: "She was told you were going to write a book. She seemed pleased." However, it is clear in the *Recherche* that only in the context of this fantasy does the narrator manage to find any answer to the questions raised by the loss of his *grand-mère*, to the mystery of her drastic alienation from him in death.

By way of his dream, Proust articulates as well the equivalence between memory and writing that he will explore at greater length in *Time Regained*. The authentic means of mourning is to be found in the creative process of writing, the only kind of work adequate to the task of bereavement. In learning this lesson, the narrator elevates his grandmother to the position classically reserved for the poet's Muse. Yet in an odd way his new knowledge comprises at once a response to loss and its further deflection. Not only do we not encounter grief where we would have expected to find it, immediately after the event of the grandmother's death, but even when the narrator finally intuits her loss, the redirection of his sorrow into mourning is still delayed: "I did not know whether I should one day distill a grain of truth from this painful and for the moment incomprehensible impression, but I knew that if I ever did . . . it could only be from such an impression and from none other" (2:786).[53]

The hesitation expressed by the narrator in this passage of the *Recherche*, as Leo Bersani has pointed out, constitutes one of the few moments of the novel in which doubt clearly arises as to whether the text we are reading is actually the same one that the narrator sets out to write at the end of the narrative.[54] The narrator's involuntary mourning of his grandmother suspends the novel's development of a mystified idea of art, exposing the one aporia in the logical argument of the narrative. Thus, if we find the possibility of art as a redemptive practice already articulated in "The Intermittencies of the Heart," such a possibility nonetheless arises here at the price of a mysterious, "incomprehensible" moment of suffering and certainly not in the form of a controlled mise-en-scène of involuntary memory.[55] This encounter with grief will be short, however, as the narrator soon after reestablishes his bearings in the wake of his "transitory grief" [*chagrin passager*] (2:795; JYT 3:165).

When the narrator becomes convinced at the end of the *Recherche* that he has found his vocation as a writer, he professes the consolation and even "happiness" involved in "extracting from our grief the generalities that lie within," while nonetheless confessing in a revealing moment his reluctance to fully embrace his own philosophy:

> I was ready to believe that the supreme truth of life resides in art, and I could see, too, that I was no more capable by an effort of memory of being still in love with Albertine than I was of continuing to mourn my grandmother's death, and yet I asked myself whether a work of art of which they would not be conscious could really for them, for the destiny of these poor dead creatures, be a fulfillment . . . a book is a <u>huge cemetery</u> in which on the majority of the tombs the names are effaced and can no longer be read.[56] (3:939–40)

The drama of the *Recherche* might be described as the effort to keep at bay the thought that the dead should be the transcendental subjects of the narrative by assuming an increasingly artificial and aestheticized relationship to memory in which grief is allowed to dissolve into the solipsistic exercise of the production of a literary style.

In contrast to the narrator's belated but successful mourning, the novel represents his mother as afflicted by an endless and pathological grief. The grandmother's death gradually precipitates her daughter's drastic and thorough identification with her. At first, the typically realistic and irreverent voice of the narrator's mother is still distinguishable in the novel from the idealistic, uncompromising rhetoric of the dead grandmother. But it becomes increasingly impossible to detect any trace of the mother's personality in her own words and deeds. She begins to carry the grandmother's purse, reading and quoting Mme. de Sévigné as was the other's practice, pausing whenever out of doors to take in with enthusiasm each landscape, natural vista, or panorama as the grandmother liked to do. Traveling to Balbec with her son means to her mind the performance of a sort of pilgrimage, recapitulating her mother's experience and greedily absorbing every trait of the deceased.

The evidence of "The Intermittencies of the Heart" at first glance might appear to suggest that, more even than the Freud of *Mourning and Melancholia*, Proust recognizes the mourning process as the ultimate, traumatic confrontation with the Other in the form of the dead. Whereas

Freud conspicuously fails to include any reference to dreams in his 1915 essay on mourning, Proust develops a phenomenology of mourning that highlights the crucial role of the subconscious by focusing on painful and anxious dreams. Indeed, involuntary memory seems to function as a traumatic event in "The Intermittencies of the Heart," in accordance with the rhythm described by Freud in *Beyond the Pleasure Principle* that divides sorrow into two moments: an initial loss (the death of the grandmother), followed by a second moment of "repetition" (the delayed epiphany in Balbec).[57] However, the rapid resolution of the narrator's "traumatic mourning" relative to his mother's bereavement signals Proust's unwillingness to dwell on the traumatic and desire to imagine an incongruously quick resolution. When the narrator experiences his succession of involuntary memories in the last volume, we witness the displacement of the traumatic model proposed by Freud in 1921 and to an extent reappropriated by Proust in "The Intermittencies of the Heart" by its benign parody.

Above all the other, evident warning signs of his mother's pathological condition, the most telling in the narrator's eyes is her quickly adopted habit of citing, as her own mother used to do, Mme. de Sévigné's letters. The mother's quotation of the grandmother's quotations of Mme. de Sévigné brilliantly illustrates the mechanism of incorporation at work in the mother's behavior, the ventriloquization of the living by the dead *en abîme* in the narrative (2:797–98; JYT 3:167). Throughout his sojourn in Balbec, the narrator will bear witness to his mother's obsession, usually with sympathy but at moments with condescension: "Daily after this my mother went down and sat on the beach, in order to do exactly what her mother had done, and read her two favourite books, the *Memoirs* of Mme de Beausergent and the *Letters* of Mme de Sévigné" (2:798).[58]

Even though the *Recherche* sustains an epistemological instability surrounding the question of whether the narrator and the author are one and the same, and though, as we have seen, the grief for his grandmother briefly accentuates the instability, the novel also clearly upholds by design the viability of the affirmative answer. Unlike his mother, the narrator will write about the event of the grandmother's death, assuming an active role in confronting his own feeling. Writing then would represent in his case the mystified outcome of a successful mourning, a proof of pain turned to productive ends. If the narrator truly believes in this elegiac function of writing, why does he feel compelled in *Time Regained* to elaborate an abstract, general principle of involuntary memory that by implication retrospectively recontextualizes the narrative? Interestingly, the narrator in "The Intermittencies of the Heart" compares himself to an actor or "*récitant*" who learns his role in order to improvise more adroitly on the topic of grief, a vocation, it might be added, that he wholeheartedly embraces in *Time Regained* (2:796; JYT 3:165). The narrator's defensive comparison of himself to an actor at the very moment his grief gains in urgency presages his later, fully articulated view of writing as a form of simulation, an ironizing of the subject's relation to the object in order to keep anxiety at bay.[59] More importantly, the simile anticipates the thorough transformation of the object of mourning into a likeness of the subject under the aegis of involuntary memory. Whereas in "The Intermittencies of the Heart" the object still represents a problematic Otherness, it appears to signify a domesticated alterity in the final volume, where the narrator embraces the aesthetic of the *involontaire*. It is himself that he comes to mourn in the novel's climactic pageant of involuntary memories. Although such a fluid conception of subjectivity is one of the most sophisticated and arresting effects of the *Recherche*, it is also, from the perspective of memory and mourning, the narrator's means of renegotiating and moderating the complicating difference of the Other and the ethical demands of loss.

As we have noted, Proust assigns the pathetic task of illustrating the mechanism of identification at work in melancholia to the narrator's mother. The absolute devotion with which she attends his grandmother during the latter's malady continues well beyond the brink of helpfulness. She is doomed in fact to transform herself into a ghost of the dead woman, as her son finally realizes at Balbec.

As soon as I saw her enter in her crepe overcoat, I realized—something that had escaped me in Paris—that it was no longer my mother that I had before my eyes, but my grandmother. As, in royal and ducal families, on the death of the head of the house his son takes his title and, from being Duc d'Orléans, Prince de Tarente or Prince de Laumes, becomes King of France, Duc de la Trémoïlle, Duc de Guermantes, so by an accession of a different order and more profound origin, the dead annex the living who become their replicas and successor, the continuators of their interrupted life.[60] (2:796–97)

Curiously, when it comes to mourning, Proust seems uncharacteristically faithful to a restrictively traditional gender politics. Women (from Françoise to the narrator's mother) are expected to play the socially prescribed role of mourners; unlike the narrator, they perform their task with obliging and unreflective devotion. The gendering of mourning in the novel, it should be noted, is not unrelated to the sociohistorical problematic of class that the passage explicitly thematizes. The simile likening the narrator's mother's pathological incorporation of the grandmother to the sterile transmission of aristocratic entitlements points to the emptiness of the nobility as a world-historical force, its phantasmatic irrelevance to the larger, living culture. Mourning in its most debased form may be seen to manifest itself in the superstitious rites of peasants such as Françoise and in the degenerate, conservative pomposity of the ruling class. As an artist, the narrator's task is to overcome such mindless reverence of the past, a task that he undertakes by surrendering to the cool self-alienation of the involuntary.

The difference between the narrator and his mother with regard to mourning is never more evident than when both face the daunting task of scrutinizing a picture of the deceased taken during her illness.[61] After her death, a sudden feeling of estrangement afflicts him as he gazes at the portrait she has left behind: "She no longer knew me . . . she was a stranger to me. This stranger was before my eyes at the moment in the photograph taken of her by Saint-Loup" (2:803).[62] The alienation elicited by the photograph derives from its interruption of the flow of sentimental associations that generally circulates around the figure of the beloved. However, as he continues to gaze at the picture, the narrator undergoes a surprising and inexplicable change of heart: "I kept my eyes fixed . . . upon the photograph that Saint-Loup had taken, and all of a sudden I thought once again: 'It's grandmother, I am her grandson,' as a man who has lost his memory remembers his name, as a sick man changes his personality" (2:803).[63] The accidental recognition of his grandmother and his proper relation to her, a defining psychic event that in its effect resembles a total supplanting of identity, prepares him for that moment when, at last, "he could look with pleasure at the photograph" (2:807; JYT 3:176). As described by the narrator, the moment bears more than a passing resemblance to the process of mourning in the Lacanian sense, a mobilization of the symbolic order that allows the subject to fill the hole in the Real by finding the proper measure and order of the relation between grandson and grandmother. As in Lacan's theory, however, the narrator's magical resolution of the problem, his facile, instantaneous act of remembering his name "as a sick man changes his personality," begs the question of mourning by highlighting its emotional capriciousness.

The narrator, unlike his mother, gradually arrives at an acceptance of his grandmother's picture, eventually finding in it a source of comfort and managing somehow to look beyond the tragic expression betrayed by his own description of her image:

A few days later I was able to look with pleasure at the photograph that Saint-Loup had taken of her. . . . But by contrast with what I imagined to have been her grave and pain-racked state that day, the photograph, still profiting by the ruses which my grandmother had adopted, which succeeded in taking me in even after they had been disclosed to me, showed her looking so elegant, so carefree, beneath the hat which partly hid her face, that I saw her as less unhappy and in better health than I had supposed. And yet, her cheeks having without her knowing it an expression of their own, leaden, haggard, like the expression of an animal that feels that it has been marked down for slaughter, my grandmother had an air of being under sentence of death, an air involuntarily sombre, unconsciously tragic, which escaped me but prevented Mama from ever looking at that photograph, that photograph which seemed to her a photograph not so much of her mother as of her mother's disease, of an insult inflicted by that disease on my grandmother's brutally buffeted face.[64] (2:807)

The narrator's shift from anxious mistrust to calm admiration of her picture marks the completion of his mourning for her and distinguishes his outlook from his mother's pathological grief. What is striking in the passage is the narrator's staged admission of naiveté, his belated and dramatic recognition that the "involuntarily" somber air of his grandmother had eluded the notice of his "involuntary" mourning. The passage might be understood as a warning, an aside to the reader suggesting the narrator's limited capacity for emotional experience. Beyond the question of Marcel's personal grief, however, what is at stake is also an allegorical mourning of the pathos of modernity. By not turning away from the grandmother's portrait as his mother did, by remaining open to aesthetic or hermeneutic curiosity, the narrator permits himself to complete a successful mourning. In this sense, the narrator's receptivity toward the photo betokens his ability to absorb the shock of alienation, the emergence of a new historical horizon.

The narrator's acceptance of the depersonalizing procedures of mechanical reproduction, his capacity to "look with pleasure" on the modernity exemplified by a photographic image, sharply contrasts with his mother's aversion to the portrait. Her inability or unwillingness to come to terms with the death of the grandmother logically coincides with a refusal of the fact of photography itself. It is as if, by recording the grandmother's "disease," the camera were responsible for inflicting the true, fatal "insult" on her face. The severing of the bond between mourning subject and dead object thus threatens to be repeated ad infinitum in the alienating alterity of the image. The fact that his mother cannot come to terms with the photograph signals her skepticism toward the modern photographic mise-en-scène. As Barthes has explained, one of the most striking characteristics of photography is the desperate effort by means of the mechanical image to "*faire vivant*," an effort that invites the spectator to deny the authority of death over both the taking and viewing of the picture.[65] The narrator, on the other hand, shows no qualms regarding the simulacrum of life that the photo of his grandmother achieves.[66] He defines his anguish as "transitory" in nature, as different in kind from his mother's "real grief" to the extent that his own involuntary memory of loss is "slow in coming" and cannot be retained:

But in reality there is a world of difference between real grief like my mother's—which literally crushes the life out of one for years if not for ever, when one has lost the person one loves—and that other kind of grief, transitory when all is said, as mine was to be, which passes as quickly as it has been slow in coming, which we do not experience until long after the event because in order to feel it we need first to "understand" the event; grief such as so many people feel, from which the grief that was torturing me at this moment differed only in assuming the form of involuntary memory.[67] (2:795–96)

Marcel unexpectedly ascribes a structure of deferred repetition to what he claims is a transient suffering, establishing a distance between loss and the comprehension of loss that only makes sense if loss is indeed traumatic. Why, then, the sudden, self-professed forgetfulness? The narrator's description of his "chagrin" offers a radical contrast to the Freudian conception of the sorrow work insofar as the latter regards the problem in cases of "ordinary" grief not as one of "understanding," but rather of dissolving the libidinal attachment. What is noteworthy here is the narrator's insistence on the commonness of his belated anguish, a universality that confronts its end limit in the sign of the "*souvenir involontaire*," the aesthetic supplement of the mourning process that represents the narrator's private anteriority. The narrator's conviction of the finitude of his grief is precisely what makes such a grief available as a narrative commodity, something not to be further examined, but merely subsumed under the category of the involuntary. What we may define as the narrator's paradoxes of mourning will become clearer and more evident in the concluding section of the novel.

Eventually, we will find that even the grief endured by Marcel on learning of Albertine's death will come safely, as Freud would have put it, to a spontaneous end. He will not, in other words, encounter or undergo anything like an "unforgettable" experience, particularly because Proust carefully avoids raising the possibility of the death of the narrator's mother in the novel. It appears simply that she will persist in rehearsing the past with such obsessiveness that, in compliance with *la loi générale de l'oubli*, she will finally disappear from the narrative altogether. In Balbec, at the end of his visit, the narrator momentarily confuses her with his grandmother; later in Venice, a little more than two years after Mme. Bathilde's death, when we see her again for the last time, she is behaving like her mother's ghost.

After the events of Venice, she drops entirely out of sight; only one reference is made to her by the narrator in *Time Regained* on the day of the Guermantes party, when his mother is supposed to be attending a little tea party chez Mme. Sazerat. At that point, near the conclusion of the novel, the narrator himself has become rather old and his mother, at best, cannot have long to live (3:888; JYT 4:435). In this sense, to understand the politics of memory at work in the *Recherche*, it is necessary to pay attention to the gradual "dissolving" of the narrator's mother, the character who is first responsible for his anxieties with regard to loss and grief. Her disappearance is cynically subsumed by the narrator under his grandmother's death, allowing him to escape the daunting obligation to mourn successfully or at least involuntarily the one object within his psychic universe whose loss could radically jeopardize his cool autonomy.

The Law of Oblivion: Proust as a Cynic

The narrator's forgetting of Albertine hastens the advancing deconstruction of his sense of identity and ultimately enables the establishment of those laws and principles that in the last volume appear to promise the triumph of the symbolic order. The representation of the psychic activity of memory and mourning grows increasingly abstract in the novel, until the development of the theme leads in *Le temps retrouvé* to the promulgation of a full-blown poetics of involuntary memory, the antithesis of the "general law of oblivion." But before the staging of this final *coup de théâtre*, the narrator appears to aim at proving the validity of a cynical equivalence between lost and wasted time.

Not much attention has been paid to the expressions of skepticism and cynicism in the *Recherche*. Unlike Baudelaire's flair for melodramatic effects culminating in moments of heightened cruelty and intensity, Proust's less histrionic rhetoric of nihilism can seem incongruous and provisional within the context of his overall project because it ultimately is overtaken and displaced in the novel by the competing discourse of aesthetics and *mémoire involontaire*. Interestingly, Martha Nussbaum, who has given the most thorough attention to Proust's stoicism, which is to say his faith in the acquisition of knowledge through suffering, neglects to explore his equally evident debt to cynical philosophy, which he encounters via the rhetorical influence of the French *moralistes*.[68] Not to consider the more pessimistic aspect of the *Recherche* would be a mistake not only because the narrator's final artistic epiphany is highly problematic, but also because any reading that overemphasizes Proust's commitment to a chronicle of rational progress must ignore the novel's actual narrative scheme and facts of production.

As is widely known, Proust's opus was written not in a linear fashion, but by commencing with the novel's opening and conclusion and then by accruing subsequently the remainder of the episodes including the Albertine cycle. The formal composition of the *Recherche*, in other words, throws into doubt the applicability of an Hegelian hermeneutic to the novel, according to which the plot structure mirrors the advance of a dialectical march toward order. *The Fugitive*, the segment devoted entirely to the mourning of Albertine, was in fact the last section to be written by Proust. Establishing an equivalence between love and mourning, the narrator reaches new heights of solipsism, even if in the end the work of mourning does not lead to a consolidation of the self, but rather to its fragmentation. Forgetting Albertine will become for the narrator the experimental proof of the validity and consistency of the "general law of oblivion," will affirm the nihilistic conviction that melancholia is impossible.[69]

Despite the novel's ostensible devotion to the problematic of memory, the narrator's conviction that he will forget Albertine is never in doubt in the *Recherche*. As he puts it, he knows he will admit the "first comer" to her place in his affections. Although the process of mourning coincides with an epistemophilic instinct evinced by his jealous investigation of Albertine's sexual preferences, it also occasions a mystifying and self-eradicating detour in the course of the narrative:

It is the tragedy of other people that they are merely showcases for the very perishable collections of one's own mind. For this very reason one bases upon them projects which have all the fervour of thought; but thought languishes and memory decays: the day would come when I would readily admit the first comer to Albertine's room, as I had without the slightest regret given Albertine the agate marble or other gifts that I had received from Gilberte.[70] (3:569)

In *The Fugitive*, Proust seems intent on writing the cynical corollary to Stendhal's *De l'amour*, replacing the latter's emphasis on the different stages of the "crystallization" process of love with a depiction of the gradual, inexorable advance of the process of decrystallization. The process of mourning in *The Fugitive* thus functions as a parodic exaggeration of the work of mourning imagined by Freud because the detachment of the libido in Proust ultimately coincides with the erasure of the object. Yet the narrator's mourning of Albertine still poses the enigmatic question of the Other, albeit in a complex and equivocal sense. On the one hand, his preoccupation with the mystery of Albertine's sexual preference suggests an anxious recapitulation of the question. On the other, even this fixation provides no stable framework for the "perishable collections" of his memories involving her because, as he declares, "thought languishes and memory decays." The ethical claims of the past thus seem doomed to lose their force or integrity, to regress into an exercise in epistemological futility.

After Albertine's death, when the question of mourning returns with renewed violence, the narrator will give the name "aura" to the stubborn survival of the dead in our consciousness notwithstanding the demise of the beloved in the actual world: "If this curiosity was so tenacious, it was because people do not die for us immediately, but remain bathed in a sort of aura of life which bears no relation to true immortality but through which they continue to occupy our thoughts in the same way as when they were alive" (3:521).[71] Clearly, the economic limits of mourning in Proust's view come to light via the narrator's insistence that aura bears no resemblance to immortality, an accentuation of the short-lived nature of memory consistent with his belief in *la loi générale de l'oubli*. The novelist's great achievement is to have transformed "the aura of life which bears no relation to true immortality" into the aesthetic ideology of involuntary memory, an ideology that cannot entirely mask the ephemerality of the "*aura de vie*" beneath art's illusion of timelessness. Indeed, his very definition of aura as an emotional attachment that prevents the subject from "immediately" [*tout de suite*] admitting the beloved's death only guarantees the belated, secondary death of the attachment itself. The fulfillment of such an aesthetic ideology thus entails a complete deconstruction of the subject, a task the narrative dramatizes through the narrator's successful mourning of Albertine.

At first, the process of mourning Albertine follows a seemingly Freudian course in as much as the narrator, before he can fully forget his beloved, is compelled to traverse in the opposite direction all of his fragmentary memories related to her (3:569; JYT 4:138). The task, however, appears to be at the same time easier and more destructive in the narrator's case than in the classic Freudian scenario because the succession of memories parallels the process of disintegration of his former self and its replacement by a new identity. Much more than Freud, Proust seems convinced that in order to mourn successfully, the subject must abandon its own identity, embracing with Ovidian gusto a continuous metamorphosis of the self. It is as though the capacity to mourn the object always entails a mourning of oneself, which proposition the narrator readily intuits, as he revels in his changed or renovated perspective, once Albertine has been forgotten: "No doubt this self still maintained some contact with the old, as a friend who is indifferent to a bereavement speaks of it nevertheless to the person present in a suitable tone of sorrow" (3:608).[72]

Opening a vertiginous *mise en abîme* of mourning, he suggests the best indication of a successful mourning is the subject's cynical indifference toward the loss of his former identity, a loss that to Proust looks undeserving of prolonged grief.[73] Freud's suggestion in *The Ego and the Id* that the very formation of the ego might be contingent on mourning—that is to say, on the successful introjection of lost objects—thus finds no narrative corroboration in the *Recherche*. No similar historical consolation or residual attachment to the object is possible in Proust's novel, in which, once achieved, the obliteration of the object does not leave behind any residual traces. In this sense, Proust, like Lacan and unlike Freud, fundamentally denies the importance of the object, sacrificing it to a conception of the subject premised on the radical solipsism and narcissism of desire. The proper perspective when reading Proust, Anne Henry rightly has argued, is not the attitude enforced by Rimbaud's celebrated assertion, "*Je est un autre*" ["I" is another], but the more extreme and contemporary position intimated by the question, "*Je est-il vraiment quelqu'un?*" [Is "I" truly someone?].[74] This is to say that Proust affirms the total fluidity of the subject, a condition fundamentally equivalent to that of an empty container that exists outside of history. According to Taylor, the modernist as opposed to romantic recovery of experience entails a reworking of received ideas of temporality and identity that ultimately points up or highlights a contradiction between interiority and antisubjectivism.[75] In Proust's narrative, there is more than contradiction because we witness the utter dissolution of subjectivity and the triumph of an interiority whose "voice" becomes impossible to position.

Proceeding from the first principles of his private, subjective experiences, the narrator reasons to general laws of psychology. Elaborating a sustained ironic simile between feelings such as "regret for a lost mistress" or jealousy and catastrophic physical illnesses such as tuberculosis or leukemia, he quips that in the case of mourning the "prognosis" is always positive, adding: "At the end of a given period after which a man who has been attacked by cancer will be dead, it is very seldom that the grief of an inconsolable widower or father is not healed" (3:659).[76] From this observation, arrived at in the course of his matter-of-fact acknowledgment that he no longer loves Albertine, he at last deduces the paramount authority of "the general law of oblivion" [*la loi générale de l'oubli*] (3:659; JYT 4:223). On a number of levels, this passage strikes me as perhaps Proust's most unrelieved exercise in cynicism. First, he stages a contest between corporeal and mental imperatives that, in circular fashion, is decided by appeal to the material truths of the body. Second, his heavily ironic rhetorical strategy, which is to push the central simile of the passage to logically absurd extremes, conveys a sense of dourness that is quasisatiric in its exaggeration, as if Proust surreptitiously were engaged in caricaturing the writings of the French *moralistes*. Finally, he betrays an indifference to suffering verging on contempt through his deployment of the adjective "inconsolable" as a mere *façon de parler*. Proust demonstrates here that for a writer the sublime act of cynicism is to adopt a parodic view of language itself, a position that in certain respects might consort with a Lacanian outlook in its affirmation of language's hold on us beyond any claim of emotional truth or weight.

Unlike the case of his grandmother, the end of his mourning for Albertine seems to compel the narrator to new degrees of skepticism with respect to the durability of memory. Whereas at Balbec he had still trusted, however momentarily, his grandmother's revisitation of him through memory, when he mistakenly comes to believe in Venice that Albertine is still alive, the thought has little impact and brings no feelings of happiness because she no longer holds for him the compelling fascination of an enigma: "Albertine had been no more than a bundle of thoughts, and she had survived her physical death so long as those thoughts were alive in me; on the other hand, now that those thoughts were dead, Albertine did not raise again for me with the resurrection of her body" (3:656).[77]

The narrator skeptically concludes that if he cannot resuscitate Albertine, this is because he is incapable of resuscitating himself. At this point, in other words, Proust's conception of mourning ceases to revolve around the enigma of the Other and instead begins to center increasingly around the self. Although the self as Proust conceives it is inherently unstable, its vicissitudes do not pose the sort of ethical challenge for the narrator that true loss represents. In the concluding volume, the narrator's rediscovery of the lost paradise of involuntary memory indeed transforms the anguished, ethical responsiveness of mourning into a coolly aesthetic and narcissistic detachment. The moral of the story seems to affirm the validity of a "weak" solipsism, according to which the subject or ego abandons its prerogatives in order to resign itself to an inherent state of transience. Insofar as the narrative regards the workings of memory as a function of the skepticism and self-alienation of a historically arbitrary subject, the *Recherche* might be said to exemplify the peculiar ideological configuration that generally typifies contemporary culture. Indeed, by taking a cynical position with regard to the resolution of mourning, Proust does more than to promote involuntary memory as a strictly aesthetic ideology, for the formation of this ideology opens a space in turn for the establishment of a consumerist economy of loss. By the postmodern epoch, this system will become nothing less than a full-blown, radically externalized commerce of nostalgia.

The Aura of Mourning

In order to understand the significance of the dialectical movement in the *Recherche* from the intermittencies to the involuntary, it is necessary to examine the central procedure of *la mémoire involontaire* as Proust describes it in the final volume, *Time Regained.* The procedure consists of the opening of memory to the accidental return of a "purer air" of the past that, as a result of "the work of oblivion," has retained its uncanny aesthetic distance from the subject and thus evokes all of "the paradises we have lost," the grounds of our solipsistic emotional reality (3:903; JYT 4:449). Such an emphasis on the sublime value of the past, on its resistance to duplication or recovery by conscious means, implies a nostalgic longing completely at odds with the narrator's calm obedience to "the general law of oblivion" in the face of Albertine's death, his chilling acceptance of her mortality and even forgetability when describing her as "bathed in a sort of *aura* of life which bears no relation to true immortality" [baigné d'une espèce d'aura de vie qui n'a rien d'une immortalité véritable] (3:521; JYT 4:92).

The dissonance between Marcel's professed feeling of bereavement at his alienation from the abstract "paradise" of the past and demonstrated indifference with respect to the real loss of loved ones such as Albertine is exacerbated by a further, decisive self-contradiction in the rhetorical premises of the novel's conclusion. Proust sets out in *Time Regained* to explain how the quest for lost time works as if it were a transcendental principle, to codify the rules of the game of the involuntary by construing in expository terms the preceding narrative instances of *la mémoire involontaire*, rather than to continue or elaborate the narrative account itself. In so doing, he drops the task of poetically or aesthetically evoking the phenomenology of lost time and instead attempts to distill for analytic purposes the essential "method" of its retrieval. The organic poetics of recollection ostensibly espoused by Marcel thereby reveals itself to consist of a repertory of artificially stylized gestures.

My reasoning may seem controversial to anyone who accepts at face value the narrator's own account of his intentions in the novel. However, I will argue in the remainder of this chapter that Proust's ambivalence with respect to the past, his equivocation between aggrieved mournfulness and clinical impassivity toward loss, his dividedness between modern seriousness and postmodern lightness is revealed in large part by Walter Benjamin's complex response to the final volume of the *Recherche*. That Benjamin's own definition of the concept of aura as formulated in the "Little History of Photography" (1931) and "The Work of Art in the Age of Mechanical Reproduction" (1936) and significantly revised in "On Some Motifs in Baudelaire" (1939) derives practically verbatim from Proust is a fact rarely acknowledged as fully as it ought to be. The German critic's famous call in "Work of Art" for the emancipation of art by technological reproduction from its cult value is predicated on the identification of such value with the artwork's "aura," the definition of which he lifts directly from the description in *Time Regained* of the "air" of involuntary memory. In this sense, Benjamin's initial exuberance over the destruction of aura may be aligned with the cool, antinostalgic, postmodern Proust. It is no accident that this essay by Benjamin has become the cornerstone of an entire subindustry of postmodern writing celebrating the ascendancy of mass media and popular culture.[78] Much more than Adorno or any other members of the Frankfurt School, Benjamin realized that the new conditions of production had altered the very concept of art. Forsaking its traditional, quasireligious function, the artwork increasingly becomes the locus of a less structured, more open-ended and consumerist experience consonant with a world saturated by the influence of mass media.[79]

However, an apparent discomfort at the implications of such a radical transformation of culture replaces the critic's early exultation by the time of "On Some Motifs in Baudelaire." In this essay, Benjamin abandons his earlier, nondialectical approach because of its unacceptable erasure of tradition and the past and concludes that the course of modernity is not necessarily redemptive, and indeed risks veering toward a nihilistic end. On this view, he nominates Baudelaire, not Proust, as his exemplar of the historically aware artist who succeeds in articulating "the change in the structure of . . . experience" typical of modernity.[80] For the German critic, Baudelaire's achievement resides in his having "indicated the price for which the sensation of the modern age may be had: the disintegration of the aura in the experience of shock" and in his representation of that price in suitably tragic terms.[81] As I will maintain, Benjamin anxiously tries throughout the essay to assimilate the Proustian doctrine of involuntary memory to the Baudelairean vocabulary of *correspondances* in order to resuscitate Proust's mournful, nostalgic, modernist aspect, but by his own admission the effort is doomed to failure, due to the limiting conditions the *Recherche* itself imposes on any such reading.

The new definition of aura that he proposes in "Some Motifs" once again derives from the *Recherche*, although now the Proustian original is quoted and attributed to its author. This time, Benjamin emphasizes not the question of the sublime distance of the artwork, but rather, in what seems like a subtle self-reversal, its capacity to return the gaze of the viewer. Given his declaration in "Some Motifs" that the aura appears when the object shows "the ability to look at us in return" and his celebration of Baudelaire's tragic anguish at the extinguishing of such an ability, we might think the German critic would praise Proust for supplying Benjamin with the terms of this thesis.[82] Yet, as we shall see momentarily, he instead quotes Proust with some distrust, observing that the explication of the auratic in the *Recherche* is an instance of "theory" and strongly implying that it therefore cannot enact or exemplify what it describes. Without quite saying so,

Benjamin suggests a suspicion that Proust's definition of aura neutralizes the very spectrality it promises because it seeks to categorize and close off a process of mourning that purports to be spontaneous and thus genuine.

In a sense, the critic's unease in "Some Motifs" regarding the explication of *la mémoire involontaire* that Marcel delivers at the end of the novel indicates precisely how far Proust advances toward postmodernity. For rather than poetically redescribing the tragic collision between the aura of tradition and the experience of shock, Proust claims to develop a language in which aura is ironically reproduced as the simulation and thus the mastery or taming of shock. As we shall see, Benjamin recognizes that the true auratic moments of *In Search of Lost Time* are related to such technological innovations as railway stations, photography, and telephones. In this manner, the critic shows that the unacknowledged foundations of the auratic in Proust's *chef d'oeuvre* are the sensational or spectacular forces of mass culture that promote commodification. Although pretending to eternalize a romantic conception of art, the novel proceeds de facto to undermine the very basis of such a conception. We might surmise, then, that the theoretical appendix of *Time Regained*, which consistently reaffirms the truthfulness of art, fulfills the ideological function of disguising and concealing the changed nature of the artistic enterprise. In this light, Proust's performance of nostalgia, his definition of aura in terms of a *paradis perdu*, prefigures the irreverence of present-day mass culture toward the past in order to avoid confronting the historical and social entropy that the work of art has undergone. Benjamin's own ambivalence toward the task of cultural mourning reflects the reversals and contradictions of Proust's theory of involuntary memory.

Loss of Halo

One of the most popular images of Proust is that of the "auratic" novelist who observes the transience and mystery of emotional experience by cultivating a poetics of epiphanic memories. To what extent is such a strategy genealogically related to postmodern production of artificial nostalgia? A serious reading of Proust's *chef d'oeuvre* might wish to address this question because if mourning in the narrative operates like an engine of emotional deglamorization or disenchantment, the reader ultimately must determine whether "aura" is not merely the obfuscatory ideal of an artistic practice that vainly aims to escape the catastrophe of history and personal experience. To understand Proust's somewhat affected resurrection of an auratic conception of art, it is important to compare his project to that of his predecessor, Baudelaire.

On this score, Walter Benjamin's essays on the two French authors are crucial to establishing their genealogical relationship but also to highlight Proust's deviation from the Baudelairean idea of memory. Benjamin's text, although it praises Proust, cannot hide a final discomfort with the "coolness" of the involuntary. Benjamin recognizes a continuity between Baudelaire's notion of *correspondances* and Proust's of *la mémoire involontaire*. The question of the link between the writers however soon reveals a fundamental discrepancy between Proust's philosophy and Baudelaire's aesthetics: one is "positive," affirming the necessity of aura, the other negative. In "On Some Motifs in Baudelaire," Benjamin argues that the poet's chief achievement was to have renounced the prophetic aura of the romantic or classical *vates*, to have relinquished his "halo."[83] Adorno, in *Aesthetic Theory*, echoes Benjamin's observation that Baudelaire's fundamental contribution was to disenchant or deaestheticize art itself.[84] Proust, on the other hand, might be said to pursue a mock reenchantment of art by promoting the shock value of experience through the work of art. Although from a traditional perspective he dilutes the meaning of art as a concept by equating the artistic process with the exploration, collation, and replication of experience, Proust gives us a foretaste of what becomes in commodity culture a received wisdom about the function of art. However, in the *Recherche*, this dissolution of art into shock is carefully disguised by the auratic theory of the involuntary. If it is true, as Vattimo suggests, that shock is all that is left of art in the epoch of mass media, we can say that the awareness inaugurated by Baudelaire and validated by Benjamin is mystified by Proust.[85]

In "Perte d'auréole" ["Loss of Halo"], one of the most striking and celebrated of the so-called poems in prose that make up *Le spleen de Paris*, Baudelaire on an allegorical level sets out to perform nothing less than the mourning of art's metaphysical autonomy. The poem recounts the poet's experience, while out for a stroll on the boulevard, of losing his *auréole* when he recoils abruptly to avoid being run over by a carriage. But instead of retrieving the dropped accouterment, as a friend urges him to do, the poet enjoys his newly liberated status as a humble, incognito pedestrian, secretly relishing the thought of bad poets crowning themselves with his relinquished badge of office.[86]

At the climactic moment in *Time Regained* when the narrator relates his epiphanic cognition of the phenomenon of involuntary memory while walking in the street, Proust in a sense appears to be picking up the *auréole* abandoned by Baudelaire.[87] The well-known passage in the *Recherche* reappropriates the central image of the Baudelairean prose-poem—namely, that of the writer accidentally thrown off balance: "I had entered the courtyard of the Guermantes mansion and in my absent-minded state I had failed to see a car which was coming towards me; the chauffeur gave a shout and I just had time to step out of the way, but as I moved sharply backwards I tripped against the uneven paving-stones in front of the coach-house" (3:898).[88] However, the consequences of Marcel's disequilibrium are notably different from those of the Baudelairean narrator's misstep. The bold, cynical self-sacrifice of the poet is superseded by the "happiness" of the novelist who, at the very moment of distress, recovers his occult vocation. Benjamin concludes his essay on Baudelaire with the quotation (in its entirety) and interpretation of "Perte d'auréole,"[89] observing that Baudelaire articulates in the prose-poem his heroic ideal, his determination to give to every lived experience [*Erlebnis*] the weight of wisdom: "He indicated the price for which the sensation of the modern age may be had: the disintegration of the aura in the experience of the shock."[90] In *The Arcades Project*, Benjamin pauses to consider Baudelaire's renunciation of aura as a sign of the poet's awareness of his susceptibility to the conditions of the marketplace.[91]

Proust's poetics of involuntary memory hinge on an apologetic and mystifying theory of aura that stands in sharp contrast to the ethic of self-ironic, renunciatory cynicism that Baudelaire promotes under the name *spleen*. For Proust, the essence of modernity is to be found in the attempt to recover or renovate the auratic, the experience of which, as Benjamin points out in "On Some Motifs in Baudelaire," corresponds to the "data" of *la mémoire involontaire*.[92] His nostalgia for what looks like an obsolete transcendental category, however, threatens to color Proust as a *mauvais poète* or cultural reactionary, the sort of person who, as I have suggested, would have stooped all to quickly to pick up the Baudelairean fallen halo. It is rarely acknowledged by scholars that Benjamin's very definition of aura is a near-verbatim quotation or translation of an important passage in the *Recherche* describing the work of involuntary memory. We should remember, however, that he collaborated with Franz Hessel on a German translation of *Le Côté de Guermantes*.[93] As we shall see, Benjamin in a sense continued in his critical work to grapple with the task of translating Proust's masterpiece. Given the undeniable influence of Proust on a constellation of related moments in Benjamin's writing, the German critic's investment in the French novelist's account of *la mémoire involontaire* ought to be regarded as only to a small degree justifiable in terms of Benjamin's well-known fascination with occultism and theosophy.

Proust does not use the word "aura," but in his description of the emotional weight of involuntary memory, he emphasizes the importance of "air" to the sense-data that provide the basic material for the work of memory:

Yes: if, owing to the work of oblivion, the returning memory can throw no bridge, form no connecting link between itself and the present minute, if it remains in the context of its own place and date, if it keeps its distance, its isolation in the hollow of a valley or upon the highest peak of a mountain summit, for this very reason it causes suddenly to breathe a new air, an air which is new precisely because we have breathed in the past that purer air which the poets have vainly tried to situate in paradise and which could induce so profound a sensation of renewal only if it had been breathed before because the true paradises are the paradises we have lost.[94] (3:903)

If we remember that the word *aura* derives from a Greek etymological root meaning "air" or "breeze," we realize that Benjamin's preferred term for the surplus value of art bears more than a passing resemblance to the core concept of Proust's aesthetic ideology. In this passage, Proust presents the "purer air" of the past as the metaphysical ground of a reverential nostalgia or *pietas* for the past, albeit a nostalgia that has nothing to do with the values of tradition, history, or ritual that Benjamin ascribes in "The Work of Art in the Age of Mechanical Reproduction" to the domain of the aura, but that revolves instead around what Benjamin will categorize in a tantalizing footnote in "On Some Motifs" as Proust's "private show."[95] In spite of the discrepancy between a poetics of the involuntary that idealizes in quasi-mystical terms the lost "paradises" of the past and the banal, quotidian shock value of such data of the involuntary as the sensation of tripping in the street, Benjamin accepts Proust's description of the auratic at face value.

In "The Work of Art in the Age of Mechanical Reproduction," the German critic indeed establishes his concept of aura [*Begriff der Aura*] by means of a pastiche of Proust's language in *Time Regained*. Benjamin's adoption of the novelist's key words such as "distance," "mountains," and "breath" makes the object of emulation unmistakable: "The concept of aura . . . with reference to historical objects may usefully be illustrated with reference to the aura of natural ones. We define the aura of the latter as the unique phenomenon of a distance, however close it may be. If, while resting on a summer afternoon, you follow with your eyes a mountain range on the horizon or a branch which casts its shadow over you, you experience the aura of those mountains, of that branch" [die Aura dieser Berge, dieses Zweiges atmen, literally "*breathe* the aura of these mountains, of this branch"].[96] Strikingly, both Proust and Benjamin seem to imagine the auratic in the language of a quotidian natural sublime, a sort of domestication of Kantian categories.[97] Whereas Proust locates this quotidian sublime in a general recovery of the past, which is the starting point of his aesthetic ideology, Benjamin refers it specifically to the "historical objects" of art, which makes his use of a nature-based vocabulary of description the more remarkable. The difference between the two writers in this regard, it should be noted, is one of degree rather than kind; both adopt a naive and anachronistic terminology as the insignia of their "modern" poetics as if, at the very moment they had to define their relation to culture, they were reduced to offering a performance or simulacrum of the sublime. In the *Recherche*, the definition of *la mémoire involontaire* as an epistemological distancing of the subject from the object follows the narrator's final epiphanies regarding memory and writing in *Time Regained* and functions as a somewhat contrived theoretical summation of ideas that the novel already has recounted in narrative form. As has been well noted, "The Work of Art in the Age of Mechanical Reproduction" is one of the few places where Benjamin looks on the technocratic "progress" of mass society with something like unequivocal historical optimism and appears to embrace the losses or costs exacted by the advance of modernity.

That his ostensibly triumphant rejection of the cult value traditionally ascribed to the work of art occurs through the Proustian description of *la mémoire involontaire* is important. The critic's rhetorical vehemence and nihilism in the 1936 essay, his pretended renunciation of the autonomy of art, might be interpreted more appropriately as enacting an allegorical mourning, the equivalent in prose exposition of Mlle. Vinteuil's sadistic acts of remembrance. Proust's description of the auratic fetishizes the artwork as a transcendent reproduction of the past, all the while disguising the fact that by indulging so much the insights of involuntary memory, he is de facto dissolving art into a simulation of experience. Benjamin at first incorporates Proust's language in order to describe "aura" as the projection of a regressive ritualistic impulse that has to be overcome. However, the critic's unquestioning liquidation of the historical problematic of art atypically places utter faith in the benignity of the technologies of mass production. Benjamin's overdetermined and uncritical adoption of Proust's description of the auratic certainly facilitates the essay's elaboration of a naive logic of binary opposition between "magical" art and mechanical reproduction.

That Benjamin was thinking quite overtly of Proust's example when writing the essay is made even clearer by the existence of a Proust dossier or scrapbook, discovered in the *Bibliothèque Nationale*, which Benjamin compiled in preparation for the composition of "The Work of Art in the Age of Mechanical Reproduction." Entitled "Prouststellen zum Kunstwerk im Zeitalter," the scrapbook amasses quotations from the *Recherche* for use in the essay.[98] In his choice of passages from the novel, the critic focuses particularly on what he calls "auratic moments" at which the novel uncovers the sublimity and strangeness of the latest breakthroughs in technology.[99] What eventually becomes apparent from an examination of Benjamin's notes is his conviction that throughout the *Recherche*, the genuine auratic moments have nothing to do with Proust's explicit theory of involuntary memory, but rather with the novelist's indefatigable ability to capture the uncanniness of recent technological innovations such as the telephone, photography, and railway stations.

Interestingly, in both the "Prouststellen" and *The Arcades Project*, when Benjamin identifies a "decisive passage" in Proust concerning aura, he does not mention the climactic epiphany in the Guermantes courtyard that occurs in *Time Regained*, but rather an extended disquisition regarding traveling and the Gare Saint-Lazare that occurs in *Within a Budding Grove* [*A l'ombre des jeunes filles en fleurs*].[100] In this passage, Proust observes that the special attraction of the railroad lies in its ability to expose the difference between arrival and departure, in occasioning the imperceptible emergence of new forms of consciousness. Proust thus defines railway stations as loci of transience and loss, as inherently tragic places (2:694; JYT 2:6). According to Kahn, Benjamin paid special attention to this passage because of the influence of the Proustian problematic of distance on his own conception of the auratic: "For Proust's and Benjamin's analyses coincide on this fundamental point: the new technologies bring to light aura at the same moment that they condemn it."[101] Technology, then, is responsible not for the destruction of aura, but for its very unveiling or appearance.

Benjamin thus seems to surmise, if not quite to come out and admit, that aura in the *Recherche* arises out of experiences of transience rather than out of theoretical manifestoes about the eternity and truthfulness of art.[102] If Benjamin is right to identify the auratic in Proust's work where we least expect it, that is to say where the new, rather than the past, intrudes to modify life, then Proust's definition of aura in terms of a "lost paradise" sounds hollow and coy.

On this view, his exposition of the distancing or alienation effect of involuntary memory in *Time Regained* functions as a theoretical supplement, an ideological mise-en-scène in which we encounter only the reified simulacrum of the aura that the novel authentically effects when it addresses the reader most indirectly—that is, via the periphrastic conceits of fiction or metaphor rather than the pedagogical devices of criticism. If Benjamin's examination of the autonomous work of art at points seems lacking in nuance and sophistication, relying on a hyperschematic opposition between mechanically reproduced and magical works (an opposition that, for example, could not be applied to literature), it does so to some degree because of his not always acknowledged point of departure—namely, Proust's already overdetermined and mystifying definition of the auratic. As has been documented, Adorno reacted sharply against Benjamin's "liquidation" of the autonomous work of art, observing that such absolutism manifests an undialectical and politically naive methodology.[103] Benjamin's desecration of high art in "The Work of Art in the Age of Mechanical Reproduction" appears not to take into account Proust's own ambiguous politics of the auratic. Although in his preparatory notes to the essay, the German critic identifies the auratic as an eminently "involuntary" by-product of the *Recherche*, he ultimately takes Proust's "theoretical" definition of aura at face value and makes this formula the point of departure for his own critique of the autonomous work of art.

It is only in "On Some Motifs in Baudelaire" (1939) that the German critic to an extent will be able to overcome his previous uncritical and unattributed "incorporation" of Proust's definition of the auratic, exposing for the first time its limits and contradictions. He becomes increasingly aware, in other words, that the narrator's final rhetorical strategy is not to perpetuate the novel's fictive premises, which in turn might give rise to aura as the "involuntary" by-product, so to speak, of the narrative. Instead, Marcel undertakes the willed manufacture of aura in *Time Regained*, an aporetic enterprise on which Benjamin can only look with skepticism. In so doing, the critic adopts a position from which it becomes possible to denounce the nihilist aspects of modernity, thus complicating his earlier triumphalism in "The Work of Art in the Age of Mechanical Reproduction," as well as the essay's apparent celebration of the prospect of culture beyond the horizon of mourning.

The Comfort of the Involuntary: Proust Between Baudelaire and Benjamin

If, in "The Work of Art in the Age of Mechanical Reproduction," Benjamin momentarily exaggerates the revolutionary potential of mass media and in particular of film, his outlook in his subsequent writings soon returns to his more customary historical pessimism and melancholia. It is not surprising that at this time, Benjamin reevaluates and finally criticizes Proust's approach to the auratic. In fact, in 1939, when Benjamin sets out on a rehabilitation of aura and the autonomy of the artwork in his essay, "On Some Motifs in Baudelaire," he turns not to Proust but to Baudelaire as his model of the historically conscious writer. Proust nonetheless keeps resurfacing throughout "Some Motifs" and, as in "Work of Art," supplies Benjamin once more with an ur-text for the German critic's own definition of aura, albeit to an overall effect that differs significantly from that of the earlier essay. Under the pretense of innocuous reflection on the similarity of the two writers, moreover, Benjamin in "Some Motifs" sets the terms of an ideological confrontation between the French poet and novelist that in the end decides the direction of his argument. Although Baudelairean *spleen* represents for Benjamin a dynamic response to the suffering entailed by cultural reification, Proustian involuntary memory affirms what the German critic defines as an "attempt to produce experience synthetically . . . under today's conditions, for there is less and less hope that it will come into being naturally."[104] Although he initially maintains that Proust does not evade the question of the artificiality of experience, Benjamin punctuates the essay with equivocations regarding the novelist's aims and goals, equivocations that eventually will undo his original claim.[105]

Benjamin had already observed, first in his 1929 essay, "The Image of Proust," and then again in "Some Motifs," that the narrator's description in the *Recherche* makes *la mémoire involontaire* seem closer to an act of forgetting or obliviousness than to recollection. Benjamin, however, does his best in "Some Motifs" to uncover the auratic value of the Proustian model as he emphasizes the traumatic quality of involuntary memories and their capacity to provide access to past experience.[106] Consequently, he develops a psychoanalytic interpretation of involuntary memory commensurate with his own view of modernity as a form of historical shock.[107] Invoking Freud's view that fragments of memory are most enduring when the event occasioning them is unconscious, Benjamin proceeds by attributing to Proust's involuntary memory a traumatic and unconscious quality that would allow access to a sphere of integrated, internalized, significant experience [*Erfahrung*] as opposed to the fleeting, instant gratification of lived sensation [*Erlebnis*].[108] His efforts, however, encounter a limit in Proust's own conceptual logic because, according to the narrator's revelatory exposition in *Time Regained*, involuntary memories function to domesticate and mystify shock for the purpose of its consumption as spectacle, hardly constituting the traumatic events that Freud and Benjamin seem to have in mind. Indeed, if the equivalent of what Benjamin is affirming is to be found in the *Recherche*, it ought to be looked for in the intermittencies of the heart rather than in involuntary memory.

Compared to the simplistic explanation of aura in "Work of Art," the new account set forth in "On Some Motifs in Baudelaire" is more sophisticated and nuanced. Once again, Benjamin's point of departure is *Time Regained*, that final section of the *Recherche* in which Proust provides a sort of "objective," theoretical formulation of the idea of *la mémoire involontaire*, after having furnished in earlier sections the "subjective," narrative representation of individual involuntary memories. Unlike "The Work of Art in the Age of Mechanical Reproduction," however, "Some Motifs" acknowledges its quotation of material from the *Recherche*, focusing on a passage that occurs a few pages after the narrator's first subjective description of an encounter with the involuntary and interspersing the citation with intermittent commentary of the critic's own. Benjamin's critique of the second Proustian investigation of "aura," as I have already suggested, comes at a moment when the German critic is revising his own initial understanding of the concept. In fact, in "Some Motifs" Benjamin abandons his first, somewhat reckless assault on autonomous art and starts to adopt a more complicated, melancholic tone when considering the social value of the object. What looked to him in the earlier essay like the triumph of modernity and its techniques of mass production is reinterpreted in terms of loss;

what looked like a forward step beyond tradition and mourning becomes instead a dialectic at a historical "standstill."[109] Proust's forced, contrived marketing of the principle of *la mémoire involontaire* cannot but strike Benjamin as quite the opposite of the articulation of an auratic moment. The "wistful fantasy" that constitutes the novelist's ideology of involuntary memory presumes a successful mourning of modernity of which the critic by contrast proves incapable.[110]

More importantly, it is in "On Some Motifs in Baudelaire" that Benjamin at last brings himself to censure the fictitious universality of the French novelist's central tenet, which he seems compelled to acknowledge, despite an insistence on what he calls "Proust's great familiarity with the problem of the aura."[111] Here Benjamin overtly cites Proust in translation, using quotation marks and interspersing his own commentary between citations: "'Some people who are fond of secrets flatter themselves that objects retain something of the gaze that has rested on them.' (The ability, it would seem, of returning the gaze.) 'They believe that monuments and pictures present themselves only beneath the delicate veil which centuries of love and reverence on the part of so many admirers have woven about them. This chimera,' Proust concludes evasively, 'would change into truth if they related it to the only reality that is valid for the individual, namely the world of his emotions.'"[112] The French novelist's conclusion strikes Benjamin as evasive [*ausweichend*] because, as he points out, notwithstanding the writer's evident grasp of the dubiousness of any attempt to interpret artistic autonomy as a transcendental category rather than as a function of the emotions, Proust alludes to aura in terms that "comprehend its theory" [*Theorie in sich schließen*].[113] At this point, Benjamin raises the suspicion that what he had unequivocally defined in the first part of the essay as Proust's successful solution to the risk of a "synthetic" production of experience in the novel might turn out to be a mystification after all.[114] Benjamin's castigation of Proust seems all the more damning, given that the novelist himself just a few pages before the incriminating passage ridicules those creative works that are unable to resist the temptation of theory: "A work in which there are theories is like an object which still has its price-tag on it" (3:916).[115]

More than a price tag, Proust's theory of *la mémoire involontaire*, with its insistence on the auratic value of the involuntary, might be said to resemble an advertising campaign in as much as it gives the *Recherche* an almost pop-culture veneer of fetishized self-promotion, strangely at odds with the dream of artistic purity that the novel ostensibly pursues with such ambition. Benjamin appears to recognize in "Some Motifs" that Proust's doctrine of the aesthetic operates in the manner of a marketing strategy devised by the *Recherche* to publicize its own cultural capital; the logic of this strategy provides the positive counterpart to the German critic's own "liquidation" of aura in "The Work of Art in the Age of Mechanical Reproduction."[116] If in "On Some Motifs in Baudelaire" Benjamin relies on an alternate, more dialectical and ethical definition of aura, it is certainly in order to escape the solipsistic spell of the first "subjective" formulation, elaborated in "Work of Art," which affirms art's uncanny ability to return the scrutiny of the beholder: "To perceive the aura of an object we look at means to invest it with the ability to look at us in return."[117] Dropping the attitude of the critic whose mourning of culture is completed or "successful," Benjamin regretfully elegizes this critically reciprocal dimension of the work of art, a dimension that has been lost as a result of the impoverishment of experience brought about by modern life. Yet even as he borrows this second definition again from Proust's text, he is now aware that he embraces it and reads it in a different spirit.[118]

In fact, the German critic raises one central objection to the ethical and historical logic of involuntary memories and their connection to authentic experience when he observes that the experience of involuntary memory is contingent on chance and derives its power from complete isolation, from its radically private character.[119] In a footnote to "Some Motifs," Benjamin can defend Proust's strategy only through a "nihilistic reading" of the *Recherche*: "The deterioration of experience manifests itself in Proust in the complete realization of his ultimate intention. There is nothing more ingenious or more loyal than the way in which he nonchalantly and constantly strives to tell the reader: Redemption is my private show."[120] Nevertheless, Benjamin is convinced that where there is real experience [*Erfahrung*], the personal or individual content of one's memory is always contaminated by participation in the collective, according to the rhythms of ritual and ceremony that are "quite probably nowhere recalled in Proust's work."[121] The discrepancy between collective and individual memory, the ritualized and the involuntary, is such as possibly to obstruct the critical recuperation of Proust's work within the larger project of a historical rehabilitation of art. In this light, Proust's self-professed reclamation of the ground of artistic authenticity looks suspicious if compared to Baudelaire's sacrificial renunciation of aura.[122] Benjamin's growing ambivalence toward the Proustian auratic, incorporated in his commentary of the quotation from the *Recherche*, becomes even more evident if we pay attention to the critical distance he establishes between Proust and Baudelaire.

The comparison of Baudelaire and Proust in "On Some Motifs in Baudelaire" establishes a very problematic continuity between the two artists within the larger dramatic pageant of modernity. Benjamin concludes his essay by observing that Baudelaire paid dearly for "consenting" to the disintegration of aura in exchange for access to the experience of shock.[123] Proust's example, however, prompts us to think about the logical consequences of such an exchange and to ask what comes after disintegration? To what extent does the role-playing dictated by the spectacle of modernity ultimately come to seem artificial and mannered in Proust? Whereas allegory in Baudelaire's poetry works as a destructive apparatus, a renunciation of auratic distance in favor of a sudden eruption of meaning, art functions in Proust's fiction as a literary and ideological machine for the production of meaning, a meaning that remains, however, quite respectful of the economic and social status quo.[124]

Benjamin argues that Proust faces "more elemental and powerful [historical] counterforces" than does Baudelaire and that the novelist's will to restore cannot count on the metaphysical solution of "*correspondances*," having to content itself instead with the quotidian limitations of involuntary memory.[125] But the critic also acknowledges in the end that Baudelairean *spleen* enforces a keener and more tragic sense of the passage of time than does *la mémoire involontaire*.[126] Although on balance he insists on the similarity of Baudelaire and Proust's ideas of temporality and memory, his argument reveals a crucial blind spot when he discusses a section of the *Recherche* in which the narrator, after having pondered the role of retrospection in Nerval and Chateaubriand, praises Baudelaire: "Above all in Baudelaire, where they are more numerous still, reminiscences of this kind are clearly less fortuitous and therefore, to my mind, unmistakable in their significance. Here the poet himself, with something of a slow and indolent choice, deliberately [*volontairement*] seeks, in the perfume of a woman, for instance, of her hair and her breast, the analogies which will inspire him" (3:959).[127] Benjamin identifies this encomium as a "confessional motto" for the novelist's work, suggesting a correspondence between Baudelaire's "days of remembrance" and Proust's involuntary memories.[128] What is problematic about the critic's argument is the fact that here, in a fit of self-contradiction, the narrator singles out for approval an expressly "voluntary" poetic of reminiscences, the "crucial importance" of which is that such acts of remembrance are not "occasioned by chance." The narrator in other words is celebrating a quality he claims to deplore in his own literary enterprise.[129]

The homage to Baudelaire in the *Recherche* is so uncharacteristic that it has provoked one of the most egregious misreadings of Proust's novel. Making reference to the passage, Deleuze in his last chapter of *Proust and Signs* unwittingly reverses the sense of the Proustian quotation. "When Proust seeks a precursor in reminiscences," writes Deleuze, "he cites Baudelaire, but reproaches him with having made too 'voluntary' a use of the method, which is to say, with having sought objective articulations and analogies which are still too Platonic, in a world inhabited by the *Logos*."[130] Deleuze somehow convinces himself that Proust is chastising Baudelaire and expressing a preference for Chateaubriand's inorganic, arbitrary reminiscences in accordance with a taste for a more modern form of memory, "an associative, incongruous chain [that] is unified only by a creative viewpoint which itself takes the role of an incongruous part within the whole."[131] Deleuze's misreading of the passage exemplifies in more blatant fashion the critical bias that also prevents Benjamin from recognizing a crucial moment of Proustian bad consciousness with respect to the ideology of the involuntary.

What is most striking about the passage in the *Recherche* is Proust's choice of a criterion by which to judge his literary predecessors, a criterion that logically ought to disallow his contribution to the very tradition he is ostensibly promulgating. By way of contrast to these predecessors, he remains intent throughout the *Recherche*, from the initial occurrence of involuntary memory in the first volume to the series of epiphanies that punctuates the last, on exploring the irrational, arbitrary character of remembrance while disregarding ethical intentionality, politics, and historical change. Although it originates in the private sphere of the subject, the concept of the involuntary may be said in this sense to anticipate the later romanticizing of passivity and detachment that facilitates the subject's eventual surrender to the mystifying cultural logic of postmodern society.

On this score, we might have to consider Proust's rather than Baudelaire's work as the watershed, the geological catastrophe of modernity, insofar as the *Recherche* manages to transcend the ethical and political values of mourning and to escape a melancholy fixation on the pathos of loss. Benjamin helps to clarify the distinction between the two writers when he observes that *Les fleurs du mal* is a masterpiece not only because of its successes, the *correspondances*, but because of its well-documented failures, which he points out are symptoms of a devotion to something "irretrievably lost."[132] The fictive operations of the *Recherche*, by way of contrast, thrive on the fiction of time regained.

In his essay "The Paris of the Second Empire in Baudelaire," as well as repeatedly in section J of *The Arcades Project*, Benjamin exhibits a clear fondness for Baudelaire's characterization in his *Salon* of 1846 of the modern hero as dressed in black, in an attitude of "constant mourning":

As for the garb, the outer husk, of the modern hero . . . is it not the necessary garb of our suffering age, which wears the symbol of perpetual mourning even on its thin black shoulders? Notice how the black suit and frock coat possess not only their political beauty, which is an expression of universal equality, but also their poetic beauty, which is an expression of the public soul—an endless procession of hired mourners, political mourners, amorous mourners, bourgeois mourners. We are all of us celebrating some funeral.[133]

Benjamin considers Baudelaire's depiction of modern heroism to be a euphemism, the "monstrous provocation" of an imagination unable to turn away from the "universal" utopia of death.[134] In Proust, however, the overpowering sense of historical finitude that in Baudelaire is presented as "modern heroism" loses its provocative status. No longer recognized as a potentially subversive collective practice, mourning is recuperated inwardly as the fiction of a perpetually successful mechanism: "the law of oblivion."[135] If Baudelaire, as Benjamin suggests, may still hold in his hands the fragments of genuine historical experience, Proust in his own day will find nothing to grasp and so must make a principle of letting go.[136]

In a revealing fragment of a methodological introduction to "The Paris of the Second Empire in Baudelaire," Benjamin identifies Baudelaire as a writer who is not "esoteric," that is to say, who is still concerned by his own class position. And he proposes Mallarmé's poetry instead as an example of the sort of purity that may be achieved in a literature that has lost its object.[137] We may revise the terms of this comparison to ask to what extent can Proust be called esoteric, relative to Baudelaire? With what politics is the doctrine of involuntary memory aligned? What stands behind the dream of an art that is also the most cogent form of knowledge? Benjamin in "The Image of Proust" makes an initial foray at answering these questions when he discusses the novel's social occult:

Proust describes a class which is everywhere pledged to camouflage its material basis and for this very reason is attached to a feudalism which has no intrinsic economic significance but is all the more serviceable as a mask of the upper middle class. This disillusioned, merciless deglamorizer of the ego, of love, of morals—for this is how Proust liked to view himself—turns his whole limitless art into a veil for this one most vital mystery of his class: the economic aspect.[138]

Benjamin's attempt to ameliorate Proust's indifference toward politics by ascribing a prophetic character to the novelist demonstrates how ill at ease the critic was with an aspect of Proust's work that reflects the principal cultural problematic of modernism, namely its historical passivity.

It ought to be observed that Proust himself was well aware of Baudelaire's "tenderness" for the poor, a trait he emphasizes in one of his last essays, "Concerning Baudelaire" (1921), in order to revise the poet's reputation as a dandy.[139] Comparing Baudelaire favorably to Victor Hugo, Proust continues, "These feelings of which I have been speaking, for suffering, for death, for a humble fraternity, make of Baudelaire the poet who has spoken the best of the common people and the beyond."[140] On the evidence of this depiction of Baudelaire's compassion for the "humble" and of Proust's surprising esteem for the voluntary character of the poet's lyric reminiscences, we might conclude that Proust looked on Baudelaire as a sort of uncanny alter ego, the repository of his good conscience, his sense of ethical duty. In his endorsement of the poet, the vision of the natural unity of "the common people and the beyond" commends a social comprehensiveness of the imagination that Proust's own fiction never evinces.

Involuntary memory is part of the Proustian effort "to turn his limitless art into a veil," to borrow Benjamin's memorable formulation. The role of the involuntary in the *Recherche* is to mask the disintegration and decline of the aura via the spurious production of an artificial ideology of nostalgia. This ideology cannot be dismissed as illusion or false consciousness insofar as it approaches Slavoj Žižek's notion of "fantasy construction," which is to say the fictive or narrative elaboration of the traumatic kernel of the "Real," what Benjamin defines in "Some Motifs" as a "synthetic production of experience."[141] As a true postmodern strategist, however, Proust accepts the decline of the auratic at the very same time that he engages in an "artificial" production of nostalgia that is the ultimate expression of the wish to get rid of the messy problems of history. Proust's work anticipates in this respect a postmodern dialectic between historical forgetfulness and the spurious, staged mise-en-scène of nostalgia. Proust's concept of *la mémoire involontaire* might seem at first sight to represent the aesthetic corrective to the logic of postmodernity, but it ultimately provides no grounds on which to resist such a logic. Involuntary memory moreover displays its ideological orientation in the course of its "marketing" of the past as an exclusive, private, impromptu event. Inevitably, this insistence on the asocial composition of memory complies with the self-absorbed detachment of hegemonic, consumerist postmodernism: the free-floating of the subject within the auratic space of the image. Consequently, Proust's ideology of nostalgia cannot really be said to prompt a quest for an alternate temporality. On the contrary, the collapse of present and past effected by involuntary memory flattens the particularities of discrete moments, deconstructing the notion of historical difference and hence of nostalgia itself.

If the process of modernity coincides for Benjamin with the genre of the *Trauerspiel,* for Proust it might be said to coincide with that of an advertising campaign. The *Recherche* envisions the utopian space of its own future, functioning as the "trailer" of itself. On the one hand, the touchstones of *la mémoire involontaire*—a madeleine, an uneven pavestone, the clatter of a spoon against a dish, *François le Champi*—appear to radiate the uniqueness of the narrator's personal experiences. On the other hand, the accumulation of these passive souvenirs may be said finally to achieve the effect of spectacularizing or glamorizing the narrator's lifestyle. The narrator's spontaneous reminiscences in fact are supposed to evoke decidedly picturesque geographical locales: Combray, Venice, Balbec. Each memory is supposed to deliver the truth of a particular place, stamped with the seal of authenticity: the involuntary. Combray's coziness, sublime Venetian splendor, the enchantments of Balbec are all phantasmatic images produced by a subject whose internalization of the reality principle of time ultimately gives the impression of a performance or simulation. Indeed, the mode of presentation at work in involuntary memory is one of spatialization or materialization, whereby the very ideal of inner time, of a Bergsonian *durée,* has been de facto abandoned.[142] That Proust's idea of time is so radically externalized only confirms the suspicion that in his work the theme of memory is removed from the phenomenological dimension and transformed into a gesture of aestheticized passivity.[143] The aesthetic espoused by the *Recherche* is hardly innocent when it comes to the ideological effects of such a mise-en-scène. If mere references to madeleines or magic lanterns carry with them a suggestion of kitsch, this is due in part to the "involuntary" success of the novel as an engine of self-glamorization.[144]

After the sublime exploration of loss in "The Intermittencies of the Heart" and poetic evocation of a mourning deprived of any defensive strategy, Proust finally realizes a narrative teleology that celebrates the most synthetic and artificial appropriation of experience, a mode of production that by reducing the past to its most objectified, spectacular, and readily consumable properties has delighted legions of readers, particularly those who embrace the political compromises of pop culture.

Like Benjamin, Fredric Jameson, in his analysis of modernism, defines its classics as failures insofar as they consistently profess, while failing to achieve, the ideals of monadic self-enclosure, autonomy, and totality.[145] Nevertheless, he ascribes to high modernism a sincere aspiration to perform aesthetic and philosophical investigation beyond the "space of the commodity," outside the culture of mass consumption, on the advance toward the revelation of new "zones of being."[146] I, too, believe that the *Recherche* ought to be regarded as a failure, although in a different sense. That is to say, it is a failure not only because the novel evades its own monadic destiny by imposing a false narrative circularity upon experience, by confining itself like other modernist *chefs d'oeuvres* within a space whose boundaries admit their own arbitrariness. The more compelling reason to view Proust's project as a failure is on the ground of its inability to escape the very space of the commodity that it is supposed to denounce in preparation for the uncovering of "new zones of being." If the section of the *Recherche* devoted to the intermittencies of the heart explores and identifies such "new zones," the novel's finale embodies an easier strategy. Rather than confronting the pain of loss, the enigmatic image of the absent Other that represents the ultimate hermeneutic challenge, Proust leaves us with fully decoded, glossily explicit images, fetishized souvenirs recovered by involuntary memory beyond the grievous necessity of mourning. His private reenchantment of the world thus invites the dilution of the subject and its agency into a free-floating phantasmatic space of the "fulfilled" image. In this gesture, we find the genealogical connection between the Proustian poetics of memory and the postmodern.

PART TWO

FRAMES OF MOURNING

Heretical Specters

Fireflies

Pier Paolo Pasolini is arguably one of the most important Italian artists of the second half of the twentieth century. Although best known around the world for his films, he is also the author of numerous collections of poems, several novels, theatrical plays, and many essays in cultural and political criticism. Indeed, he started his career as a poet, but instead of following an orthodox path within the elitist Italian literary establishment, he changed course and idiom a number of times, finally coming to describe his own intellectual character as "heretical." Pasolini's brand of hereticism values tradition enough to want to revise or reconfigure it, an aspiration that evinces itself in his work through his recurrent invocation of both the phantoms of the past and of the future.[1] He invokes these apparitions in the name of a variety of concerns, including the indictment of the spread of sameness throughout contemporary culture (a full-scale anthropological mutation he referred to as *omologazione*), resistance to the genocide of local cultures, and reconsideration of the equation of progress with modernity.[2] Pasolini's disillusioned, reflective fixation on history and tradition thus sponsors a certain resistance to the postmodern appeal of the merely retro. Those impatient with his project might feel that Pasolini's irrational attachment to a mythical, arcadian, and barbaric *Kultur* places him on the fringes of any realistic political debate and relegates his more polemical views to the domain of poetic utopianism. However, it may be replied that precisely the singularity of his voice within Italian culture, a perspective suspended between the memory of tradition and hope in the political future, gives to his poetics a critical value. By transforming nostalgia into a critical weapon, Pasolini, in accordance with his own playful self-description in the poem "Poet of Ashes" [*Poeta delle ceneri*], eventually demonstrated himself to be "more modern than all the moderns" [*più moderno di tutti i moderni*].[3]

The interest of Pasolini's artistic development resides in his epitomizing of a cross-disciplinary, multimedia creative ideal that resists the modernist and avant-garde quest for the purity of the medium without succumbing to the glibness of a hedonist aestheticism. Pasolini fulfilled this ideal by working to explore new artistic languages through the commemoration of the old (the inventive framing of shots and original visual composition of his movies, for example, derive from his admiration of the Italian painters of the fifth and sixth centuries). Yet he adamantly refused to become, to recall the title of one his plays, merely a "beast of style" [*bestia da stile*].[4] If his poetic writings initially betray symbolist and even decadent affinities, his overall artistic history may be viewed as a sustained effort to achieve an eclectic mannerism sufficiently comprehensive to reproduce in an almost ontological sense the complex and changeable phenomenology of existence. Indeed, some critics have argued that his poetics of contamination ought not to be viewed strictly as a response to the technical problem of the choice of artistic languages, but rather enlarged to include broader conceptual and ethical questions such as are raised by his conflation of the sacred and the profane and, ultimately, of art and life.[5] Pasolini at any rate pursued a kind of art that might encompass simultaneously two radically different spheres of experience: the *trasumanar* [messianic transcendence] and the *organizzar* [organization].[6] We should note as well that he aspired to an art compatible with a perceptual pragmatism that finds in the language of the body its ultimate expression.

With respect to his repudiation of avant-garde formalism, his embrace of different media, and his poetics of contamination, his work might be judged as anticipating many of the elements of mainstream postmodernity's skepticism toward architectonic or universal methodologies. However, we should be careful to observe that he introduces an original note into postmodernism's emphasis on the freedom to explore new language games outside the boundaries of the metanarrative of progress that constitutes modernity's primary legacy, namely an engaged note of ethical and political critique.[7] As Carla Benedetti rightly points out, Pasolini has no interest in the postmodern lightness classically exemplified by Italo Calvino's delightful fictions, but in a more arduous and iconoclastic spirit of experimentation. Benedetti maintains that Pasolini's dissection of the fallacies of modernity is far more radical than any hegemonic, self-proclaimedly "postmodern" exercise in populism because his ethos of contamination persistently confronts us with the "paradoxical" difficulty and alterity of the past, thus eschewing the self-congratulatory purity of aestheticism.[8]

If we wish to further differentiate Pasolini's work from the most hegemonic strains of postmodernism, we might consider his original approach to a poetics of quotation. Unlike most postmodern artists, he does not indulge in an ironic superficiality of citation. Instead, he is interested in recreating and bringing back to life "the substance" of the cited work itself. This interest is particularly evident in his films. Even the most mannerist quotations of Pontormo and Rosso Fiorentino in *La Ricotta*, for example, enact a dialectical tension between past and present, rather than the light consumerism of past styles epitomized by "nostalgia films."[9] Pasolini's ambition was to "reanimate" a certain mode of perception, as he himself proclaimed when he described his use of Masaccio's paintings in *Accatone* not as "quotations," but as an attempt to resurrect the very substance of the paintings: "I believe for *Accatone* I often was thinking of Masaccio. Not to imitate him in certain frames, but thinking of the very substance of his work as a way of looking at certain faces, at the gravity of matter."[10] In this light, we may say that Pasolini's approach to cinematic quotation is "spectral" to the degree that it seeks to evoke a past language not through rote memorization of its grammatical rules, so to speak, but through creative recovery of its uncanny "substance" and "gravity."

The concept of a "spectropoetics," a term introduced by Jacques Derrida in *Specters of Marx* to name both the tropology of ghosts and phantoms inherent in Marxist language and the contemporary necessity of mourning Marxist ideology, aptly characterizes Pier Paolo Pasolini's various creative activities as poet, novelist, essayist, and filmmaker.[11] Indeed, it is precisely in the mode of mourning that his cinematic imagination, which has been the source of his most widespread international recognition, conjures up such spectral personae as Medea, Oedipus, Christ, the messianic guest in *Theorem*, and Saint Paul. The pertinence of Derrida's terminology to Pasolini's overall project grows clearer if we observe that although reflecting on the fate of communism in the 1990s after the fall of the Berlin Wall, the French philosopher identifies the true apocalypse of this system in the 1950s during the period of de-Stalinization and rightly suggests that an epoch of mourning for Marxism begins at that moment.[12] Against this background, Pasolini surely must be acknowledged as one of the earliest and most important exemplars of leftist mourning—as a "spectator," to borrow Derrida's word, an intellectual whose duty is to address the specter of communism.[13]

I wish to concentrate in this chapter on the most original aspect of Pasolini's heretical "spectropoetics"—that is, his elaboration throughout his career of a political imaginary, a political attitude that is immanent in its anthropological, religious, and phantasmatic components and that finds in cinema its most original phenomenological manifestation. I will propose that we understand Pasolini's unique mode of intellectual heresy as a subtle but also fundamental iconoclasm by focusing on Pasolini's stubbornly mournful relation to the past, a melancholic devotion to certain intellectual traditions that simultaneously unites a defiance of the modernist, avant-garde aesthetic of the new with a refusal to indulge a reactionary, sentimental nostalgia.

In his mournful imagination, in fact, we encounter not the inclination toward a regressive and consumerist nostalgia symptomatic of populist postmodern culture, but the critical, experimental bent of an intellectual determined to offer hospitality to an array of "impure," spectralized subjects. Accordingly, I will define Pasolini's poetic and cinematic works as instances of a critical postmodernism that repudiates the empty formalism of the modernist avant-garde, eschewing a triumphalist abandonment of memory and the canon in favor of a phenomenology of posteriority that keeps alive a sense of ethical and political commitment. Unlike the postmoderns who wish to escape the anxieties of contemporary culture either through stylistic games or populist bravura, Pasolini propounds a radical politics of the hospitality of the Other, which is his most important legacy.

We might say that for Pasolini, even melancholia is a form of hospitality to a fundamental Otherness at the core of modernity, particularly if we think of his insistent representation of the assertion of sexual identity as a kind of melancholy. Pasolini, as is well known, was openly gay. In his most interesting work, however, we do not find either a kitschy celebration of queerness or the more cliché and regressive association of homosexuality with depression. Instead, he articulates a more idiosyncratic and problematic "spectropoetics of gender." His poems and films repeatedly affirm,

in agreement with Judith Butler, that the formation of heterosexual identity takes place by means of a melancholic repudiation of homosexual desire.[14] Consequently, some of the most iconically "eroticized" figures in Pasolini's work are not even queer. Accattone, the straight protagonist of the
eponymous film, exudes the kind of melancholy we might ascribe not only
to his poverty and dejected social status, but also to his repression of homosexual desire. One of the most important of Pasolini's achievements is
his exposure of the need for postmodern society to welcome sexual Otherness, to extend a mournful consideration to those whom it hitherto has
banished from its libidinal economy.

Pasolini's merits as a cultural critic are manifest in his thorough understanding that modernity in Italy is a belated phenomenon, giving to his
own version of postmodernism a historical specificity. Yet his anxious relation to the present does not culminate in a repression or avoidance of crisis. I agree with Zanzotto, who maintains that to believe Pasolini genuinely desires a return to an archaic, rural society is absurd, that the past
in his work is not to be viewed as a historical truth, but rather as a
metaphor for a radical new beginning.[15] Accordingly, I would contend that
his noted fascination with an arcadian, peasant existence must be construed as an imaginative response to a messianic, rather than pragmatic or
empirical, potential. In his poetic encounters with the specters of history,
Pasolini encounters not only the *revenants* of the past, but also the *arrivants* of the future.   The ghosts of the future –

What is most original and fascinating about Pasolini's unrelenting exposure of the spectrality of culture is the tension he maintains between art
and politics, ghostly figuration and ethical pragmatism. On this score, one
of his most significant images of the spectral occurs in an essay published
toward the end of his life in *Il Corriere della Sera* and revolving around the
disappearance of fireflies in Italy. He depicts the anthropological mutation
of society in the 1960s, Italy's passage from an agrarian to an industrialized
society, by means of the following trope: "In the first years of the '60s, because of pollution in the air and, in the country, particularly of the water,
the fireflies have started to disappear. The phenomenon has been sudden
and traumatic. After a few years, there were no more fireflies. They are now
a rather crushing souvenir of the past."[16] To choose fireflies as an index of
cultural loss is telling because it appears that Pasolini is mourning at once
their minute particularity, their spectral luminosity, and, above all, their
nonutilitarian, fragile marginality. His insistence on the "traumatic" and

"crushing" reality of their absence implies that the explosion of mass production in Italy may have ecological consequences far more serious than may be registered by the measures of the capital markets. Confronted by the prospect of the fireflies' utter eradication, he seems to bear in mind the fading importance of his own artistic mission.

In what follows I will examine Pasolini's spectral language in his poetic and cinematic productions, the two complementary halves of his critical engagement with postmodern culture.

Pasolini, Poet of Ashes

Pasolini's poetic career began in 1942 with a collection written in the Friulian dialect and entitled *Poesie a Casarsa*.[17] This first effort might be said to represent an experiment in a linguistic, rather than sentimental, nostalgia. The author's resorting to his native dialect represents neither a populist gesture nor an attempt at regionalist realism, but rather the expression of a hermetic, symbolist desire to reanimate a "dead language" through the mediating influence of Pirona's Friulian–Italian dictionary.[18] To Pasolini, the weakest feature of Italian poetry was its adherence to a debased *crepuscolarismo*, a kind of provincial, self-indulgent elegism.[19]

For all of its interest from the standpoint of symbology, however, the collection manifests a "narcissism of memory" and a stylistic reliance on ambivalence and chiaroscuro mannerism that he will later abandon.[20] To the politically engaged writers of the 1960s such as Asor-Rosa, Ferretti, and Moravia, Pasolini's Friulan lyrics looked like expressions of adolescent excess. After 1947, Pasolini composed his poetry and other writings exclusively in Italian. His concurrent migration from Friuli to Rome dramatically marked his transition from youth to maturity and, with this passage, the relinquishment of the elegiac tone of *Poesie a Casarsa*.[21] His mature poetry instead enacts a drama of mourning, a scenario in which Pasolini struggles to emancipate poetry itself from its traditional lyric solipsism to achieve a new, rhetorical "vitalism" by means of a sustained spectralizing of language that opens the word to the interlocutory or interrogative sway of resonance. As becomes even clearer in his movies, Pasolini not only gave expression to a phantasmagorical vision of culture, but also treated his reader as the implied, ghostly "spectator" of his poetic explorations of paradox and contradiction. Striving to transgress the conventional boundaries of aesthetic purity, Pasolini achieves the poetic contamination of high and low, art and politics.

Critics often have responded with bafflement to the elusive meta-phorical web of his watershed poetic volume, *The Ashes of Gramsci* [*Le ceneri di Gramsci*] (1957), some recognizing in the collection the conscientiousness of the civil poet, others the indulgent self-mythologization of the romantic subject.[22] This seems to me a false dichotomy inasmuch as Pasolini presents himself in the book as haunted by history, as simultaneously conscious of the past and of its ghostly unreality, thus collapsing the distinction. His intellectual and artistic courage consists in opening the authorial presence to a ghostly reverberation or referentiality, in abandoning the poetic purity of hermeticism or the solipsistic refinement of personal memory exemplified by Montale's *Arsenio* or *La casa dei doganieri* for the besmirched, historical world of the political.[23]

If Pasolini already deploys phantoms and apparitions in his Friulian poems, their role seems to be strictly limited to the representation of the subject and its linguistic *Bildung* and reveries.[24] The identification between poetry and individual memory that Pascoli had perfected in Italian poetry becomes increasingly impossible to sustain for Pasolini.[25] According to the critic Rinaldi, however, Pasolini creates in *The Ashes of Gramsci* an imaginary world that constitutes a "*zona franca,*" where the figures of the past seem quite independent of authorial intervention.[26] By reinterpreting the question of ideology in terms of the phantasmatic, the Friulian poet brings to light anew the intricate negotiation between the subjective and intersubjective sphere of the mournful imagination, according to which political ideology informs an original poetics of spectrality. Pasolini adopts a Gramscian approach to the problem, maintaining throughout the 1950s a view of ideology as a social experiment with potentially significant benefits. Yet he clearly identifies the operations of superstructure less with the world of historical fact than with a haunted universe in which both Marx and Gramsci are revenants to be regarded at times with fear and distress. It would be naive, then, to take at face value the supposed antithesis of the title, *Passion and Ideology* [*Passione e ideologia*], which he assigns in the 1960s to a collection of critical essays.[27] The ideology of *The Ashes of Gramsci* is enacted by a phantasmagoria of allegorical figures ranging from Gramsci himself to the mythic boys of the Roman underclass such as the youth described in "The Popular Song" [*Il canto popolare*] as "the joyful seed at the heart of the melancholic popular world" [*allegro seme in cuore al triste mondo popolare*].[28] This symbolic vocabulary defines the boundaries of Pasolini's poetic ideology through a transformation of conventional political images into incantatory, sacred myth. As he points out in "Il canto popolare," the human world he wants to depict is not "dazzled" by modernity because it is already "always the most modern" [*sempre il più moderno*].[29]

No doubt the fabrication of this spectropoetics is a symptom of Pasolini's intentional distancing of himself from "referential politics" in the 1950s, a moment of ugly Italian consumerism and disgraced Russian socialism. Nevertheless, Pasolini's deliberate exploration of the territory of the taboo, the heretical, and the semiotically impure unveils to the poet and to his readers important new modes of ideological and political engagement. I do not think that we should consider Pasolini's poetic strategy escapist because I believe he single-handedly opens a new space for the contamination of the aesthetic, the ethical, the sacred, and the political. This space provides a more ample forum for public discourse than the desultory tones of the so-called *poesia civile*. Pasolini eschews the project of this literary movement, which was to inspire Italians with positive admiration for the appropriate civic virtues, in favor of a more self-questioning mode of political meditation that at best can hope only for the uncertain resolution of a weak messianism. In "The Tears of the Excavator," for instance, the poet laments in the last stanza that "The light/of the future does not cease for even an instant/to wound us" [*la luce/del futuro non cessa un solo instante/di ferirci*] even as he voices, almost in spite of himself, a sense of expectancy while gazing at a group of workers and their "red rag of hope" [*rosso straccio di speranza*].[30] Pasolini bears witness through the establishment of his spectropoetics—thus, through acts of cultural mourning—to the loss of the sacred, on the one hand, and of political intentionality, on the other. As a poet, we might say, he aspires to discover a form of elegy that exists beyond the private sphere and that can come to encompass ideology, the red rag of hope.

Such an untimely perspective promises nothing less than an epochal revelation in the criticism of culture. In fact, rather than a lesson in the civic virtues, Pasolini's poetry enacts the contamination of the sacred and profane by propounding an allegorical reinterpretation of an *imitatio Christi*. Yet Pasolini's sense of the sacred always remains continuous with a notion of the heretical or blasphemous. Not for nothing did he give his collected poems the title *Bestemmia*. Philippe Sollers, in "Pasolini, Sade, Saint Matthieu," identifies Pasolini's chief heretical impulse with his inability to resist competing against his predecessor, Rousseau, and thus in the refusal of any intellectual middle ground, in his final renunciation of Rousseau, Voltaire, and Plato in favor of the extremes of Sade and the Gospel.[31]

Sollers's pronouncement draws our attention to Pasolini's most sensation-alistic and thus compromised heretical impulse—that is, his refusal of an ethics of compromise and bourgeois accommodation. Another way of defining Pasolini's hereticism might be to point out his diffidence toward the empty logic of formal innovation offered by modernism and the avant-garde.

There is no doubt that the most influential figure of twentieth-cen-tury Italian intellectual life is Antonio Gramsci.[32] To this day, his intuition that culture does not function as a mere reflection of the economic base and his analysis of the relations of force in terms of hegemony and ideol-ogy continue to dominate cultural theory. The first edition of Gramsci's *Prison Notebooks* or *Quaderni del carcere* was published in Italy in the late 1940s and early 1950s.[33] This event is likely to have prompted much of the thinking behind the work collected in Pasolini's 1957 volume *The Ashes of Gramsci* as well as behind his other expressions of mourning for the radical Sardinian philosopher. Pasolini's refusal of poetic lyricism after the early, Friulian period of his literary career opened new avenues of reflection. By means of frequent recurrence to the language of the body and an insistence on the relation between sexuality, the sacred, and the political, Pasolini tried throughout his career to introduce "the impure" into art.[34] We may then view his endeavor to bridge the gap between aesthetics and practice, the artistic and the nonartistic, as a move in the direction of Gramsci, away from Croce (whose philosophy stressed the distinction between "poesia" and "nonpoesia"), and ultimately away from traditional western episte-mology, which from Kant onward emphasizes the separation of aesthetics from ethics, religion from politics. The affinity between Pasolini and Gramsci, in other words, is surely to be located in their common interest in the relationship between class and power and their shared faith in the pedagogical responsibility of the intellectual. Moreover, Pasolini's perpet-ual feeling of exile within his own culture may be viewed as a sympathetic response to Gramsci's exile, jailing, and eventual death under fascism.[35]

Ultimately, Gramsci's alterity with respect to the dominant forces of mass society, which is to say his spectrality, was the overriding point of fas-cination for Pasolini. In a way, we can say that Gramsci's political philoso-phy invites or encourages the practice of mourning. His removal from everyday life as a consequence of his long years of imprisonment conferred on him the privileged status of an outsider and a martyr, and the dire tone of his posthumously published notebooks lends his voice a spectral quality, and hence the crucial space he occupies in Pasolini's political imaginary. The figure of the Sardinian radical acts in fact as a catalyst for the political and ideological argument of *The Ashes of Gramsci*, inducing epiphanies and revelations that punctuate the poems in the collection from "Canto popolare" to "Comizio" and "Una polemica in versi," in addition to the magisterial elegy that gives the volume its title (P 2–23, B 1:222–35).

Although Gramsci holds an undeniably central position in that eponymous poem, "The Ashes of Gramsci" is in fact crowded with other ghostly presences whom Pasolini invokes in the English cemetery where the revolutionary theorist lies buried. Amidst "the bones of millionaires/ from mightier nations" [le ossa dei miliardari di nazioni/più grandi] and "princes . . . and pederasts . . . /their bodies in their scattered urns" [principi . . . e pederasti/i cui corpi sono nell'urne sparse], the poet summons both the shades of Wordsworth, whose "Immortality Ode" Pasolini quotes to describe the setting ("And O ye Fountains . . ."), and Shelley, whose "anima" or spirit Pasolini apostrophizes, recalling the British poet's own description of the same Roman burial ground in "Adonais," his elegy for Keats (P 5, 7, B 1:224–25). Contriving a sort of ghostly "carnivalesque," the Friulian poet stages a pseudodialectic between passion and ideology that appears doomed to remain suspended in a scandalous ambivalence. Such indecision ensues at least in part from his aspiration to a sort of visionary poetic praxis whereby the poet abandons the strictures of objective or scientific reason in order to be "possessed" by history:

> But while I possess history,
> it possesses me. I'm illuminated by it;
>
> but what's the use of such light?[36] (P 13)

The question begs rephrasing: What sort of meaning can we attribute to the weak referentiality of a ghost, an apparition who, in Gramsci's case, persists in "The Ashes of Gramsci" only via the trope of his ashes, the intangible traces left in the wake of a nearly total cultural and ideological disintegration? Gramsci indeed seems practically absent as a real, historical individual, complicating any reading of the poem as politically engaged in the usual sense. Yet its paucity of overt historical reference may be viewed as a source of the poem's originality. Instead of revisiting the well-trodden road of *poesia civile*, Pasolini follows a more idiosyncratic path to the "political unconscious," to use Jameson's celebrated formula, reappropriating the signifiers of Marxist ideology along the way and redeploying them at the level of the imaginary.

"The Ashes of Gramsci" presents the Sardinian thinker as an allegorical figure of heresy in a precise sense, construing his phantasmatic value as synonymous with his exemplification of the category to which postmodern philosophy generally refers as "the Other." In other words, Gramsci stands for those who have been proscribed from the traditional metanarrative of western civilization and hence from history in its institutional or disciplinary aspect. His spectralization within the linguistic precincts of the poem thus recapitulates in the form of critique his actual, historical exclusion from the legitimating social order of the state.

> There you lie, banished, listed with severe
> non-Catholic elegance, among the foreign
>
> dead: The ashes of Gramsci.[37] (P 7, 9)

Ostracized even in death through his burial among foreigners, he is doubly removed from the poetic speaker inasmuch as the dead man's very physical remains have been annihilated, leaving behind only the synecdochic reminder of his "ashes" in place of a body. In this manner, the elegy's pivotal trope of *le ceneri* comes to signify the tragic condition of delegitimation or alienation, of being exiled from culture. Yet it is precisely as a result of his erasure from the annals of the nation that Gramsci becomes visible as an object of mourning and, as a consequence, spectralized.

As Derrida cogently reminds us in *Specters of Marx*, a Marxist spectropoetics is necessitated by the very metaphorical economy of Marx's rhetoric itself.[38] It is imperative to recognize the crucial role of the ghostly and the apparitional in the language of Marxist argument from *The German Ideology* to the *Manifesto* and *Capital*. At the moment of its inception in his theory, Marx depicts communism as a specter roaming through Europe. From the function of the commodity, to the mechanisms of production, to the uses of ideology, many of his key notions seem to draw on the linguistic resources of a phantasmatic logic.

A spectropoetics moreover is requisite, Derrida points out, in the sense that the task remains of mourning an ideology that after the collapse of Eastern-bloc socialism, threatens to sink into obsolescence. What is at stake is nothing less than the survival of the spirit of Marxism, which is to say the survival of a peculiar faith in the ideal. As early as the 1950s a critical awareness of the horrors perpetrated by the soviet state in the name of communism raised doubts as to the continued viability of the ideology. Within this context, we may recognize Pasolini's fascination with the specter of Gramsci as an occasion for an act of mourning that precludes the possibility of false consciousness, of manic historical triumphalism.

Whether the mourning of Gramsci's heretical precedent is still possible after the loss of faith in the Enlightenment narrative of historical progress, however, will remain the overriding, open question of "The Ashes of Gramsci." Addressing the dead man, Pasolini encapsulates this dilemma with one of the sharpest expressions of his tormented ambivalence, of his genius for dialectical self-contradiction, in his entire oeuvre:

> The scandal of contradicting myself, of being
> with you and against you; with you in my heart,
> in light, but against you in the dark viscera.[39] (P 11)

This is a scandal Pasolini explicates more fully at the end of the poem's third section:

> Yet without your rigor I survive because
>
> I do not choose. I live in the non-will
> of the dead post-war years: loving
> the world I hate it, scorning it, lost
>
> in its wretchedness—in an obscure scandal
> of consciousness. . . . [40] (P 11)

The scandal, in other words, consists in the poet's inability to uphold unquestioningly a political doctrine that, before the war, Gramsci develops as a means of opposition in response to the pragmatic needs of the oppressed. In the ghostly postwar years, Pasolini finds it impossible to direct his enthusiasm toward the ideological. Part of the discrepancy is circumstantial; Gramsci was untouched by historical disillusionment, whereas Pasolini has suffered through the apathy of an ensuing period that at one point he labels "this vacuum of history" [*questo vuoto della storia*] (P 19, B 1:233). Nevertheless, the repeated reference to his detachment as a "*scandalo*" suggests that his sympathies reside with Gramsci—indeed, that he may learn to overcome his apathy via the mourning of the dead revolutionary.

In a sense, the tragedy of the poet is that of a modern, male incarnation of Antigone who finds himself in conflict with society as a result of his obligation to the dead—"traitor to my paternal state" [*del mio paterno stato traditore*], as he puts it in section 4 (P 11, B 1:228). Significantly, when he addresses Gramsci in the poem for the first time, he calls him "not father but humble brother" [*non padre ma umile fratello*] (P 3, B 1:223). Yet the fraternal relation, based not on kinship but on a common ethical vocation, is not sufficient for Pasolini to explain to the larger community why he insists on taking responsibility for the dead man's commemoration and attempting to enforce the laws of the heart over those of the state.

In section 3, the poet redescribes his predicament as a function of erotic impulses that bourgeois society inevitably represses or otherwise marginalizes:

> And if I happen
>
> to love the world, it's a naive
> violent sensual love, just as I
> hated it when I was a confused
>
> adolescent and its bourgeois evils
> wounded my bourgeois self. . . . [41] (P 9, 11)

In the same section, he announces to his phantom addressee: "between hope/and my old distrust, I approach you" [*Tra speranza/e vecchia sfiducia, ti accosto*] (P 9, B 1:226). Such an approaching or "accosting" of Gramsci, the poet avows, ultimately requires the confrontation of a consciousness who represents an "adolescent/symbiosis of sex and death" [*simbiosi/d'adoloscente di sesso con morte*] (P 9, B 1:226). In this sense, Pasolini's identification with the dead man readily admits its nature as libidinal attachment. Yet such an identification, vacillating as it does between hope and distrust, compounds rather than resolves the difficulty of being "with you and against you" [*con te e contro te*], as if the poetic subject's libido had become attached to an object that was categorically barred or denied to him (P 11, B 1:227).

On this score, it ought to be noted that the society depicted in the poem is almost exclusively male, populated by figures such as the "apprentice" [*garzone*], the "Roman peasant . . . [with] penis swollen" [*col membro gonfio . . . il giovincello ciociaro*], the "bunches of soldiers" [*gruppi di militari*], the "boys/light as rags" [*ragazzi/leggeri come stracci*], and "young men with tan sweaty faces" [*i giovinetti madidi/nel bruno della faccia*] (P 5, 17, 21, 21, 17, B 1:223, 231, 234, 234, 232). No female presence appears in the poem, save for an isolated reference to the "nests of whores" [*rintanate zoc-colette*] in the slum of Testaccio (P 21, B 1:234). Pasolini's mourning of Gramsci thus is inscribed within a homoerotics implicit to the poem but never explicitly declared. Precisely in his stigmatization as a gay man, in the impropriety of his sexual desires in the eyes of the dominant social order, Pasolini finds the basis for an admittedly equivocal expression of solidarity with the martyred Sardinian pariah.

Ultimately, Pasolini's very ambition to mourn the radical Otherness of Gramsci's thinking precludes "The Ashes of Gramsci" from fulfilling the traditional public functions of poetic elegy. Indulging the personal, subjective sentiments of loss, abandonment, and nostalgia, the speaker uneasily validates a constellation that his own political conscience cannot avoid regarding as reactionary. As a result, he finds himself implicitly contradicting his own idealized image of Gramsci, the uncompromising radical. It is clear that Pasolini is not capable of a psychic work that brings him to a progressive and synthetic "surmounting" of melancholy. Rather, his grief represents a distorted form of aggression, in keeping with the classic Freudian conception. Gramsci's grave, instead of inspiring altruistic civic and moral sentiments in the high, classical tradition of Foscolo, only occasions personal anxiety for Pasolini. He is absorbed in melancholy recriminations of those imaginary objects (such as the world and society) that refuse him love and attention. He does not try to capitalize on the pain of loss, to derive an aesthetic benefit from it, but rather to indulge his interminable suffering in an onanistic fashion.

Whereas the majority of Pasolini's poetry up to the volume *The Ashes of Gramsci* may be read as unselfconsciously elegiac, the eponymous poem decisively relinquishes the customary offices of the mode, acknowledging the problem of elegy's diminished legitimacy in the twentieth century. Pasolini's confusion reflects in fact a discomfort with the increasingly indefinite value of the elegy. At the same time, the collection inaugurates a new way of writing poetry.[42] More fully than the lyric effusions of Pascoli and Montale, Pasolini's antipoetic poems exemplify the idea that in modernity the only true elegy is, as Jahan Ramazani puts it, "an elegy for elegy."[43] Although he avoids the "crepuscular" aesthetic of mainstream Italian lyric elegy, he also maintains his distance from the funereal monumentalism of Ugo Foscolo, whose *Sepolcri* (1806) is the most influential text in Italian poetry to solemnize the heroic cult of the dead.[44]

Pasolini's affinity for the word "ashes" [*ceneri*] is renewed toward the end of his poetic career in the autobiographical poem in which Pasolini gives both to the text and to himself the title "Poet of ashes" [*Poeta delle ceneri*] (1966). Pasolini composed the volume *The Ashes of Gramsci* during the same years in which Adorno, responding pessimistically to Hölderlin's elegiac interrogative in "Brot und Wein" ("wozu Dichter in dürftiger Zeit?"), professed his skepticism regarding the writing of poetry after Auschwitz.[45] These were also the years in which Paul Celan obsessively reevaluated the meaning of the German word *Aschen* in the mesmerizing refrain "dein aschenes Haar Sulamith" of his "Todesfuge" and again in "Aschenglorie," memorably broadening the allegorical horizons of the trope.[46]

Pasolini authored the poem "Poet of Ashes," according to Siciliano, on the occasion of the premiere of the film *Uccellacci e uccellini* (1966) in New York. Indeed, in the poem, he envisions himself responding to the questions of an American journalist.[47] At the same time, the poem was written to furnish an appendix to an anthology of his writings that opened with the essay "Al lettore nuovo." More of an epitaph than a schematic chronology, "Poet of Ashes" rehearses Pasolini's Rimbaud-like memories of his early poetic career of seven years, his flight to Rome (the only romanticized chapter of his life), and his subsequent "lyrical" period. The reminiscence resolves the dichotomy between life and literature in an appealingly naive vitalism. Yet perhaps because of such idealism, the poem fails to render a convincingly Wordsworthian "growth of a poet's mind" or account of imaginative enlargement.

At first glance, it might appear Pasolini takes himself as a poet of "ashes" insofar as, during the mid-1960s, he believes in the necessity of working through a mourning of the resistance. On further consideration, though, it should be noted that his political commitment is destined to be "lived as a parasite on the glory and grief of those cemeteries" [vissuto da parassita sulla gloria e il dolore di quei cimiteri]. In spite of the initial pathos of his confession, "I weep again, whenever I think of it, / over my brother Guido" [Piango ancora, ogni volta che ci penso, / su mio fratello Guido], Pasolini finally denies any feeling of sympathy or solidarity when he declares, "I do not wish to return to those hills / neither as tourist nor as visitor of tombs, it should be clear, / them also I have forgotten" [Io non voglio ritornare a quei colli, / nè come turista nè come visitatore di tombe, sia chiaro / Anch'io li ho dimenticati].[48] Far from the Testaccio and from the English Cemetery, after his confessions at Gramsci's gravesite, Pasolini appears to be newly reconciled to his own insignificance. On the secular altar of mass culture he decides to sacrifice his trade of poet because poetry in any case "never counts."

This conviction, however, cannot be interpreted in the dignified sense of another modern poet's famous affirmation, "For poetry makes nothing happen."[49] Auden in fact concludes his elegy for Yeats by exalting the role of the poet, declaring, "In the prison of his days / Teach the free man how to praise."[50] Pasolini seems ready at ten years' remove from "The Ashes of Gramsci" to grant poetry a different and subsidiary value from that which Auden's encomium confers. Notwithstanding his pretense to "hurl his body into the fray" [*gettare il suo corpo nella lotta*] after the fashion of Aeschylus, Pasolini, in the faded urgency of his complicated political faith, apparently wishes to claim a more exquisite object of nostalgia: "I will always have regret for a sort of poetry / which is action in itself" [*Avrò sempre il rimpianto di quella poesia / che è azione essa stessa*]. It is in the wake of this disillusionment with the possibility of a performative poetry that Pasolini in the 1960s turns to cinema.

From Poetry to Film

In Pasolini's turn to the celluloid medium, we should recognize not only his strenuous commitment to an ethos and aesthetic of impurity, but also the intention of raising the stakes of his heretical venture. The commodification and spectacularization of visual culture are the paradoxical premises of Pasolini's attempt to explode capitalist culture from within, reversing the function of the image toward its spectral and messianic potential. In this sense, Pasolini's cinema of spectrality ought to be regarded as a radicalization and intensification of the spectropoetics developed in his lyric texts. More than poetry, cinema seems to offer a chance to renegotiate the boundaries between subjective and intersubjective experience, thus preparing the way not for a merely aesthetic recovery of collective memory and tradition, but for the projection of the past into the future of ethical and political hopes.

In his final devotion of himself to a cinematic career, however, we should recognize an engrossment in the phenomenology of the spectral that prevails over and above any late-coming fascination with the ultimate mass medium. In fact, Pasolini's films function throughout his directorial career as spaces of cultural haunting or repetition within which the camera resurrects, among other things, the pictorial tradition of Masaccio and the mannerist painters (we may think of *Accattone* and *La ricotta* in this regard). Moreover, Pasolini will elaborate his conception of spectrality as a poetic form of ideology throughout his cinematic oeuvre from his first feature, *Accattone*, which tells the story of a character endowed with a gift for proletarian evangelism, to the hallucinatory body-consumerism of his final movie, *Salò*. As in his poetry, Pasolini's use of religious iconography in his motion pictures should be read not in opposition to, but in continuity with, the political, as an experiment in contamination that perhaps yields its most fully achieved result in *The Gospel According to Saint Matthew*.

If Rinaldi's assertion is correct that already in "The Ashes of Gramsci" Pasolini presents himself as a "cinematographic spectator," a subject lost in the darkness in contemplation of the projections of an imaginary history, it is all the more true that he comes closest to embodying the ideal spectator of the past in his cinematic productions.[51] Indeed, his chief accomplishments as a director consist in his demonstrations of hospitality not only to the revenants of ideological and religious history, but more importantly to what Derrida defines as the "*arrivant*" or future restitution of justice, the apocalyptic event of a Marxism to come.[52] For example, Pasolini's late-blossoming interest in the so-called third world, registered in films such as *Appunti per un film sull'India* (1968), *Appunti per un'Orestiade africana* (1970), *Il fiore delle mille e una notte* (1974), and *Le mura di Sana* (1974), ought to be understood in the context of his effort to discover a contemporary locus of messianic, utopian potential. Not by chance does he give to the two movies set in India and Africa, which are among his most imaginative and moving documents, the title *Appunti* ["notes"], suggesting not fully developed feature films but rather impromptu sketches or drafts for future revision.[53]

As I will argue in the second part of this chapter, however, the most crucial mythologization of the figure of the spectral *arrivant* in Pasolini's filmography occurs in *Theorem*. The narrative, layered with Marxist overtones, concerns a mysterious guest who, upon entering the household of a bourgeois Milanese family, converts each and every member to a new order of life and then vanishes, apparently moving the father to renounce all his material possessions, including a factory operation belonging to the family. Through a virtuosic reconceptualization of the grammatical elements of the medium—from narrative structure to mise-en-scène, montage, sound, and even color—Pasolini achieves in *Theorem* a phantasmatic contamination of religious and political ideology that ultimately is grounded in the ontology of film. The movie represents, in other words, a spectralization of messianic time. Before considering this particular production, however, I wish to turn to Pasolini's theoretical essays in order to examine his notion of film as a mode of mourning and to investigate how this notion shapes his directorial practices.

Cinema, the Messianic Hope

Pasolini's theoretical statements regarding cinema are important not only to an understanding of his discussion of the inherent, technical spectrality of cinema, but also to identifying the emergence in Italy in the 1960s of a mode of critical reflection that may be opposed to the light-hearted approach of the postmodern exemplified in the 1970s by the writings of Calvino and Eco. In fact, film supplies Pasolini not only with a new technology, but also with a new logic, freeing him from the generic dead ends of elegy and lyric at which he had arrived in his poetic development.

Pasolini's interest in directing movies arose at the end of the 1950s as a consequence of his authoring several successfully produced screenplays, either by himself or in collaboration with established filmmakers.[54] Neither his early pastoral verses in the Friulian dialect nor his later spectral elegies of *The Ashes of Gramsci* appeared to satisfy Pasolini's need to find an original and historically transparent mode of mourning. The film medium provides him with the possibility of translating his nostalgia at once into a more intangible, spectacular, and allegorically complex production, enabling him to incorporate the most iconographically elaborate compositions of the past such as the tableaux vivants of Massacio or Pontormo and to evoke as well the looming ghost of Italian cinematic neorealism.[55] Pasolini's directorial practices and theory thus represent the supreme achievements of a lifelong effort of cultural mourning. It is by contaminating the latest technologies of the motion picture and of multimedia production with the religious and political signifiers of more historically remote eras that he escapes from the obsolescent poetics of *il crepuscolare* that dominated Italian modernist literature. As a line of European critics had done, Pasolini credited film with the potential to revitalize political and artistic expression within modern capitalist society. Cinematic language for Pasolini calls into question the entire semiotic of tradition constructed by the dominant social order for the purpose of self-legitimation. In essays such as "The Cinema of Poetry" (1965) and "The Written Language of Reality"

(1966), the Friulan director constructs a semiotics of cinema during the 1960s that offers an original conjunction of spectropoetics and messianism.

Although he identifies Pasolini's example as an important source of inspiration for contemporary cinema, John Orr evasively concludes that the filmmaker's oeuvre can be seen either as a cornerstone of the phenomenon of postmodern film or as its categorical repudiation, depending on one's point of view.[56] Although it may be true that Pasolini's filmmaking does not exemplify the triumph of surface over depth typical of a certain postmodern style of cinema, the question of nostalgia remains overwhelmingly urgent in all of his movies. Jameson has famously introduced the definition of a genre he calls the "nostalgia film" in order to name the translation of certain feelings of longing or yearning for the past into an exclusively commercial value system, according to which history can be viewed only as a product to be exchanged, without any further dimensionality.[57] The Friulian director's movies, however, appear to embody a notion of postmodernity that is antithetical to Jameson's insofar as they perform a spectralization of the past that, far from mystifying the relation of cinema to the means of production, exposes the inherently nostalgic function of film precisely as a form of critical mythopoesis, but not of the mere stylistic consumerism of the past. In this sense, if the cinema of nostalgia defines the area of a fashionable, populist postmodernism, Pasolini's poetics of spectrality fulfills a political and critical function, encompassing not only the horizon of the past, but that of the future, critically dwelling in a condition of cultural belatedness.

Pasolini's spectropoetics of film may be categorized as "postmodern," then, as long as we care to distinguish between a postmodern glibness that ratifies the commercialism of mass culture and a postmortem mournfulness that reproves the capitalist logic of consumption. From *Accattone* onward, all of the director's films mobilize the distinguishing stylistic signifiers of cinematic postmodernism, particularly the blending of the highbrow and the lowbrow, in the name of social nonconformity. Another way of thinking of his heretical postmodernity becomes apparent if we notice the exaggeratedly sexualized vision of the body he achieves on screen through a pseudofetishistic use of the camera that parodies and deconstructs the accepted visual erotics of "mainstream," commercial motion pictures. It is through mourning for the ontological ground of the body, in other words, that Pasolini depicts a position outside the limits of orthodox sexual decorum.

On this score, the gender politics of his movies are exemplary of a larger attitude. The ambivalent outlook of his films suggests a horizon within which the mundanity of the real and the excess of the poetic may coincide, thus obliging the viewer to ask to what extent Pasolini was committed to a historical "realism" that recapitulates or accedes to the status quo. Such an inquiry helps to establish the ideological premises that underlie his nostalgic poetics of film as well as his eventual abandonment of the modernist faith in the historicity of form. For critics such as Viano, Pasolini's creative allegiance as a filmmaker ultimately appears to be to some form of realism, which is to say at least to "a certain realism" tempered by lyricism and ambiguity.[58] For others such as Rohdie, what is more significant is the irrational, regressive aspect of Pasolini's movies, an aspect Rohdie reads as closer to Crocean idealism than to a banal primitivism.[59]

In an interview with Oswald Stack, Pasolini proposes the following definition of the medium:

In my view cinema is substantially and naturally poetic . . . because it is dreamlike, because it is close to dreams, because a film sequence and a sequence of memory or of a dream—and not only that but things in themselves—are profoundly poetic: a tree photographed is poetic, a human face photographed is poetic because the physical is poetic in itself, because it is an apparition, because it is full of mystery, because it is full of ambiguity, because it is full of polyvalent meaning, because even a tree is a sign of a linguistic system. But who talks through a tree? God, or reality itself. Therefore the tree as a sign puts us in communication with a mysterious speaker.[60]

What is evident from this quotation is Pasolini's attention to the ontological and "reverential" quality of cinema, a quality I wish to differentiate from that of realism and which is present in all of his motion pictures. Even in his first feature, *Accattone*, he achieved a startling contamination of sacred and profane experience by depicting the life of a member of the Roman underclass as reverentially reinterpreted through visual quotations of Italian religious painting, in particular the work of Masaccio. From his earliest movies onward, Pasolini aspires to an intensity in close-up shots that is reminiscent of Dreyer, employing 57- and 70-millimeter lenses to dramatically emphasize the contrast between light and shadow, hollowing the eye sockets and deepening facial shading as if to transform an actor's natural physiognomy into a kind of death mask.[61] Although the director's persistent focus on the Roman underclasses and incorporation of regional dialect helps to maintain a certain illusion of realism, particularly in his first films, he also clearly experiments from early on with the rhetoric of a visionary or "dreamlike" idealism. His stylistic evocation of the grand neorealist films of Italy's past thus does not seek merely to recapitulate a historicist enterprise that Pasolini perhaps had come to feel was already exhausted in the manner of literary "crepuscularism." Over Italian neorealism's nostalgic regret for local or regional forms of community, he will prefer a ceaseless mourning for the specters of history that culminates in a sweeping reconception of the social order.

The most influential theories of realism, namely those of Bazin and Kracauer, present certain points of contact with Pasolini's poetics but remain significantly different. For Bazin, cinematic realism originates with the ascendancy of Italian neorealist directors, who demonstrate that "every realism is profoundly aesthetic."[62] According to Bazin, neorealism consists of an immanent phenomenological approach to reality, an approach characterized by emphasizing certain visual elements, such as "depth of focus," while deemphasizing others, such as editing.[63] Bazin also stresses the "revolutionary humanism" implicit in Italian neorealism. By the time Pasolini embarked on his directorial career at the end of the 1950s, the revolutionary humanism espoused by neorealism already had run its course, complicating his struggle to elaborate a viable cinematic aesthetic. He may be said to retain Bazin's confidence in the "ontology of the photographic image," the ability of the image to recollect the subject and thus to preserve him or her from a second death.[64] But unlike Bazin's theory, Pasolini's approach involves a thorough consideration of the technical and philosophical role of editing in the economy of a motion picture. He draws a parallel between editing and death that establishes film as a means to a ghostly mourning.[65]

In realist cinema, Kracauer perceived the potential source of an aesthetic and epistemological awakening: "We literally redeem this world from its dormant state, its state of virtual nonexistence, by endeavoring to experience it through the camera."[66] Both Bazin and Kracauer located the aesthetic validity of film in its ability to reveal reality, to capture the continual flux of life. To reduce their theories to the mere valorization of the indexical dimension of film, the motion picture's operation as a trace of the world, would be to oversimplify the case.[67] Cinema's aptitude for visualizing contingency, ambivalence, and transience is also recognized by the two foremost theorists of film realism. Pasolini by contrast warily reappropriates some of the techniques of realism in order not to affirm film's centrality to the modernist episteme, but to formulate a regressive poetics of spectrality that fulfills the promise of an aporetic critical catharsis elicited by the end of modernity. By means of a paradoxical reanimation of realism, in other words, he renounces the aim of a comfortable aesthetic resolution to the haunting imperative of cultural mourning.

It is necessary, I would argue, to distinguish between such an effort and a sincere attempt to continue the imaginative project of realism. In recent years, the critical consensus has placed special emphasis on the role of the corporeal in Pasolini's films. Without denying the originality of his view of the body and its importance to his enunciation of a cinematic homoerotics, I think it is necessary to recognize in his insistence on the "spectrality" of cinema an unwavering opposition to the illusory false consciousness of a naturalist aesthetics.[68] Pasolini's poetics of spectrality, however, does not represent a new form of "spiritualism"; quite the contrary. In this light, we may say the Friulian director partially forsakes the classical vocation of poetry for that of film because film allows immediate access to the bodily. Yet another side of Pasolini's "literal," "material" poetics of spectrality ought to be recognized in his assumption that, according to Cocteau's dictum, cinema represents death at work, revealing in its wake the afterlife of things.[69]

Pasolini's conviction that death is analogous to a cinematic montage of our lives represents a literalization of the Freudian position that every organism wants to die its own death. Like an organism, film resolves and gives expression to the death instinct through editing. Almost all of Pasolini's movies conclude with a death, a motif that intervenes not only at a microstructural level to effect the homeopathic regulation of the death instinct through montage, but also at a macrostructural level as the annihilation of the narrative drive.[70] Pasolini's cinema therefore constantly threatens, through an aesthetic regression into the territory of the death instinct, to become metahistorical and mystical. However, by accepting the complexity of the challenge, he manages to envision at times new forms of mournful, critical imagination.

We should not fail to observe, then, that the mortuary aesthetic of Pasolini's movies endorses a posthistoricism that raises the ironic hope of a mystical, revolutionary afterlife of history. The decisive importance of film to Pasolini's overall artistic project resides in the capacity of the cinematic image to depict the poetic figure that in more recent years Derrida has termed the *revenant–arrivant*, meaning thereby the sign of the second coming of the radical spirit of Marxism. Achieving its most iconic incarnation in the visitor of *Theorem*, this figure appears in various guises throughout the Friulian director's filmography. Like Ettore in *Mamma Roma*, for example, the eponymous protagonist of *Accattone* is both a *revenant* in the sense of reincarnating the iconic subjects of Italian Quattrocento painting and an *arrivant* in the sense of belonging to the mythical world of the Roman subproletariat. The messianic subtext of Pasolini's films is dependent on the inherently "regressive," oneiric nature of cinema, a spectrality that questions and successfully undermines the false clarity of the symbolic world.

Real Specters

In what follows, I examine the spectral logic informing Pasolini's different essays on cinema, paying particular attention to the paradoxical and contradictory meanings that he assigns to the notion of "realism." In conclusion, I propose a reading of *Theorem* [*Teorema*] as Pasolini's most complex and sophisticated allegory of mourning.

As is well known, Pasolini was not only a filmmaker but a "semiotician" of cinema who authored a substantial body of essays from 1966 through the 1970s in which he consistently highlighted the necessity of examining the "ideology" of cinema:

It is necessary to create ideology; it is necessary to destroy ontology. Audiovisual techniques are in large measure already a part of our world, that is, of the world of technical neocapitalism, which moves ahead, and whose tendency it is to deprive its techniques of ideology or to make them ontological; to make them silent and unrelated, to make them habits; to make them religious forms. We are lay humanist . . . we must therefore fight to demystify the "innocence of technique" to the last drop of blood.[71]

This statement, which concludes one of Pasolini's most important essays on film, "The Written Language of Reality," may be understood not only as one of the critic's principal theoretical manifestoes, but also as the declaration of a radical political agenda that the director was unable to realize fully by the time of his murder in 1975. In the same essay, he contends that the fulfillment of such an agenda depends on acknowledging the tension between an increasingly obsolescent humanism and the evolving technology of cinema, a medium that abolishes the art product's customary obfuscation regarding its own means of production:

... We cannot ignore the phenomenon of a kind of a downgrading of the word, tied to the deterioration of the humanistic languages of the elites, which have been, until now, the guiding languages. . . . From the great poem of action of Lenin to the small page of action prose of an employee of Fiat or of a ministry, life is unquestionably drawing away from the classical humanistic ideals and is losing itself in pragmatics. The film (with the other audiovisual techniques) appears to be the written language of pragmatism.[72]

A paradoxical reconciliation of humanism and pragmatism through cinema was the utopian horizon Pasolini initially outlined in his "semiological" essays on film. Although these essays, written for different magazines at different occasions, fail to offer a systematic philosophy of cinema, they nevertheless evince their author's devotion to the "logic" of spectrality, to the language of the subjective, the phantasmatic, and the poetic.

Perhaps the most enigmatic moment of Pasolini's reflections on film coincides with his introduction of the argument for a poetic cinema rooted in a concept of free indirect subjectivity.[73] Pursuing this argument, he posits a correspondence between "free indirect discourse" or "reanimated speech" and its visual counterpart, which he calls the "free indirect point-of-view shot." This technique of visualization inheres in the camera's reproduction of the sensory perceptions and experiences of its subjects, in an intermingling of the directorial gaze and the dramatized consciousness.[74] In a manner similar to the literary device of indirect discourse, free indirect point-of-view shots allow the director-auteur to enunciate a character's inner thoughts and feelings without direct citation. Whereas in literature the dialectical positions of author and character may be recovered by parsing their respective linguistic acts, in cinema, the natural distinction made possible by language disappears.[75] The plurilinguism that Bakhtin argues is intrinsic to free indirect discourse and thus to literature cannot be replicated by the more homogeneous medium of the moving image.

Pasolini offers a novel solution to this problem. In his judgment, the method of free indirect point of view, the cinematic equivalent of the linguistic device of "free indirect discourse," should be identified not with a single category of speech act but rather with the total visual style of a particular auteur. Nothing less than the director's personal mode of depiction opens itself to being haunted by his character's "vision" and thus provides a lyrical synthesis of the two perspectives. The camera becomes the representative of a consciousness suspended between the subjective and the objective, witnessing the "historical" events of the narrative from a vantage that cannot claim the authority of the historically critical or disinterested.

In his essay, Pasolini points to the movies of Antonioni, Bertolucci, and Godard as the principal examples of a cinema of poetry. It is modernist sound-cinema that not only supplies the paradigm of "poetic" film, but also suggests the limitations of a category that may be implicated in the reactionary perpetuation of the program of high culture.[76] A crucial, tacit concern of Pasolini's argument, then, is whether the techniques of free indirect point of view can be mobilized in the service not of the modernist ideals of abstraction and impersonality that risk assimilation to a high-cultural agenda, but of the concrete and personal necessities of those discourses that have been suppressed by such an agenda.

Pasolini identifies two major visual "stylemas" that enable the film-maker to represent the subjectivity of a "sick, abnormal protagonist," thus achieving the poetry of the free indirect point-of-view shot.[77] The first consists of "obsessive framing," of the juxtaposition of multiple iterations of the same image that are differentiated only by the merest shifts in angle, lens, or distance. The second stylema consists of highlighting the transience of characters through a recurrent focus on their entrances into and exits from the frame, a stylema the director will apply holistically, as we'll see, to the narrative structure of *Theorem*. Indeed, the movie *Theorem* (1970), which tells the story of a mysterious guest who enters the lives of the members of a wealthy Milanese family only to vanish after upending their complacent domestic routine, provides the very "theorem" of Pasolini's aesthetics of film insofar as it exemplifies a poetics of haunting.

Pasolini's spectropoetics achieves eloquence in his espousal of an empty frame, in his proposal that the absence of human figures from the cinematic field of vision brings about a greater gain in meaning than their presence: "The world is presented as if regulated by a myth of pure pictorial beauty that the personages invade, it is true, but adapting themselves to the rules of that beauty instead of profaning them with their presence."[78] The motion picture provides the best medium for the spectralized performance of mourning because, as the Friulian critic concludes, the "pretext of the visual mimesis" of a character implies the presence of a "second film," a "subterranean" double that haunts the ostensible pretext and can only be discerned through its traces in "obsessive shots and editing rhythms."[79] It is interesting that even in a separate essay on the art of the screenplay, he identifies the specificity of the form with its nature as a "structure that wants to be another structure," suggesting that the two different languages of the verbal and the visual haunt one another.[80]

Pasolini first demonstrated an interest in the ideological foundations of discursive "style" in his literary-critical essay, "Comments on Free Indirect Discourse" (1964), a review of Giulio Herczeg's book, *The Free Indirect Style in Italian*.[81] Pasolini ascribes the author's need to "reanimate" a character's speech to a "mysterious need for intercommunication with his character."[82] What the essay ultimately asserts is a politics of plurilinguilism based not on an identification with the sameness of the character, but rather on an attitude of openness and hospitality to the difference of the other. The most crucial objection to Herczeg's text for Pasolini in fact concerns the suggestion that free indirect discourse can simply reanimate the thoughts of the characters according to a sort of "ontological phenomenology" that effects a transparent "rapport of sympathy" between the author and the character, "as if their life experiences were the same."[83] The Friulian critic dismisses this line of reasoning as a form of bigotry: "The most odious and intolerable thing, even in the most innocent of bourgeois, is that of not knowing how to recognize life experiences other than his own: and of bringing all other life experiences back to a substantial analogy with his own."[84] Pasolini clearly conveys the ethical stakes involved in the usage of free indirect discourse, a practice that is tantamount to a poetics of possession by the foreign, an incorporation of the Other's speech and thoughts that greets the unfamiliar with hospitality while acknowledging its alterity and hence its unknowability. Beyond any merely sympathetic identification with a character, what Pasolini advocates is recognition of the difference of his or her voice, a recognition that has definite political and ethical consequences.

Pasolini's investigation of the free indirect point of view in film therefore has to be considered first of all in the context of his search for zones of freedom secured by the incongruity of discrete semiotic regimens, as opposed to the osmosis enforced by technology. His notion of free indirect point of view thus transcends the strictly sociological and psychological horizons of interpretation to catalyze a poetics of haunting that presupposes acceptance of the impossibility of an ethically adequate work of mourning in contemporary culture.

Gilles Deleuze is the reader who has given the most serious consideration to Pasolini's theoretical efforts. Indeed, he contends that the "linguistic" bias of the Friulian author's film criticism evinces an idea of the motion picture as a new semiotic praxis of signs and images that advances beyond a traditional distinction between *langue* and *langage* toward the conception of cinema as a form of thought.[85] For Deleuze, the director's insistence on free indirect point of view represents a crucial attempt to explode the conventional analogy drawn between subjective and objective frames of reference in favor of what might be defined in the language of Jean Mitry as a "half-subjective" image, an image produced by a camera not within, but with the character's consciousness.[86] According to the French philosopher, Pasolini's solution to the dichotomy between cinematic subject and object leads to the discovery of a pure form.[87]

Although Deleuze correctly assesses the aesthetic importance of the technique of free indirect point of view, he fails to acknowledge the openness and ethical responsibility to the Other that such a method demands. Pasolini was deeply suspicious of the idea of art as a purely psychological or formal mimesis. At moments, he regards such a notion as an effect of the "anthropological evolution of capitalism," a metanarrative that pressures the artist to uphold the myth of form in an "international style."[88] Consequently, his vision of a "cinema of poetry" is deeply ambivalent because he thinks of film as a less flexible medium than language for the construction of metaphor and hence for the enactment of a poetics of hospitality. "The pretextual characters," Pasolini asserts, "cannot be chosen from outside the cultural limits of the filmmaker; that is, they are analogous to him in culture, language, and psychology—they are exquisite 'flowers of the bourgeoisie.'"[89] His insistence on the bourgeois character of cinematic representation manifests a fear that the resemblance between the directorial and fictional gazes may be merely a form of reification. The threat, in other words, consists of a film poetry that is too elegiac and hence incapable of a sufficiently critical work of incorporation.

Through reference to Pasolini's filmography, we may more sharply define the correspondence between a movie's auteur and protagonist as grounded in an ethical or political, as opposed to psychological, sympathy. The central characters of his features often perform a simultaneously heretical and messianic social function. The classic Pasolinian hero is a ghostly figure, a *revenant–arrivant* who embodies a Christlike combination of stigmatization and revolutionary potential, as is evident throughout the director's oeuvre from *Accattone* to *The Gospel According to Saint Matthew*, *Theorem*, and *Saint Paul*. Unlike the films of Antonioni, Godard, and Bertolucci, Pasolini's movies endeavor to establish a more complicated language with which to reinterpret the voice of the Other, a discourse that defies the limits of formalist aesthetics and of neocapitalism's relegation of the poet to the role of archivist of a humanistic reverence for form.[90] Pasolini, it might be said, strives throughout his career to honor the fundamental principle of his poetic hero, Rimbaud: "'I' is another" [Je est un autre]. To the degree that it sums up an idea of poetic self-redescription as an act of challenge or dissent, this motto guides the director's quest to avoid mimesis of the entrenched conditions of reality and to mourn the unfulfilled, utopian promise of the future.[91]

His disavowal of a mimetic cinematography in order to preserve the heterogeneity of subject and object is the foundation of an original film poetics, a methodology that differs from the approach of Antonioni, Bertolucci, and Godard in its refusal to assume the common neurotic history of auteur and character. What Pasolini finally proposes is a distinctive practice of spectrality: nothing less than a mourning of realism and modernism that acknowledges its incommensurability to either practice while undermining the spectacularized visual culture that is characteristic of populist postmodernity.

Editing and Death

In "Observations on the Sequence Shot" (1967), Pasolini equates the decisive intervention of editing with that of death, thus introducing a quasiexistentialist proposition into the project of film criticism. Overcoming his fascination with the phenomenological value of the long take, he names the editing process as the proper philosophical locus of cinema, albeit not without a touch of trepidation:

At this point, then, I must say what I think of death (and I leave readers free to ask themselves, skeptically, what all this has to do with cinema). . . . Death effects an instantaneous montage of our lives, that is, it chooses the truly meaningful moments (which are no longer modifiable by other possible contrary or incoherent moments) and puts them in a sequence, transforming an infinite, unstable, and uncertain—and therefore linguistically not describable—present into a clear, stable, certain and therefore easily describable past.[92]

Pasolini's theory of cinema helps to evince a specific cultural necessity, namely, that of finding a viable mode of mourning beyond any nostalgia for a poetics of genre or the formal consolation of elegy. Cinema provides the ideal solution to the necessity of honoring the past as an unresolved, "mysterious" (to use a term Pasolini frequently applies to the medium), and spectral presence. With deathlike finality, editing transforms the ineffable, abstract idea of cinema into the descriptive legibility of a film, thus enabling a paradoxical renewal of the ritual value of mourning within the very domain of technology that threatens to abolish cult or ritual practice. Films embody a "clear, stable, certain and easily describable past" and thus the promise of a restoration of our capacity for successful mourning. The temporal transmutation of the present of the sequence shot into the past of the edited film arrives as a hermeneutic event, the shift from an endless, indiscriminate accumulation of all moments to a final arrangement of the significant few. As the Friulian director readily observes, the aim of editing is not to erase the present, but "to render the present past."[93]

Pasolini's theory bears more than a little resemblance to Benjamin's argument in "The Storyteller" that death sanctions the very act of storytelling: "Just as a sequence of images is set in motion inside a man as his life comes to an end . . . suddenly in his expressions and looks the unforgettable emerges and imparts to everything that concerned him that authority which even the poorest wretch in dying possesses for the living around him. This authority is at the very source of the story."[94] Note that the German critic describes the symbolic moment of death by means of a vividly filmic trope as a series of images "set in motion." In a passage strikingly similar to Benjamin's declaration, Pasolini writes: "Death effects a rapid synthesis of a past life, and the retroactive light that it shines on that life highlights its essential moments, making of them actions which are mythical or moral outside of time. Well, this is a way in which a life becomes a story."[95] It should be noted, however, that for Benjamin the motion picture was not the proper medium of transmissible experience, but rather modernity's crucial means of technological reproduction and thus a sort of dialectical antithesis of the *Erfahrung* brought to light through storytelling.[96] Benjamin's melancholic assessment of the declining art of storytelling is controverted in Pasolini's opinion by the discovery that film is actually the most effective type of storytelling insofar as it guarantees through editing the presence of the past as a poetic trace. Even more importantly, the medium thereby acknowledges its contingent relationship to reality, dissolving the present in order to reveal a "mythical or moral" level of meaning "outside of time."

Pasolini's final pair of critical essays regarding cinema, "Theory of Splices" and "The Rheme," confirm his turn away from structuralism and semiology and toward a film poetics that aims at the mournful, phantasmatic "deconstruction" of reality.[97] In "Theory of Splices," he redefines cinema not in the audiovisual terms he usually adopts, but in the mystical terms of spiritualism or the supernatural: "All that I have described and analyzed linguistically and grammatically is nothing more than an 'appearance' in which another language and another grammar are 'embodied,' which, in order to be, need—like the spirit—to descend into matter."[98] His recourse to a "spiritualist" vocabulary, if superficially suggestive of the tradition of Crocean aesthetic idealism, also notably deviates from such rhetoric insofar as Pasolini's discourse insists on the need for "incarnation."[99] By this last term, he means the filmic translation of spatial perception into temporal rhythm, a metamorphosis in which he locates the origin of the "mysterious relationships of space" between shots and the evocation of the "lingering spirits" of memory.[100]

In these last essays, Pasolini introduces into his technical vocabulary the concepts of "rhythmeme" and "splice." The first term designates the theoretical possibility of charting the relationship between the spatial and temporal dimension of a film.[101] The second term indicates the link between shots, the point at which the editor attaches one shot to another. However, as Pasolini defines it, the splice is a negative duration: "the meaningful nonexistent."[102] By means of these concepts, Pasolini establishes the initial premises of a grammatology of cinema, a poetics of splices and rhythmemes in which the structuralist dialectic between cinema and film unveils its "spiritual," deconstructive side. Even if his initial reliance on semiotics seems somewhat antiquated, Pasolini's theory of cinema maintains an enormous interest for us, insofar as it represents an important effort to reinscribe the question of mourning within the contemporary language of the image. Through the intersubjective, spatiotemporal aspects of cinema, his nostalgia for tradition, myth, and the past finds its most compelling expression as an ethical spectropoetics through which imagine a renewal of culture.

Theorem

In *La ricotta*, one of his most celebrated films, Pasolini inserts a voice-over in which Orson Welles recites one of the director's poems. This lyric voices its author's regretful longing for the past in hyperbolically self-dramatizing language:

> I am a force of the Past.
> Tradition is my only love.

I come from ruins, from the churches,
from the altarpieces, from villages
forgotten on the Apennines and the Pre-Alps
where my brother lived. . . .
An adult fetus, more modern than all the moderns,
I roam in search of brothers that are no more.[103]

The interest of the poem lies not in the fact that it expresses Pasolini's nostalgia for the past, but rather in the way such nostalgia is displaced by the irony of the author's self-portrayal as "more modern than all the moderns," thus puncturing his own reverential solemnity. Yet there is a grain of truth to the self-parody; to achieve a cinema more modern than all the moderns might well be regarded as one of Pasolini's defining directorial ambitions, an impulse that leads him from *Accattone*'s poetic reinterpretation of the sacred to *Theorem*'s allegory of quasireligious mourning. In the story of a mysterious stranger who visits, transforms, and then abandons a bourgeois Milanese family, Pasolini propounds a symbolic rewriting of the quintessential myth of modernity, namely, the death of God.[104] At the same time, the Friulian director takes pains to eschew the claims to autonomy of the self that typically ensue from the mourning of metaphysics, a manic triumphalism evident in the rhetoric of post-Nietzschean writers such as Bataille. Indeed, he drops entirely the Nietzschean goal of superhuman self-perfection, preferring instead to contemplate what might be described as the all-too-human problematic of hauntedness or unresolved mourning.

In a passage from an early draft of the novel, Pasolini makes clear that the true moral of his story concerns the necessity of living with radical, tragic ambiguity: "The true moral of these events—as the reader will realize at the end of this operetta—will be once again ambiguity: not an agnostic ambiguity, no, but, insofar as the style of these pages might allow it, a tragic ambiguity."[105] Although he wishes to highlight the impossibility of restoring the sacred to contemporary society, however, his parable stops short of reaching an utterly negative moral conclusion. The first interpretive challenge *Theorem* poses, then, is to make sense of its equivocal nature as a parable that is also a "report" [*referto*], a revelation that simultaneously manages to be both emblematic and "enigmatic" [*enigmatico*].[106]

Theorem is one of Pasolini's most significant films not only because, unlike *Oedipus Rex* or *Medea*, it succeeds in finding a contemporary narrative framework for its allegorized content, but also because the movie is emblematic of the modern condition of cinema as a "time-image." Deleuze has suggested, in fact, that the cinema of the time-image is inherently "theorematic" insofar as it replaces a premodern emphasis on the association of images with a new stress on the thought immanent to the image.[107] In its achievement of a quasimathematical rigor of thought manifest in the image, *Theorem* represents in Deleuze's eyes the most exemplary but also most problematic of Pasolini's films. Far from typifying the dogmatic attitude its title seems to imply, *Theorem* for the French philosopher restores the "unthought into thought" by interpolating an uncanny event into consciousness from the outside: "Thought finds itself taken over by the exteriority of a 'belief' outside any interiority of a mode of knowledge. Was this Pasolini's way of still being Catholic? Was it on the contrary his way of being a radical atheist? Has he not, like Nietzsche, torn belief from every faith in order to give it back to rigorous thought?"[108]

Deleuze's likening of Pasolini to Nietzsche helps to define *Theorem*'s philosophical concerns inasmuch as the film proposes, as I have already mentioned, a reinterpretation of the disappearance of God; yet the simile also overlooks a crucial disparity. As Sam Rohdie acutely observes, what distinguishes Pasolini is his interest in mourning a loss he himself not only stages, but also celebrates, a form of self-alienation that Rohdie, quoting Umberto Eco, labels the "way of finding oneself in the other."[109] The Friulian director is never simply nostalgic for a lost object. Consequently, his anguish cannot be categorized as decadent, romantic, or modernist in any strict sense. An acute awareness of the contingency or nonuniversality of human "nature," Rohdie argues, instead finds its correlative in the overdetermined artifice of the director's cinematic style: "To watch Pasolini's films is to watch a parable, a type of non-fictional fiction, evidently made up and false, yet whose falsity is there to express a truth. . . . His language cites itself as well as the other languages it contains."[110]

Renouncing both the naturalism of sorrow still prevalent in romanticism and the manic denial of grief maintained by the avant-garde, Pasolini's movies constitute poetic simulacra and allegorizations of loss that ultimately situate his theory of mourning in the territory of a critical postmodernity.[111] Even before the publication of the novel in 1978, the film, which was released in 1968, could be said to straddle two artistic disciplines, as Pasolini was well aware. Originally composed as a play for the theatrical stage, the story of *Theorem* was successively rewritten by Pasolini until its eventual transposition to the screen. When Garzanti finally published the novel, Pasolini prefaced the narrative with a few instructions regarding the reading of the text in which he rehearsed the genealogy and aims of the work: "The book, *Theorem*, was born against a golden background, painted with the right hand, while with the left hand I was work-ing to paint a large wall (the homonymous film). Of such an amphibious nature, it cannot really be said which is more prevalent: that of literature or that of film."[112] In the same preface, Pasolini acknowledges having perhaps overindulged in dialogical mimesis of the bourgeoisie via "free indirect dis-course," but asserts that in the film he kept such a risk at bay by maintain-ing "an extremist visual angle, perhaps a little sweet . . . but in compensa-tion without alternatives."[113]

Pasolini's decision to issue both the novel and the film thus appears to have originated in his desire to supplement the politically acquiescent verbal realism of free indirect discourse, which typically relies on measure and distance, with the more uncanny and subversive visual simulation of the free indirect subjective. In this light, the film may be regarded as the specter of the novel, which is to say the ghostly double that the most "real-ist" of literary forms represses and is haunted by, the phantasm that can have no legitimation in the ideological domain that the book's verbiage re-produces. *Theorem*, then, must be understood as a hybrid, as the tension or dialectic between novel and film. Accordingly, although I refer mostly to the film in what follows, I also will discuss by turns the novel's own "indi-rect" gestures toward heterogeneity and incommensurability, its eccentric mixture of literary narrative exposition, vernacular stream of conscious-ness, and lyric verse.

One of the director's few films to take the bourgeoisie as its ostensi-ble topic, *Theorem* abandons the sort of analogical approach he attributes to the general conventions of the point-of-view shot, whereby a character of bourgeois origin is evoked in the equally middle-class terms of a com-modified visual rhetoric. Pasolini refuses such complacent transparency by introducing a heavily encoded moral allegory through the use of religious and political iconography, by overtly thematizing the confrontation with Otherness in the person of the mysterious visitor-guest, and by sublimat-ing this theme into the film's effort to bring about a reestrangement of artistic form. Without pretending, as in his earliest films such as *Accattone* and *Mamma Roma*, to give voice to a "mythologized" subproletarian class, *Theorem* reformulates the question of mourning not in terms of the loss of the object, but rather in terms of the difference of the Other. The guest's visual association with Rimbaud throughout the film is to be understood in this sense as reinterpreting the perspectivism of free indirect subjective in terms of the poetic principle, "'I' is another."

The very hybridity of *Theorem*, its embodiment of the supplemen-

tary relation between text and image, indicates the extent of Pasolini's distrust of speech and language, his perpetual mourning of an ideal *logos* that
drives him to experiment with new forms of expression. On this score, he
is one of the first artists to adopt a recognizably postmodern methodology
inasmuch as he aspires to find hospitality in new mediums that offer
bridges or alternatives to the untranslatability of language and promotes an
aesthetic of fierce, self-consciously theatrical performativity.[114] By virtue of
its very "amphibious nature," as Pasolini puts it, *Theorem* enlarges on its
own explicit topic of hospitality to problematize the function of artistic
genre as a "welcoming" of the artist. His ethical achievement and originality, then, should be located precisely in his willingness to suspend the rules
of discrete language games.[115] In *Theorem*, the operation of hospitality occurs at all structural levels, affecting not only the central theme of the plot,
but its artistic and creative ramifications.

Given the essential conflict of the narrative between messianic iconoclasm and bourgeois conformism, the relentless effort to question formal
first principles in *Theorem* must be understood, insofar as it represents a
means to self-exposure, as a response to the ethical agon of mourning. This
is to say that the film's own openness to loss—its mourning of what cannot be presented—ironizes the anguish of the bourgeois characters as they
confront the disappearance from their lives of the sacred or ecstatic ideal
embodied by the visitor. Mourning not only is dramatized at the
macrostructural level of theme, therefore, but also is incorporated into the
microstructural, stylistic procedures of the film. Pasolini's antinaturalistic
style—his predilection for frontal shots, flattened surfaces, a static camera,
and sustained editing—represents in *Theorem* a virtuosic and pervasive incorporation of the mysteriousness of the unseen. By shunning long takes,
Pasolini repudiates the kind of cognitive ambiguity typical of neorealism
inasmuch as that particular cinematic language attempts to resist the grammatical interventions of close-ups and editing. Instead, he embraces a more
radical metaphysical distress that strikes the viewer apropos not of the content visualized on screen, but of the very spectrality of visualization itself.
This last point is driven home in the film by the director's continual recurrence to the two stylistic modes he had observed particularly in Antonioni's
films in his essay on the "cinema of poetry." These two stylistic traits, the
obsessive reframing of shots and the imaging of the characters' exits from
the frame, synecdochically reassert the two thematic poles of the film: repetition and mourning.

The conceit of a contemporary messianic visitation is pursued by Pasolini to its extreme, traumatic conclusions in the lives of the members of a bourgeois Milanese family composed of Paolo, the paterfamilias and the owner of a local factory; Lucia, the mother; Odetta, the daughter; Pietro, the son; and Emilia, the maid.[116] The film is visually divided into two parts. The first and shorter portion, which takes place before the stranger's arrival, is printed in a monochromatic sepia tone, whereas the second portion is printed in full color. The plot largely consists of the guest's wordless, serial seduction of each one of the family members, starting with Emilia, before his eventual vanishing from the household. What distinguishes the film's framing of this plot from the novel's is the unfolding of action in the movie according to an indefinite and nonlinear chronological structure. In fact, the movie relates the story in a decidedly nonsequential order; the opening shots ostensibly derive from an interview with employees at Paolo's company after he has decided to give the factory and its business to the workers in the wake of the visitor's disappearance. These images are interspersed with shots of a desert that appear to constitute a further flashforward. But the visual interpolation of the desert subtly complicates the diegesis of the narrative, making it tricky to fix the present tense of the action and confronting the viewer with a disorienting loss of hermeneutic foundations, with the aftermath of the action appearing before its commencement.

Images of the desert are intercut with the action of the characters throughout the movie until the final shots, when the denouement of the main storyline concerning the fate of the family transpires in the desert, thus joining the two visual motifs. As a result, almost the entire film must be regarded as a flashback from the *nunc stans* of this conclusion, including the first scene of the interviews of factory workers conducted by a television news crew (we might note, by way of contrast, that the novel's equivalent of the movie's opening is an investigative report that Pasolini situates toward the end of the book).[117] However, if the desert represents the present tense of the movie, it does so in a highly ironic sense because the allegorical evocation of biblical archetypes that punctuates both the novel and the film locates this "natural" present in a symbolic past as well. Ultimately, the desert seems to affirm a temporality of eternal repetition, as Pasolini himself hints when he writes in the novel, "And these variations of rock, stones, or sand were no more to the Jews than the sign of repetition, the possibility of perceiving a monotony that entered into the bones like the fever of the plague."[118] Pursuing the self-interrogation of an image moving through time as much as space, the film enacts an apocalyptic temporal suspension that the novel appears capable only of describing.

"The season is undefined," writes Pasolini, "it could be spring or the beginning of autumn—or both together, because this story does not follow a chronology."[119] The most enigmatic symbol in *Theorem* is the desert, the spatiotemporally mystified wilderness beyond commerce and society through which Paolo wanders at the end of the film, presumably after having renounced his business. The viewer is uncertain if a messianic future is opening or if history has finally been erased. An analogous uncertainty is rhetorically enforced in the novel by means of oxymoron, when Pasolini evokes a natural world that manages to be "inhospitable but not hostile" [*inospitale ma non nemico*] in the act of welcoming the human, to be thoroughly alien or Other and thus, in a philosophical sense, inhuman: "So the landscape of what was contrary to life repeated itself unshadowed and quite uninterrupted. It was born of itself, continued by itself and ended in itself; but it did not reject man, indeed it welcomed him, inhospitable but not hostile, opposed to his nature but not to his reality."[120]

The figure of the inhuman in *Theorem* therefore is directly implicated in the problematic of hospitality that recently has received Derrida's attention. Indeed, *Theorem* might be said to spectacularize a Derridean sense of the overlap between the concepts of "guest" and "ghost," a congruence that Pasolini's narrative brings to light with the guest's departure.[121] As Anne Dufourmantelle points out, Derrida's exploration of hospitality crucially revolves around a meditation on the questions of naming, burial, memory, and place, a constellation of topics, we might add, that in turn inevitably raises the specter of mourning.[122] The same themes are closely associated in *Theorem*, a narrative that never reveals the name of its mysterious central figure of the guest, that continually stresses his "unforgettable" influence on the rest of the characters, and that, through its imagining of Paolo's wanderings in the desert and Emilia's self-burial, dramatizes the importance of discovering the proper symbolic place of both dwelling and dying. Hospitality, we might say, comes to light in the welcoming of the radical Otherness of death and in the honoring of a stranger's sorrow for the dead.[123] In order to extend such a welcome, hospitality requires repeated ethical renewal or reaffirmation, a continuous reinscription of the topic at the furthest extremes of paradox.[124]

It might also be said that the repetition of anguish in *Theorem* ultimately usurps the place of the reality principle in a manner suggestive of Freud's classic definition of the work of mourning. Yet the consequences on the individual family members of the nameless visitor's desertion of the household seem sufficiently catastrophic as to throw into question the very notion of a finite "work." Emilia's reaction to the guest in the film, for example, immediately manifests the mechanism of repetition. She runs back and forth from the garden to the house two or three times before attempting suicide in the kitchen. When the guest intervenes to save her, we know that her fate has only been momentarily postponed. Repetition also decisively shapes Lucia's behavior after the stranger's departure, when her succession of meaningless liaisons with young men signals her sense of bereavement. In Odetta's case, the theme of repetition is played out through the allegorization of the Oedipal scenario, according to which the visitor substitutes for the father in her affection.[125]

The issue of repetition is further highlighted in the novel by the lyric interlude of the poem, "Theory of Two Paradises" [*Teoria dei due paradisi*], which hints at an interpretation of the narrative as a recapitulation of the Fall. In its valediction to the consecrated institution of the family, the poem may also be read as a parodic reiteration of the Proustian yearning for the "lost paradise" of maternal love and domestic tranquillity, even as it infers from the removal of such benefits the more radical possibility of a traumatic or symbolic death à la Lacan. Similarly, the repetition of free indirect subjective in the film, as each of the family members "falls" under the stranger's sway, betrays a peculiar ambivalence, an equivocation between censure and sympathy that never indulges in desecration or cynicism, instead encouraging a critical impartiality. Indeed, it is by recurrently exposing the ethical incommensurability of its characters that *Theorem* stakes at least part of its claim to a postmodern resistance to synthesis.

With respect to *Theorem*'s borderline status between modernism and postmodernism, the most interesting character in the story is Pietro, the son with painterly aspirations. Although some critics have perceived him as a stand-in for the director himself, I believe he actually represents the antithesis of Pasolini's creative ideal. Marcus regards Pietro as Pasolini's "self-reflexive" spokesperson, who is wary of high-cultural pretensions and whose method of painting on glass in a sense allegorizes the luminosity of the celluloid art. [126] *Pace* Marcus, however, Pietro's choice of materials more aptly may be read, it seems to me, not as an approving gesture to the cinematic (and notwithstanding the fact that most of the painting depicted in the movie was created by Pasolini's friend Zigaina), but as a more disenchanted reference to the neo-avant-garde and its ideology of deliberate but empty transparency. In the novel, the anonymous visitor shows Pietro some reproductions of Wyndham Lewis's imagist paintings and thus initiates him into the mysteries of modernism.[127] "The picture," writes Pasolini in a free indirect evocation of Pietro's response, "is strongly colorful—with pure colours: if one looks at it more closely it is like a network of outlines which leave free surfaces, triangles and rectangles that are slightly rounded . . . and it is on these free surfaces that those pure colours are applied: Prussian blue and reds—pure but extremely discreet, almost stealthy, as if veiled by the patina of age."[128] Despite the positive appeal of the composition's "pure colours," the culminating emphasis on "the patina of age" makes clear the author's skepticism regarding the validity of the image as an ideal.

In a poem that follows the passage just quoted, Pasolini assumes the role of a dramatic chorus, summarizing Pietro's fascination by declaring that "the first ones we love/are the poets and painters of the previous generations/of the beginning of the century."[129] Addressing Pietro directly, however, the poet proceeds to chastise the naive, regressive impulse toward nostalgic emulation: "Do feel nostalgia for them when you are sixteen/But begin to understand immediately that the poets and painters old or dead in spite of the halo of a heroic air you give them/are useless to you, teach you nothing."[130] Pasolini sharply suggests in this choral apostrophe the hollowness and irrelevance of the very "heroic" image of aesthetic innovation on which modernism is predicated. Consequently, we may view the director's own career in the movie industry as a literally postmodernist response to the crisis of historicity in the arts, the statement of an artist who is determined not to simply regurgitate modernist tenets in the manner of the neo-avant-garde of the 1960s.

Along these lines, it is noteworthy that in the section of the book entitled "Pietro's Corollary" [*Corollario di Pietro*], which chronicles Pietro's distressed reaction to the guest's disappearance, the painting by Lewis is referred to as a "little, useless enigma" [*piccolo enigma inutile*], a derisive characterization that reveals Pietro's sudden disaffection with modernist abstraction.[131] What he had regarded earlier as the picture's "civility of composition" [*civiltà della scomposizione*] now strikes him as "expired, devalued, disappointing, impoverished" [*scaduto, deprezzato, deludente impoverito*].[132] In keeping with the principles of free indirect discourse, opinions attributed to Pietro in the novel are dialectically bound up with and contaminated by the author's views, meaning that in the young painter's apostasy from the school of modernism, we may detect a trace of Pasolini's own disillusionment.

The chapter "Vocation and Skills" [*Vocazioni e techniche*] must be regarded in this light as crucial to an understanding of the novel. The chapter constitutes a portrait of Pietro's *Bildung* as a young artist and of his complex struggles with different technical options. The narrative unfolds as a mock recapitulation of the history of painting in which the first, figurative-impressionist stage (when Pietro vainly tries to reproduce the guest's features) is superseded by an ersatz abstract modernism (manifested in his gluing sheets of paper to a piece of cardboard, collecting "transparent materials," and devoting himself to painting a simple blue surface) that culminates in the creative dead end of "action painting" (signaled by his vertical dripping of paint onto a carefully positioned surface). In the course of this methodological odyssey, Pietro becomes convinced that the modernist mania for technical innovation sublimates or disguises an anxiety on the artist's part with respect to his or her own insignificance: "To construct a personal world, with which a comparison is not possible. About which no previous measures of judgment are offered. Measures have to be always new, like technique. Nobody should understand that the author is not worth anything."[133] The young painter's final undertaking is to introduce the element of chance into the production of his work, a move that transforms his formerly Mallarmean, idealist quest for *l'azzurro* into the accidental creative events promised by action painting.

Theorem implicitly presents itself as a diagnosis of the exhaustion of bourgeois culture after the failure of the Enlightenment metanarrative of rational historical progress, but a diagnosis that refuses any hope of stylistic, mannerist cures. It is true that in the film the clash between the old and the new avant-garde is more offhand than in the novel, and that Pietro and the guest share in a somewhat less polemical examination of Bacon's, rather than Lewis's, paintings. But even in this casual shift of subjects, we may observe Pasolini's encoded distaste for modernism's "purist" aesthetics and his preference for the figural, the body (or the specter of the body), and the return to "reality" after the triumph of abstraction and minimalism.

In an appendix to the first part of the novel, the individual family members are assigned confessional monologues in which they all express their despair of ever finding a replacement for the nameless stranger. The repeated avowals of their devotion collectively signify the capacity of these typical representatives of their class to be forever altered by the experience of the sacred, to renounce the ethic of reflexive consumerism that informs market-based capitalism. By the same token, however, their attestations to the impossibility of completing the work of mourning for their messianic visitor imply feelings of displacement and dislocation that will resist any but the most utopian of resolutions. After he vanishes, all of the household's members pursue their own personal spiritual adventures, the most extraordinary of which befall Emilia and Paolo. Lucia, Odetta, and Pietro meanwhile appear to conform to the somewhat more conventional pattern of traumatic loss, incessantly reliving and repeating the pain of separation from the visitor. Particularly moving are Odetta's measurements of the distance between chairs where the guest and her father had been sitting and her obsessive attachment to her collection of photographs. Eventually, however, she retreats into the rigid isolation of a catatonic and is brought to a clinic. Lucia compulsively picks up random men who strike her as bearing some resemblance to the guest. As we already have seen, Pietro perpetuates the artistic curiosity passed on to him as a gift by the stranger.

Theorem's allegorical designs become unmistakable, however, with respect to the mystical metamorphoses separately undergone by Emilia and Paolo. In the first case, after leaving the family and arriving at a *casolare* or old house, Emilia seats herself like a Beckettian character in an immobile, atemporal state. She refuses to eat, even when a motherly figure tries to take care of her: "Emilia, however, does not allow herself to be convinced at all, as would be the case of a neighbor in mourning."[134] More starkly than any of the other characters, she demonstrates that the impossibility of performing a ritual or psychologically meaningful work of mourning ultimately bespeaks an incapacity "to dwell" poetically in the location of one's past.

While involuntarily accomplishing miracles such as healing sick babies with her touch, Emilia toward the end of her story is shown as levitating above the local rooftops. It is important to understand that Pasolini's use of the trope of levitation does not at all consort with the ethical levity popularized by an alternative style of postmodernism. The ideal of "lightness" promoted by Calvino in his *Six Memos for the Next Millennium*, for example, seems to aspire to a free-floating aesthetic receptivity that presupposes the abandonment of ethical and political responsibility. By contrast, the image of levitation in *Theorem* symbolizes a reawakening of spiritual and social conscience that authorizes the film's eventual enshrinement of Emilia as a figure of ethical "gravity."[135] The last stop of her pilgrimage is on the urban periphery of Milan, where she submits to being buried in a hole and covered with mud by an old woman who has accompanied her along the way.[136] The film's final glimpse of Emilia presents her as a derelict human form covered with mud "almost completely" [*quasi completamente*].[137] Her eyes remain visible gazing out of her entombment, and only a few, miraculous, "real" tears (in the Lacanian sense) emerge mysteriously from her grave. The suspension of her death between a physical and symbolic death, is an original way to problematize the interminable condition of mourning for Emilia.[138] *Theorem*, like much of Pasolini's oeuvre, dramatizes the emergence of the miraculous and the spiritual as the result of a spectral encounter with the Real. As we have already seen, the ultimate representation of the Real in the film is the desert, the natural wasteland that in the novel Paolo labels "that which is indispensable of reality" [*ciò che della realtà è solo indispensabile*].[139]

Equally mysterious as Emilia's burial will be Paolo's retreat to the desert after having given the factory to his employees, "from possessor to possessed" [*da possessore a posseduto*], and undressing in the train station.[140] The poetic, miraculous shock of his transformation is conveyed in the film by a jump cut from a close-up of Paolo's naked feet at the station to the same shot set in the desert. The illusion promulgated by the edit is of an unbroken walk from the station into the wilderness, accentuating the continuity, rather than the discrepancy, between Paolo's "bourgeois" and post-conversion consciousness. The camera accomplishes a sort of Escherlike legerdemain, a collapse of the levels of signification that normally are kept in binary opposition: the diegetic and extradiegetic, the literal and the allegorical, the symbolic and the real, the profane and the religious. Unlike a Kierkegaardian hero, however, Paolo cannot be said to perform an epiphanic leap of faith from the sphere of aesthetics into that of religion. His peregrinations from the city to the desert lead to confusion, not enlightenment. It might be said, then, that Paolo's progress takes him into the territory of contemporary epistemology, in which the emptiness of the signifier is brought to light by the incompatibility of the extremes it alleges to comprehend:

Sad result, if I have chosen this desert as the real and true place of my life! Is he who was searching in the streets of Milan the same as the one who now searches on the roads of the desert? It is true: the symbol of reality has something reality does not have: *it does not represent any meaning* and yet it adds to it—by its very representative nature—a new meaning.[141]

The image of Paolo desperately screaming in the desert, on which the film concludes, undermines any potentially optimistic reading of his story as a conversion experience, as a saving transformation of the capitalist manager into a latter-day Paolo, the apostle. How we ought to take this arresting visualization of his bewilderment, his attainment of a state of inarticulateness beyond culture and history, is elaborated to some extent at the end of the novel. In the poem that ends *Theorem*, "Oh, My Naked Feet!" [*Ah i miei piedi nudi*], the solitude through which Paolo wanders is presented as a kind of utopia in the etymological sense, an absence or lack of place. Like Oedipus at Colonus, Paolo in the wilderness seems to have overcome his neurotic repressions and to signal acceptance of his destiny through its performative evocation. His outcry, we are told, might represent a demand for attention or "might be a cry where anxiety is mixed with hope, or might be a cry of absolute certainty" [É un urlo in cui in fondo all'ansia si sente qualche vile accento di speranza; oppure un urlo di certezza].[142] The omniscient narrative voice goes on to add: "In any case this is certain: that whatever this scream of mine tries to say it is fated to last beyond any possible end."[143]

In *Theorem*, because nothing is known about the visitor, his disappearance is irreconcilable with mourning. Because he has no legible, personal history of his own, he can be given no place or location in memory, and thus the desert comes to symbolize the utopia of his absence. Or to put it in Derridean terms: "Without a fixed [*arrêté*] place, without a determinable *topos*, mourning is not allowed. Or what comes down to the same thing, it is promised without taking place, a determinable place, so thenceforth promised as an interminable mourning, an infinite mourning defying all work, beyond any possible work of mourning."[144] *Theorem*'s importance, in other words, is that it exposes the operation of mourning as an "enigmatic allegory," as an impossible or aporetic "work" in which the incompleteness of sense emerges as the natural consequence of a culture informed by lack, loss, and absence.[145] In the end, this incompleteness is associated with what language cannot legitimate, what cannot be enunciated in the rational accents of modernity: the state of being, as Paolo describes it, "filled by a question which no one can answer" [*pieno di una domanda a cui non so rispondere*] and possessed by a cry that "is destined to last beyond any possible end" [*è destinato a durare oltre ogni possibile fine*].[146]

Yet the novel can achieve only a ghostly approximation of the poetic force with which this condition is spectacularized in the movie's final, wordless sequence of images. The camera confronts us with the infinite horizon of the desert that previously had been glimpsed only in flashforward. The first three or four shots frame Paolo in long focus: naked, wandering aimlessly, and stumbling. He exits the frame at one point, leaving the viewer with just the empty vista of the desert. The final shot, however, is a frontal view of Paolo returning to approach the camera, and finally the viewer, in a close-up, screaming. It is Pasolini's last attempt to accomplish through this close-up a sort of incorporation of the spectator, the ultimate cinematic representation of the Rimbaudian dictum "'I' is another" [*je est un autre*].

In Paolo's final scream at the edge of the desert, we can discern both the desperation and the vitality of a weak messianism, which is to say an apocalyptic sense of redemptive possibility that is deprived of any reassuring, orthodox theological or spiritual foundations. Pasolini's merit is to have performed a thoroughgoing, idiosyncratic contamination of ethical and artistic concerns that not only eschews, but also rebukes the kind of postmodern artifice that thrives on spectacularized reification. At the same time, he has refused to retreat into an accommodationist or reactionary mysticism. His spectropoetics ultimately constitute not an homage to the ineffability of the spectral past, but the expression of a heretical concern for the persistence of politics, ideology, life. As he puts it in one of the lyrics that conclude the volume *Trasumanar e Organizzar*, a poem ironically entitled "Propositions of Lightness" [*Propositi di leggerezza*] and written at a time when he defined his verses as "completely practical" [*completamente pratici*] (B 1:899), "Mystification is lightness/Sincerity is heavy and vulgar: it stands with the victorious life."[147]

4

Godard's *Histoire(s)*

Godard's Riddle

Writing in 1965, Pasolini identified Godard as one of the most important exemplars of a "cinema of poetry" and in the process succinctly captured the energy of the Swiss director's youthful, New Wave experimentalism: "The elegy is inconceivable to him. . . . His vitality is without restraint, modesty or scruples. . . . His formalism is . . . a technicality, which is intrinsically poetic: everything that is captured in movement by a camera is beautiful."[1] Godard's virtuosic "technicality" celebrates freedom from history and from the "inconceivable" task of elegy, thus contributing crucially to what Alain Bergala has described as the impulse of *la Nouvelle Vague* toward amnesia, toward a forgetting of historical reality in the wake of World War II.[2]

Whereas Pasolini casts in a positive light the nonelegiac attitude and aesthetic indiscriminacy of the camera that typify Godard's films of the 1950s and 1960s such as *Breathless* (1959), *Contempt* (1963), and *Band of Outsiders* (1964), other critics have taken a dimmer view of his early output. It is interesting on this score to recall Stanley Cavell's disdain for the cool detachment of these movies. For him, the interest of cinema consists in the medium's capacity to sustain a modernist enterprise when painting, literature, and music have grown incapable of such a feat.[3] Cavell alleges that after *Breathless*, Godard's films offer a bleak representation of depersonalized characters, pastless, futureless, and hence presentless, trapped in a world ruled by knowingness and the withdrawal of feeling.[4] Godard's stylistic devices thus do not achieve the alienation effect of Brechtian drama, but its mere simulation.[5] His critique of society strikes Cavell as empty and superficial, whereas the Swiss director's investigations of the formal limits of the medium seem like simulacra of previous modernist gestures. In this sense, Cavell implicitly recognizes in Godard's early corpus the outlines of postmodernism: its stylistic and temporal entropy and its critical ineffectiveness.

At first glance, such an opinion might look counterintuitive, especially to most French critics, who would consider Godard a modernist or even a classicist rather than a postmodernist, conferring on his productions the status of a high art immune from moral and aesthetic contestation.[6] However, a self-conscious skepticism regarding the philosophical metanarratives that might validate the historical and cultural singularity of his work clearly constitutes the basic problematic of his early career. Regarded in this light, Godard and Truffaut's polemic during their years on the staff of the *Cahiers du cinéma* against the rigid parameters of French classical cinema and in favor of a certain Hollywood movie-making (Hitchcock, Ray, Welles) looks like a paradigmatically postmodern gesture. Against the purity of the French tradition, Godard opens the gates to the contamination of the cinema of genres, the cinema of clichés.

Even the theorists who most convincingly press a modernist reading of the Swiss director's early films wind up begging significant questions. Deleuze, for example, finds in Godard's privileging of the interstices between images, conscious pursuit of Pasolinian "free indirect vision," and achievement of a new technical synthesis the epitome of modern cinema.[7] The French philosopher interprets Godard's style as the attempt to extract an image, specifically, a "thinking" image, from its surrounding context of clichés.[8] *Pace* Deleuze, however, it might well be said that from *Breathless* to the beginning of the 1970s, when he joined the Dziga Vertov group, Godard was mesmerized by the clichés of consumer culture. His early films constantly undertake to incorporate low cultural forms—from advertising to fashion and popular songs—resulting in a kaleidoscopic amalgamation of all the debris of the culture of spectacle. Other critics such as Annette Michelson and Colin MacCabe have held that the strength of Godard's approach is to be found in its ability to investigate the nature of representation and the quality of the image in the era of late capitalism.[9] The risk, less often noticed by such critics, is that conveying the results of his investigation in spectacularized form deprives his findings of the authority of an engaged, critical analysis, forcing the director to adopt the rhetoric of a mere bystander to the reification of late-capitalist reality as an image. Even if we find in Godard's early efforts the self-conscious exploration of the creative methods of modernism—the use of montage techniques to approximate the abstract effect of collage, for example—his attempt to overcome the strictures of genre and narrative transforms what were gestures of authentic expression under the modernist regime into a generalized fetishizing of the visible. The reinterpretive shock inherent to the editing process thus is blunted by the dehistoricized, objectified formalism of the image.

Yet the early movies do not by any means tell the complete story of his artistic project. In an astute analysis of *Passion* (1982), Fredric Jameson observes that Godard's film presents itself as a gestalt object, appearing by turns modernist or postmodernist relative to which interpretive "grids" or set of criteria are invoked.[10] Jameson proceeds to draw a categorical distinction between the director's early and later oeuvres, the dividing line falling sometime in the early 1980s. The critic keenly adds that in their fascination with canonical precursors, memory, and high art, Godard's later works ought to be considered more modernist in outlook than his earlier, New Wave productions. Affirming an aesthetic economy based on speed, the montage of "jump-cutting," and the proliferation of the image, the movies of the 1950s and 1960s betray a fundamentally postmodern sensibility, whereas those of the early 1980s onward appear to enact a sort of untimely revival of modernism: "For Godard—surely as postmodern avant la lettre as one might have wished in the heyday of auteurist high modernism—has today in full postmodernism become the ultimate survivor of the modern as such."[11]

To grasp the meaning of Godard's directorial development, then, is important to the attempt to situate modernism and postmodernism in relation to one another. Enlarging on Jameson's distinction, I will argue in what follows that over the past two decades, and particularly in recent years, Godard has abandoned his initial pursuit of a strictly "technical" (to recall Pasolini's term) mastery of the image and has devoted his attention instead to the ethical problems of memory and mourning. Consequently, he has become "the ultimate survivor of the modern" in both the senses of witnessing the passing of modernity and of remaining its faithful representative, as I will demonstrate with reference to his recent, masterly report on the medium, *Histoire(s) du cinéma* (1997).[12] His mourning of the modernist aesthetic in his later films, and especially in *Histoire(s)*, hinges on a leave-taking of the canonical archetypes of the modern, a memorializing of high-cultural aspiration and aesthetic purism that paradoxically signifies a renewed sense of what we might call the epistemological weightiness and poetic expressiveness of the works of the imagination. When taken as a whole, then, the disparate, seemingly irreconcilable moments of his career—from his sweeping reformulation of the rules of the cinematic game in the 1950s and 1960s to his exploration of videos and filmic essay form in the 1980s and 1990s and his elegiac meditation on the state of the medium at the end of the millennium—may be seen to constitute an exemplary genealogy of contemporary culture.

We ought to remember in this regard that the moment when, after a period of writing for *Cahiers du cinéma*, he starts his career as a director neatly coincides with the heyday of the society of the spectacle, as Guy Debord has identified it.[13] Godard's artistic evolution thus provides an ongoing commentary on, and eventual critique of, the growth and diffusion of the culture of spectacle as characterized by the absolute reign of the market and immersion of consciousness in an "eternal present."[14] Of course, the director's New Wave films, from *Breathless* to *Pierrot le Fou* (1965), not only mirror the vertiginously accelerating spiral of information, advertising, and the commodification of everyday life, but also contributed through their reliance on aggressive montage and an exquisite sense of the contemporary to the conscription of cinematic modernism in the service of postmodern hedonism.

The task of commemorating the modernist aesthetic in *Histoire(s)* entails for Godard the attempt at the same time to discover the paradoxical space of a critical postmodernity, one in which the "everything goes" message of his earlier phase might be replaced by a philosophy of the visual. By assuming a self-consciously mournful relationship to the past, Godard redefines his own position as a filmmaker, a role he comes to identify in the film with that of Benjamin's backward-glancing angel of history. Reacting to the cultural amnesia enforced by the mass culture of late capitalism, Godard relinquishes his earlier aesthetic of exhilarated contingency for one of lucid melancholia and in so doing recuperates the inheritance of Baudelaire, Proust (at least those aspects of Proust compatible with a melancholic ethic), Benjamin, and Heidegger, all of whom are explicitly cited, quoted, or methodologically evoked in his study. *Histoire(s) du cinéma* should be considered the final transmogrification of the Swiss director's aesthetic, a work in which the crucial question is how to mourn not only film at the dawn of the digital age, but art per se, because film for Godard represents the final chapter of art history. *Histoire(s) du cinéma* thus functions not only as a tribute to the vanishing discourse of art cinema, but as an adieu to literature, poetry, philosophy, and painting as well. What Godard achieves in this work is the nearest thing to that arrival of modernist art that Lyotard suggests will come after and through the postmodern.[15] The question remaining to be answered is whether such a weakly messianic event as the second coming of modernism has the power to disturb and put into question the politics of complacency enacted by an acritical, populist postmodernism.[16]

Cinema of Memory, Memory of Cinema

Released simultaneously in France with a four-volume book interweaving text and stills, *Histoire(s) du cinéma* ambitiously attempts to reconstruct twentieth-century history and the very development of the movies through a collage of film traces. Over a span of nine years from 1988 to 1997, Godard worked on this singular enterprise, which at once constitutes a sort of archeology of the film medium and an act of recalling the twentieth century.[17] The result is a four-and-a-half-hour work divided into eight segments or "constellations," bearing the evocative titles "Toutes les histoires," "Une histoire seule," "Seul le cinéma," "Fatale beauté," "La monnaie de l'absolu," "Une vague nouvelle," "Le contrôle de l'univers," and "Les signes parmi nous."

The different units vary in length and bear an often inorganic relationship to the central idea of the film. The titles and subtitles reappear like refrains in a litany.[18] The final product consists of a dense montage of fragmentary movie sequences punctuated by the superimposition of flashing text, color schemes, paintings, and readings of literary works. Playing the role of Virgil, Godard guides us on our meandering way through an inferno of images while commenting in voice-over on the past as if from beyond the grave. In the process, he synthesizes in *Histoire(s)* two distinct critical traditions, namely the French view espoused by Baudelaire, Malraux, and Faure that the responsibility of art history is to perpetuate the ongoing mythology of the tradition and the German view held by Benjamin and Adorno that it is to disclose the changed status of the work of art in modern culture.

Godard's first attempt to compose a history of the film medium, *Introduction à une véritable histoire du cinéma* (1977), was occasioned by the death of the director of the *Cinémathèque Française*, Henri Langlois.[19] This first, dutifully expository chronicle of the form may be said to look like what Proust would have dismissed as a voluntary memory. By contrast, the reliance of the later *Histoire(s)* on techniques of fragmentation, elision, and decontextualization bespeaks his awareness that the film image has been collectively interiorized to the point that its renewal requires the development of a cinematic analogue of Proust's "intermittencies of the heart." Godard, in other words, wishes to acknowledge not only the duty of the auteur to remember, but what he calls the "rights" of memory itself, which he honors through the resurrection of a personal selection of images.[20]

Histoire(s) du cinéma recounts the camera's pursuit of what the film alternately calls a "*monde perdu*" and a "*temps perdu*," a lost paradise that turns out to be that of modernism itself (2a:86, 92). Godard's approach renounces the "objective" logic of collective history and memory in favor of the subjective contingency of Proustian intermittencies. His quest for a lost cinematic utopia, however, is motivated by an ambition that exceeds the strictly autobiographical. Godard strives to express the physiognomy of the twentieth century through its remains. In this sense, if his aesthetic inspiration is mainly Proustian, his ideology and methodology betray a close proximity to Benjamin's last works, *The Arcades Project* and the "Theses on the Philosophy of History." Indeed, it is by developing a cinematic language capable of encompassing the Benjaminian antipodes of materialist critique and messianic hope that Godard ultimately arrives at a truly original relation to the past, at a model of remembrance that is neither mechanical nor nostalgic. *Histoire(s) du cinéma* imagines the resurrection of history through the recuperation of an idea of film that has been eradicated by the ascendancy of mass entertainment, a recovery that can only be accomplished in a new attitude of receptivity to modernism.

Melancholic in tone, *Histoire(s)* ought to be understood as a highly subjective response to the increasing obsolescence of a certain idea of the medium—call it "art cinema"—a filmmaking that above all aims at innovation in montage and mise-en-scène. Although computerized cinematography may in some sense represent the future of the form, it is evident that the digital image, as distinct from its celluloid variant, enacts a temporality of the perpetual present tense. Indeed, insofar as the digital image is removed from any ontological grounding or referent, it may even be regarded as a photograph that is atemporal in nature. What the camera produces is no longer necessarily a historical record because digital techniques make possible the creation of the image ex nihilo. Although the flexibility of the new technology opens a space for a certain type of creative experimentation, its divorce from historical reality deprives film of its function as a mode of memory and hence as a framework for critical inquiry. At the same time, the very existence of video and digital imaging changes the status of film, imposing on the medium the condition of an art that has been overcome and of which it is now possible to tell the history.[21] In this light, Godard's search for lost cinema represents not only an act of nostalgia, but the recognition that a certain time and epoch is over. What is curious about this recognition is that his sustained valediction to the modernist ideal of originality and its radical reconception of art's cult value appears to necessitate a phantasmatic resuscitation of the aura of the film image. This dynamic is articulated through the continual reappropriation of modernism's most poignant tropes of remembrance from Baudelaire's *corre-spondances* to Proust's *intermittences,* Benjamin's historicist angel, and Heidegger's *andenkendes Denken.*

Implicit throughout his quest in *Histoire(s)* is the recognition that film has furnished the twentieth century with new resources of memory, chief of which are the reorganizing procedures of montage. Montage defines the mode in which film incorporates the fragmentary into a defamiliarized experience of time, the objective counterpart to the subjective, modernist activity of remembrance. On this score, it is telling that the preposition in *Histoire(s) du cinéma* may be understood to imply both the so-called objective and subjective genitive cases because cinema represents both the object and the very agent of the inquiry. Not coincidentally, the privileged rhetorical figure in *Histoire(s)* is chiasmus (the title of the film's section 1a, for example, is "Histoire des actualités, actualité des histoires"), the constant reoccurrence of which suggests that the determining principle of the work is functional inversion. To this extent, Godard's *Histoire(s) du cinéma* patterns itself after Heidegger's philosophy of Being, however privileging the image over language as the preferred medium of *aletheia,* the operation of unveiling. The proximity is overtly highlighted at different points by the director himself, as again in section 1a, in which the sentence "Chemin qui ne menent nulle part," which translates the title of Heidegger's celebrated work, *Holzwege,* repeatedly flashes on the screen. The reference, which will be followed in section 1b by a quotation of Heidegger's commentary on the disappearance of the gods, sets an epochal tone for Godard's endeavor, which is to inscribe the celluloid image within an ideal genealogy of reason as a way of recognizing the ideal's demise. If, like Heidegger, Godard foresees the end of the grand tradition of metaphysics, the poignancy of his experiment consists in acknowledging by recourse to the increasingly outmoded technology of film the failure of the tradition, the condition of coming after the end of history. Cinema thus becomes in Godard's hands the most effective mode of a thinking that, according to the late Heideggerian ideal of *ein andenkendes Denken*, remembers and responds.

Speculating on the fate of a medium that seems about to disappear before the completion of its perceived end, *Histoire(s)* draws a parallel between the task of cinema and that of the narrator at the end of Proust's *Recherche*. The mélange of movie quotes that comprises Godard's meditation thus adheres to the idea of film as an artistic means of access to the past and to the truth, even as it proleptically mourns the death of such a notion. The originality of this posture, which I take as illustrative of the director's general outlook in his later oeuvre, may be brought into sharper focus by undertaking a somewhat more nuanced consideration of the contrast between his first and second phases.

Colin MacCabe has pointed out that of all the directors of *la Nouvelle Vague*, Godard was the most aware of the new, fundamental importance of the image, an image no longer supposed to be capable of unveiling reality.[22] In movies such as *Breathless* or *Pierrot le Fou*, *Band of Outsiders*, and *Contempt*, Godard's characters are often no more than pawns in a web of culturally prefabricated representations. From Michel Poiccard's mimicry of Bogart in *Breathless* to Arthur and Franz's clownish criminality in *Band of Outsiders*, Godard's male protagonists frequently act out a parody or pastiche of gangster violence, posturing like misfits in films unable to project the formal confidence of a conventional genre piece. In *Band of Outsiders*, Arthur and Franz at once personify the iconoclasm of their namesakes, Arthur Rimbaud and Franz Kafka, and the buffoonery of a picaresque crime drama in which references to high art and low humor coexist in a graceful, lighthearted comic impasse.[23] By contrast, if Pasolini may be said to share Godard's overall lack of faith in the continuing viability of film's prevailing visual conventions, the Friulian director devotes his effort to the endowment of images with a new degree of realism. The early Godard, on the other hand, seems more than happy to indulge a postmodern love of surfaces. Although *Breathless* and *Pierrot le Fou* both display a prodigious cinematic memory, allusions in those movies possess more of the allure of pop quotations than the dignity of poetic evocations. On these grounds, Ishaghpour is right to view Godard as occupying the sort of role within the history of the motion picture that Warhol plays within that of painting.[24] Notwithstanding their expressiveness and irony, the instantaneous, pictorial, mute quotations in *Pierrot le Fou* of diverse cultural artifacts ranging from Rimbaud's *A Season in Hell* to Elie Faure's history of art betray a certain cynicism. Such references present their contents ahistorically, as the expired currency of the past, and privilege the play of technical variations over any reflective engagement with the tradition.[25] In the films belonging to his first phase, Godard retreats from the epistemological weight of the motion picture image in pursuit instead of sheer textuality, maintaining a stance that Jameson declares "resolutely postmodernist."[26] By opting for unremitting superficiality and reflexivity, however, Godard may be said to retreat from representation itself. His relentless anatomizing of the reified image, Jameson points out, does not prevent its triumph over the film's interpretive procedures through the inherent spectacularity of the visible. In other words, the ambient cultural logic and exteriority of the visual signifier that organize Godard's early films guarantee the ultimate aesthetic victory of the image as such: "The spirit triumphs over the letter, no doubt, but it is the dead letter that remains behind."[27]

To understand how modernism and postmodernism are intertwined in Godard's career, we ought to pay special attention to one of his most celebrated works, namely, *Contempt* (1963). *Contempt* stages the equivalent of a primal scene of postmodernity, a scene in which the Hollywood producer played by Jack Palance asks the writer, Paul, to revise Fritz Lang's ethically serious screen adaptation of Homer's *Odyssey* into a more commercially appealing form. According to Lang, the *Odyssey* is the story of the conflict of an individual with his destiny. But the producer wants the accent to fall instead on Odysseus's conflict with Penelope, a topic that gradually will be absorbed into, and mirrored by, the film itself by means of its staging of Camille's final act of betrayal. *Contempt*, as Harun Farocki rightly points out, ultimately celebrates the convergence of the diegetic and extradiegetic insofar as the writer-protagonist's life is eventually bound up in his own adaptation of the Homeric epic.[28] As he is conversing with Camille (Brigitte Bardot), Lang in one scene quotes Brecht: "I create jewels for the poor" [*Je fais des bijoux pour le pauvres*]. The beauty of the declaration cannot mask, however, the cultural naiveté of the statement, underscored in the film by the overbearing commercial credo of the American producer. In this sense, the film starts by paying homage to Brecht's alienating effects, openly staging the conflict of competing interpretations, but ends without developing a metacritical, Brechtian point of view. It is noteworthy on this score that at one point in section 1b of *Histoire(s)*, the epithet "poor Bertolt Brecht" [*le pauvre Bertolt Brecht*] flashes on the screen, implying the director's anger over the betrayal of the German dramatist's legacy. In *Histoire(s)*, Godard also cites with mournful bitterness the Brechtian dictum voiced jokingly by Lang in *Contempt*, the contrast in mood driving home an understood indictment of the commercial apparatus of movie production and distribution. Godard's early productions instead generally seem content to affirm the most basic theorem of postmodernity, that reality is always already an image. The modernist quest of the film within the film, which supposedly was to have been titled "In Search of Homer," ends in a disenchanted, postmodern vacillation, and *Contempt* thereby offers an allegory for the impossibility of modernist purity and originality.[29]

Gradually, however, Godard's initial postmodern flirtation with the stylistic motifs of modernism evolves into a pained historical awareness of the deterioration and extinction of modernism, cinema, and art itself. This awareness culminates, I believe, with the Swiss director's declaration in *Histoire(s)* that the New Wave represented an end to the auteur tradition of motion pictures, rather than a new beginning.[30] Since the 1980s, he may be said to have found a new motivating theme in the phenomenon of cultural amnesia, even if, in his first attempts in this direction (*First Name Carmen* [1983], *Hail Mary* [1985], *King Lear* [1987]), his tone seems somewhat unclear. With *Histoire(s) du cinéma*, Godard's project of commemoration becomes more deliberate and finds its proper object in the film medium itself.[31] His accomplishment in *Histoire(s)* is to transform the theoretical cliché of the end of culture into poetic imagery, ultimately performing a task the director had set for himself, as Deleuze observes, since the days of *la Nouvelle Vague*. Of course, his representation of the demise of cinema as the final chapter of western art history may be viewed as an extension of what has been a philosophical topos ever since Hegel's announcement of the end of art.[32]

What is the meaning of such an event, and what is the aesthetic and philosophical validity of Godard's response remain, however, separate questions for analysis. From one perspective, the death of cinema might be interpreted as the latest instance of the syndrome Benjamin famously identifies as the decline of the aura of the modern artwork. Ironically, in his controversial essay, "The Work of Art in the Age of Mechanical Reproduction," Benjamin had identified the film medium as the principal historical threat to an auratic conception of art, in hindsight rendering an ingenuous assessment. Standing Benjamin's judgment on its head, Godard's avowal of the disappearance of the art film hints that with the ascendancy of digital technology, the magical value once assigned to the celluloid image has been superseded by its "exposition value." *Histoire(s) du cinéma* thus presents the search for a cinematographic trace or register of history as the last, most lucid means of confronting modernity's terminus. As in Benjamin's work, melancholia represents the origin of historical understanding. As in Benjamin's work, the return to the past becomes the occasion not of its simple citation, but of its allegorical recoding.[33] Unsympathetic critics have complained of the irrelevance of Godard's meditation on the waning seriousness of culture, sneering that life and the movies continue well after the New Wave is over.[34] Such commentators fail to recognize the allegorical dimension of the Swiss director's work and its messianic task of redeeming the present.

Not only does he want to update Benjamin's famous postulation of technology's destructive effect on aura, but also, and perhaps more importantly, he wishes to recuperate for film a space of sublimity and urgency, a desire partly conveyed by his stress on the medium's position as the "last chapter" of its narrative. Against the commercialism and commodifying logic of the mass-market movie industry, Godard protests by taking up the abandoned, once-transcendent project of turning cinema into an instrument of thought, as Sollers would have it.[35] While assuming the mournful air of canonical modernism, *Histoire(s) du cinéma* in this sense demonstrates full cognizance that the golden age of modernism and of cinematic masterpieces is over, thus staking out a domain beyond the possibility of a successful mourning.[36] Likened to a cubist artifact on account of its composite nature, *Histoire(s)* rehearses a litany of allusions and images in search of some sort of Heideggerian meaningful point in which the values of past and tradition might transcend the technological quest of metaphysics. The director adopts a religious tone, borrowing his motto from Saint Paul and interspersing it throughout the film: "The image will come at the time of resurrection."[37]

The critic who has most clearly understood and delineated the caesura between the first and second Godard is Serge Daney. Not coincidentally, a conversation between the director and the critic regarding the vicissitudes of the medium is incorporated into section 2a (Daney, we should note, is the only critic granted such a privilege in *Histoire(s)*). Daney is very much aware that Godard begins his career as a modern *progressiste*, only to experience the transformation into a melancholic *cinéphile*—a devotee, however, who is not content with a vacuous moroseness, but focused on accomplishing a specific act of mourning: "The morose pleasure of mourning (of 'nothing is anymore like before') is behind. Today mourning weighs. It is in process of being accomplished. In a sense, everyone is charged with the task of knowing of what his own act of mourning consists of. Godard is the only one to say why what has been attempted by cinema (and missed) is of an inexpressible importance."[38] Daney's acute recognition of the "heaviness" of Godard's manner of mourning is in contrast with the postmodern insistence on the typical aesthetical and ethical value of "lightness" and aptly characterizes the tone of Godard's project of a critical postmodernity.

What changes between the first and second phases of Godard's career is not so much his aesthetic of repetition and saturation of cultural signs, but the emergence of his melancholic awareness of the end of history as a tragic event. This awareness prompts a search for meaning that leads from the exuberance of the New Wave to the act of mourning of *Histoire(s) du cinéma*. It is telling in this respect that the director's favored method of editing shifts over time from a practice of disruptive, defamiliarizing jump cuts to the haunted multilayering of superimposition, a device that in *Histoire(s)* allows him to present his meditation on the past as a continuous palimpsest of film images.

Godard's latest opus defines a critical postmodernity through a search for the philosophical dimension of mourning, a mourning that does not consist of a "successful" work of montage, which would enable the overcoming or forgetting of loss. Godard has recently declared that "montage" distinguishes the very nature of cinema and, as a practice, implies a potential that remains as yet unrealized within the technical boundaries set by Griffith and Eisenstein.[39] Indeed, for Godard, who in this respect stands quite at the opposite extreme from Pasolini, montage amounts to nothing less than a magical resuscitation of the dead: "Above all, the object during editing is alive, whereas during shooting it is dead. It is necessary to resuscitate it. It is witchcraft."[40] Gradually, montage becomes for the Swiss director an open-ended philosophical metaphor, aimed at preparing in truly Lacanian terms an impossible encounter with the Real. Godard transfers montage, an operation fetishized at the beginning of the New Wave as the expressionistic juxtaposition of newsreel, advertising, cultural quotation, and fictional image, from the domain of the aesthetic to that of the ethical and historical. Godard in *Histoire(s)* breaks down the images into history, inspired by Benjamin's dictum in his "Theses" that history is made of images not stories. At stake is a nonmetaphysical conception of history, a conception we will now turn to investigate, paying particular attention to Godard's mode of quotation.

Histories Beyond Nostalgia

It might look strange to define Godard's newly found vocation as that of an archivist. After all, according to Alain Bergala, *la Nouvelle Vague* as a movement was predicated on amnesia, on forgetfulness of the war.[41] If his earlier films are bathed in the aura of the contingent and the contemporary, Godard's later oeuvre actively resists the imperatives of the present tense. His formal strategy of resistance to the commodification of the image, to the superficial comfort of postmodern aesthetics, has become in recent years delicately historicized. By the same token, the kind of history that Godard's work articulates cannot be said to represent the "regained" metaphysical rationality of events, but a much more complex and "projective" display of losses. Even the very use of the plural in the title *Histoire(s)*, highlighted by parentheses, signals his unwillingness to propound a credible, objective, univocal account of the birth and death of cinema, preferring instead the open-ended narrative space of multiple recollections. The plural indicates that the nature of cinematic memory and history is exquisitely intersubjective. At the beginning of section 1b, "Toutes les Histoire(s)," the word "histoire" flashes on the screen and is deconstructed by Godard into its component phonemes: "his-toi-res." To emphasize the "*toi*" (you) bound up in history means to inaugurate an historical investigation of cinema from an intersubjective point of view; it means, at the same time, the willingness to address history directly, nonmetaphysically.

In the days of the New Wave, Godard seemed more interested in how to tell a story than in the story itself. The Godard of *Histoire(s)*, on the other hand, seems to abandon his initial formalist preoccupations in order to pursue an investigation into the ontology of the projected, moving image. Essentially, his approach is to answer the notorious Bazinian question, "What is Cinema?", by evoking a plurality of historical constellations. To appreciate such an approach, it must be recognized that the director's notion of history abandons the claim of nineteenth-century historiography to metaphysical foundations. Not only is his history of the medium not a version of genetic historicism, it is not even an archeological operation à la Foucault, because for Godard the opportunity to elucidate morally the meaning of the present is more important than any potential, aleatory reconstruction of the past. Unlike Foucault, Godard is uninterested in unmasking the "hidden" historical, cultural, and legal conditions of the production of certain works; he aims rather to establish a more allusive and elusive context informed by our intersubjective memory of common events and experiences.[42] The director neatly points up cinema's function as a sort of material ground or catalyst of collective memory, a concept too often used in a vaguely metaphorical way.

Subjective and collective memory in *Histoire(s)* thus reinforce and enlarge one another in subtle ways. Godard's own personal history as a filmmaker is mirrored in the larger biography of the film medium, an effect that heightens the pathos of the simultaneous arrival of the director and of cinema itself in the twilight of old age. Ultimately, this twilight condition, as I will detail later, is represented in *Histoire(s)* as a form of cultural and philosophical convalescence, a way of taking leave of modernity. Above all, such a melancholy posture must be understood as both an implicit rebuke to the noncommittal glibness of mass culture and an admission of the jeopardized condition of ethical and historical interpretation. This fact becomes clearer if we give serious consideration to the meaning Godard ascribes to the concept of the "end" of film. Not only in *Histoire(s)* but also in many recent interviews, Godard has repeatedly located the symbolic death of cinema in the historical failure to film at length the concentration camps of World War II.[43] That moment in fact represents for him the egregious triumph of the spectacular nature of cinema over its potential to document reality, to provide what the Swiss director has called a "museum of reality."[44]

One way for him to resist the lure of the spectacular, which to an extent may be aligned with the "immanent," detached aestheticism of his earlier corpus, is to devise a critical strategy of quotation. In this sense, the fact that the composition of his later films consists almost exclusively of

quotations should be viewed not as the survival of his devotion to the superficiality of a postmodern eclecticism, but as the attempt to create a correspondence between the collective nature of the images and the memory
induced by films. The "citations" in late Godard function not as souvenirs
but as reminiscences, as subliminal visual experiences recuperated from
the patrimony of collective memory. In the economy of *Histoire(s)*, the impact of the cited image is almost traumatic, closer in proximity to the intermittencies of the heart, according to a Proustian perspective, than to involuntary memories. Unlike the use of quotation in his early films, where
classical, mythical, or high-cultural references were flattened and assimilated to a monotonous play of surfaces, Godard's later productions aim at
endowing every quotation with the uniquely haunting presence of a
tableau vivant of words and images. Already in *Passion* (1982), he allegorizes at length the problem of quotation through the story of a director
named Jerzy, who films scenes of actors posing in stances and costumes
that evoke the subjects of the most famous *chef d'oeuvres* of European
painting. Far from perpetuating a complacent postmodern mechanism of
replication, this cinematic reinvestment of the fundamental referent of
representational painting, the human body, implies a renovation of the
search for the sublime. The staging of great paintings in the film functions
not as an exercise in the production of simulacra, but to the contrary as a
regretful recognition of art's loss of aura, a recognition enabled by an
emerging temporality of the "resuscitation" of the image that Sollers labels
the "*plus que present*."[45]

The uncanny nature of filmic quotation does not entail an abandonment of critical responsibility on the part of the author. Unlike Benjamin's
dream of a book made only of quotations, Godard's dream is to claim his
right to interpret, fashion, and manipulate his references. Interestingly, he
recently has made a public plea for the establishment of the legal right of
quotation. Fearing legal action in 1997 for copyright infringement, Godard
maintains in an interview with Bergala that unlike a mere "excerpt," which
does no more than redeploy existing intellectual property and so ought to
be charged fees or duties, what he means by quotation necessarily involves
a creative contribution, such that the artist must be seen not only as "copy-
ing," but also as translating and interpreting the original.[46]

After having examined the technique of quotation within the intellectual framework of *Histoire(s) du cinéma*, we are in a position to dismiss
the notion that the horizon of the film is nostalgic in a regressive sense. It

is the communal significance of our movie-going experiences that allows
Godard to proclaim the recuperative and revisionary value of his project
while at the same time denying any cheapening nostalgia: "*Histoire(s) du
cinéma* are not nostalgic. They allow us to release nostalgia; one starts with
nostalgia and very quickly one disclaims it. In History there is no nostalgia.
Michelet has no nostalgia."[47] Indeed, the visual idiolect of *Histoire(s)* represents a complicated and self-aware expansion of Pasolini's cinema of poetry, a language game in which the poetic gesture of "free indirect vision"
acquires momentous importance by bringing to light the incommensurable diffuseness of our intersubjective, cinematic memories. Even Proust's
strong influence on *Histoire(s) du cinéma* cannot reverse or ameliorate what
Godard considers the natural inclination of film, which in contrast to literature progresses from regained time to lost time.[48]

The Swiss director's insistence on his film's lack of nostalgia defies the
recent ascendancy in postmodern culture of the genre of the nostalgia film,
a development pointed out by both Jameson and John Orr. These critics
equate the genre with a stylistically punctilious reconstruction of the past
that is consumed without any gain in historical awareness.[49] Jameson iso-
lates the defining characteristic of "nostalgia cinema" in the presentation of
the past as a commodity, a voguish token of another period that signifies
by means of a deliberate adoption of retro fashion, decor, and music. The
content of this type of movie demands a merely historicist, rather than a
historical attention to the image, a fascination with appearances that stands
at odds to the modernist interiority of longing typified by the conditions
of exile or alienation.[50]

Jameson considers some of Godard's works from the 1980s and early
1990s as studies in a new mode of aestheticism, especially in their use of
classical music. *Hail Mary* (1985) is for the American critic the paradigmatic
example of a simulacrum of religion and thus of a "nostalgia product," a
vehicle for the transformation of the religion of art into the art of religion.[51]
I would argue, however, that *Histoire(s)* ought to be considered on this
front as a qualitative departure, as a genuine breakthrough. Even if in *Passion* and more emphatically in *Scénario du film Passion* (1982), Godard had
moved toward a more self-consciously historical reflection on the aesthetics of the pictorial, it is only with *Histoire(s)* that his investigation of the
semiotics of the image contemplates a space of allegorical meaning beyond
the commodity status of the visual. In its open acknowledgment of history
and tradition, this recent work offers a possible alternative to the nostalgic

postmodern regime of sense. This alternative defines the space of a critical postmodernity that recuperates and reworks the ethical message of an outmoded modernism. It is precisely by redefining the film medium in general and the process of montage in particular as a mode of mourning that he avoids the lure of "lifestyle" nostalgia. This cinematic mode of mourning eschews the Freudian alternative between success and melancholia in pursuit instead of the traumatic–auratic dimension of remembrance.

From Bazin to Barthes, the photographic nature of motion pictures has always been understood as mournful; Bazin, in his influential essay, "The Ontology of the Photographic Image," speaks of the art of embalming the dead, of a "mummy complex" that aims to preserve the pictorial subject from a spiritual death, a function partially performed by painting and sculpture but fully perfected by photography and film.[52] Besides cinema's mournful aspect, however, Bazin's argument seeks to reaffirm the "realism" of the medium, the authority with which it underwrites epiphanies of presence: "Today . . . it is no longer a question of survival after death, but of a larger concept, the creation of an ideal world in the likeness of the real, with its own temporal destiny."[53] Godard, on the other hand, appears to come to the melancholy conclusion in *Histoire(s)* that after the death of cinema, the spectator is left only with epiphanies of absence.[54]

In the course of completing his *Histoire(s)*, Godard describes cinema in 1996 as an act of mourning that in a sense endeavors to reclaim life.[55] For the Swiss director, as he repeats throughout the film as well as in recent interviews, the lens steals from existence its very image. That is the reason why, in his opinion, film was born in black and white, the colors of mourning. For Godard, the monochromaticism of black-and-white film stock expresses the truth of the camera's "*enterprises funèbres*," a reality that the invention of color printing has only managed to make more evident through a fake, exaggeratedly vivid palette of hues that tries to mask the profundity of sorrow: "I would say in my way that starting from the moment at which the image was stolen from life, at which point representation became a theft, it was necessary to 'bear mourning.'"[56]

According to the director's quasireligious phenomenology of cinema, the goal of editing is to achieve the resuscitation of the object in accordance with a rhythm that ordains first death, then mourning, and finally representation.[57] It is doubtful, however, that, as he sometimes appears to suggest, the medium can clear a serene psychic space through a cathartic exorcism of pain, a space regulated by a successful mourning. Several crit-

ics have noted that the tone of *Histoire(s) du cinéma* is apocalyptic or catastrophic and that the director proposes an experiment that resembles the
interminable ordeal of the eponymous character depicted in Poe's short
story, "Mr. Valdemar"—that is, hypnotizing film at the moment of its
death.[58] Nor can it be said that the spectral invocations of past films
amount to a mise-en-scène of an orderly ritual of mourning; indeed, the
most striking effect of the quotations appears to be their capacity to elicit
an encounter with the real. *Histoire(s) du cinéma* is punctuated by the well-
known sequence from *Vertigo* (1958) in which Scottie saves Madeleine from
drowning near the Golden Gate Bridge (1b:267). The citation aptly allegorizes not only the possibility of resurrection for the image, but also the
traumatic context of that resurrection. Notwithstanding her very Proustian
name, Madeleine in Hitchcock's film epitomizes the return of the real, not
an elegiac memory.

In *Histoire(s)*, the elegiac mode is finally offset by the traumatic, resulting in a meditation on the nature and possibilities of cinema, rather
than a melancholic celebration of its former glories. Godard often relies on
the imperfect tense to tell and conclude his stories; in section 3b his recapitulation of the fortunes of the members of *la Nouvelle Vague* concludes
with the declaration "they were my friends" [*c'était mes amis*] (3b:165); in
section 4b, he relates a story by Ramuz in which a peddler who arrives at a
village and prophesies a storm is banished when the sun comes back. Godard gives this little parable an additional twist by enunciating his own
moral: "the peddler was cinema" [*ce colporteur c'était le cinema*] (4b:239).
The most decisive use of the imperfect tense occurs at the very end of the
film, when the director rehearses a Borges tale in which a man who crosses
paradise and is given a flower in a dream finds the flower on awakening;
the final line of *Histoire(s)* is "I was this man" [*j'étais cet homme*] (4b:311).

If the imperfect represents the melancholic temporality of regret, its
use in *Histoire(s)* coexists with what Sollers has rightly defined as the "*plus
que present*" of the quotations, their almost auratic emanation of historical
sublimity. One of the film's first intertitles or images of text is also one of
its most significant. At the beginning of *Histoire(s)*, in section 1b, the sentence "Father, don't you see I am burning?" [*Père, ne vois tu pas que je
brûle?*] (1b:14) inaugurates the chapter "Toutes les histoires." The sentence
famously belongs to a dream interpreted by Freud as an exemplification of
the relationship between the wish-fulfillment of a dream and the traumatic
reality of death. A father whose son has just died dreams of the child re-

proachfully posing the cited question. The dreamer awakens to discover the body of his son in the next room, where it is on display for the funeral wake, actually burning as a result of the fall of a lighted candle.[59] For Freud, the dream satisfies the father's wish that his son still be alive while paradoxically protecting his own sleep. Looking back on this explanation, Lacan observes in his *Seminar XI* that the dream hardly supports the Freudian theory of wish-fulfillment, because what is at work here is rather an encounter with the Real, which itself is inscribed in the traumatic temporality of repetition.[60]

How shall we interpret the reinscription of the sentence within Godard's visual argument? I think it is fair to say that in *Histoire(s)* the dream related by Freud propounds an allegory of how cinema itself operates, according to which film addresses its viewers in a tone of reproach. Throughout Godard's study, we find a metaphoric connection between consumption of the moving image and combustion. In section 1b, for example, the aim of the medium is described as an igniting of the imaginary in order to heat up "the real" [*le réel*] (1b:111). The trope of burning at work in the film's quotation of the Freudian case history moreover appears to suggest the possibility that, like the child in the reported dream, the camera might enable from beyond the grave a decisive if traumatic encounter with the Real, the domain beyond the symbolic and the imaginary that belongs to the territory of the sublime. Although the moving image has been said in a general sense to exert a "dreamlike" influence over viewers, the Swiss director proposes more precisely that rather than offering the reassurance of unabashed wish-fulfillment, cinema may serve to reorganize radically our relationship to loss and death by recovering, through the practice of quotation, the fundamental unpresentability of the past that comes to light under the aegis of the Real. His method of mourning the modernist movie tradition precludes any possibility of a successful overcoming of loss, yet at the same time resists a wholehearted embrace of the paradigmatic Freudian alternative of melancholia, arriving instead at an outlook we might call that of "sublime mourning." It is precisely this outlook he apparently is contemplating in section 2b, when he invokes Madame de Staël's romantic characterization of a remorse for the past that leads to an ephocal, revolutionary reconception of the present: "For isn't it true that it's necessary to bear mourning but in forgetting it; and Mme de Staël has told us how she wrote to Napoleon, Glory, Your Highness, is mourning blazing with happiness" (2b:191–95).[61] In contradistinction to both the relentless, mechanical, bit-by-bit working-through of mourning and the pathologically interminable suffering of melancholia, Godard proposes a new attitude of chastened ethical freedom in response to the apocalyptic collapse of the metaphysical foundations of history—an attitude, in short, of sublime mourning.

This sense of the urgency and paradoxical burden of the act of mourning is enforced in *Histoire(s)* by his confrontation, as in a contemporary version of the *Divine Comedy*, with tutelary "poets" whose problematic status within the modernist genealogy further complicates the task of mourning such a legacy. Among the multitudinous references recognizable in the film, the quotations, revisions, and reappropriations of four intellectual figures in particular—namely Baudelaire, Proust, Benjamin, and Heidegger—form a constellation that in my opinion is crucial to a genuine understanding of Godard's project. In what follows, I will seek to explicate the complex relation that the director assumes to each one of these figures in his compelling visual history of the end of modernity.

Godard as Monsieur G.

Histoire(s) du cinéma is punctuated by references to Baudelaire. In section 1b, for example, the intertitle "my heart laid bare" [*mon coeur mis a nu*] flashes on the screen numerous times, and in section 2a, the film situates its single longest quotation, which is of Baudelaire's "Le voyage." The poem is cited almost in its entirety in *Histoire(s)* (2a:53–79), and the deliberate, emblematic quality of the evocation seems to suggest that for Godard the duty of carrying on the quest Baudelaire originally assigns to language has fallen in the present day to film. Read onscreen by Julie Delpy, the excerpt from "Le voyage" is also reprinted in the book that accompanied the film's video release. Godard quotes the text without punctuation and without always respecting Baudelaire's stanzaic divisions, thus achieving a creative reinterpretation or reorganization of the literary model through the application of the art of montage, a method that results in an entirely original scheme of cinematic versification.[62] Godard moreover interrupts Delpy's recitation of the poem with a critical intervention revolving around the "projective" nature of the celluloid medium, before cutting back to the voice-over of the first stanza of the poem's sixth section. As the sequence unfolds, the director grows increasingly free with his editorial mediation, splicing together fragments from different stanzas (for instance, cutting from the middle of the second stanza of the seventh section to the beginning of the first stanza of the eighth). However, he ends the reading of "Le voyage" on the penultimate stanza, thus suppressing the unexpected, consolatory defiance of the poem's famous final lines: "We can plunge to Hell or Heaven—any abyss will do!—/ Deep in the Unknown to find the new" [Plonger au fond du gouffre, Enfer ou Ciel, qu'importe?/Au fond de l'Inconnu pour trouver du nouveau].[63] These two lines also constitute the climactic verses of the last section of *Les Fleurs du Mal,* entitled "La Mort," and their positioning within the argument or structure of the volume implies a possible equivalence between "the Unknown" [*l'Inconnu*] and "Death" [*la Mort*]. The omitted couplet might be said to represent the poetic unconscious of *Histoire(s)* insofar as the death of film is an event that presages the discovery and renewal of a messianic afterlife.

Through his aggressive editing of the poem, the filmmaker asserts the lyric value of the moving image, as if to usurp the office of the poet in an act of postmodern hubris that only reinforces the untimely pathos of his work. Implicit to this endeavor is the assumption that a truthful investigation of the medium necessarily involves the final assessment of modernism itself.[64] Godard in other words proposes himself in *Histoire(s)* as a figure who could be labeled "the director of postmodern life" and so inscribes himself within a culturally crucial Baudelairean genealogy. The filmmaker takes up his position at the end of this genealogy via his cinematic exploration of the paradox and iconoclastic value of what Baudelaire in "The Painter of Modern Life" calls the "memory of the present."[65] The essay famously presents such a memory as the proper subjective register of the eternal in the modern work of art. For Godard, the celluloid image in turn supplies the perfect ontological ground of this form of remembrance.

How, then, are we to understand his resuscitation of modernism, given the argument of his retrospective survey of the medium? My feeling is that it is not necessary to imagine a hard caesura between Godard's commitments to modernism and an ethically awakened postmodernism because, as Antoine Compagnon has observed, a kind of continuity might be established between the perpetual refusal to compromise of first-generation modernism and an alertly critical postmodernity. In fact, running counter to the avant-garde ideology of the new, both perspectives stress the necessity of reworking tradition, renouncing the logic of overcoming, and maintaining an awareness of the end of history.[66]

According to Compagnon, the kind of modernism that followed in

Baudelaire's footsteps and was epitomized at the beginning of the twentieth century by the various subcultures of the avant-garde corrupted the
ambivalent, paradoxical, and complicated notion of modernity originally
proposed by the French poet, replacing it with a superstitious worship of
the future and of progress. In this ironic light, postmodernity, by criticiz-
ing modernism's sometimes blind idealization of the new, suggests an opportunity to return to Baudelaire and to arrive belatedly at an understanding of the core problematic from whence derives his sense of existential and
cultural agon. Godard's growth over the course of his own history as a filmmaker appears to confirm Compagnon's intuition of a potential correspondence between high modernity and critical postmodernity.

Section 2b of *Histoire(s)* bears the archetypally Baudelairean title of
"Beauté fatale," which, on first thought, might be taken as a simple homage to the seductive Otherness with which the feminine confronts the male
directorial gaze, but which, on further consideration, suggests an allegorical allusion to the sublime enchantment of the very medium itself. The
French adjective connotes not only the lethal, but also the predetermined
and even the moribund, hinting that the challenge of contemporary filmmaking is to resist the diminution of visual expression to a merely ornamental, commodified value under the aegis of a populist postmodernism.
Godard seeks to restore the sublime to the postmodern, thus performing
an experiment that differs radically from the regressive attempt to retrieve
modernism for modernism's sake. The Swiss director does not pay tribute
to Baudelaire's language by adopting a retro pose, but by placing a philosophical wager.[67]

At an allegorical or symbolic level, he might be said to envision himself in the place of Monsieur G., the pseudonym Baudelaire gives in "The
Painter of Modern Life" (1859–60) to Constantin Guys, who supplies the
model par excellence of the modern artist.[68] Far from being a reverential,
classically minded painter, Guys was a draftsman and journalist for the *Illustrated London News*, a worldly, histrionic artist who, like Godard, strug-
gled with a perpetual sense of his own transience. Baudelaire describes
Guys's paintings as a "luminous explosion in space," a riot of visual details
all clamoring for justice.[69] Like the earlier Monsieur G., Godard renounces
any hope of achieving harmony, hierarchy, or otherwise systematic organization of the visual elements he splices together, in the process demonstrating the two traits that the poet considered indispensable to Guys's
practice: a messianic effort of memory that calls the past back to life, as if

commanding Lazarus to arise, and an intoxicating frenzy of synthesis.[70] The filmmaker, in other words, wishes to establish a dialogue between modernity and eternity à la Baudelaire, even as he avows the painful conviction that the movies represent the end of art. Whereas Baudelaire was intent on arguing that the variable and the transient and not merely the eternal comprised the necessary grounds of beauty, Godard, inverting the logic of the poet's argument, tries to recuperate the eternal through the now-familiar sign of the fugitive.

Another concept that might well define the director's creative effort in *Histoire(s)* is the Baudelairean notion of convalescence. "Imagine an artist," writes Baudelaire, "who was always, spiritually, in the condition of that convalescence, and you will have the key to the nature of Monsieur G. Now convalescence is like a return to childhood. The convalescent, like the child, is possessed in the highest degree of the faculty of keenly interesting himself in things, be they apparently of the most trivial [nature]."[71] According to the poet, such keenness of interest results from a heightened sense of mortality; only on returning from the shadow of the valley of death does the convalescent exhibit the "fervent desire" to remember all the essences of life: "As he as been on the brink of total oblivion, he remembers, and fervently desires to remember everything."[72] For the poet, then, the condition of convalescence does not imply a successful mourning, but a convulsive return to life accompanied by "sublime thoughts" and "violent nervous shock."[73] The Baudelairean concept of convalescence with its emphasis on the epistemological upheaval wrought by the reencounter with the past prefigures the sublime mourning achieved in *Histoire(s)*. Godard's treatise crystallizes in a particularly vivid form the conjunction of childhood, convalescence, absolute memory, and the quest for the sublime. One of Godard's recurring axioms in *Histoire(s)* is that cinema represents the childhood of art, a statement that takes on more meaning once he adds that television stands for a banal and uninteresting adulthood. Recuperation of the bits and pieces of the medium's past is a way for Godard to attain a state of artistic convalescence, a condition in which, as in childhood, it is still possible to look at all things as novelties.

Of course, there is something paradoxical about Baudelaire's harmonizing of the notions of convalescence, childhood, memory, and sublimity. This is even more so in the case of Godard. The particular pathos of his enterprise derives from the persuasion that film offers the last chance of access to the heroic potentialities of artistic expression insofar as the moving image, as we already have shown, represents to his mind the last chapter of the history of art (4A:92). In this sense, to visualize a history of the medium is not the same as to accomplish a successful mourning. Such an exercise in retrospection rather establishes an example of that "synthetic," "barbarous" mnemonic art that for Baudelaire was the cornerstone of Guys's creative originality.[74]

Espousing a poetics of eclectic, intermediating verbal and visual quotations, Godard manages to effect a sort of Baudelairean synesthesia, whereby the juxtaposition of image and sound produces a kind of philosophical dissonance, rather than a logical coherence. In this light, the extensive and singular use of citation in *Histoire(s)* might be looked at as an updating of Baudelaire's poetic of *correspondances*, an enigmatic, mysterious overlapping and condensation of different materials and epochs. Particularly telling in this respect is the montage at the end of section 3a of a black-and-white photograph of Pasolini's face and a detail from Piero della Francesca's Renaissance painting "The Legend of the True Cross." The two images are linked by the chiastic subtitle "a thinking that forms/a form that thinks" [*une pensée qui forme/une forme qui pense*] (3a:97). The artistic genealogy thus educed from the Renaissance to Pasolini is, if not analytically justified, at least poetically enforced. The sequence promotes an idea of the cultural history of Italy based on the metaphor of resurrection and a vision of Pasolini as the Christlike sacrificial redeemer of modernity. The chiasmus stresses the autonomous, paradoxically involuntary nature of that type of history expressed through montage, the operation that in Godard's latest work increasingly occupies the same position that language holds in Heidegger's philosophy of Being, becoming a sort of house of resonance.

Yet the notion of "*correspondance*" might also be said ironically to designate certain aporetical effects of Godard's mode of montage. Significant in this sense is the linking of George Stevens's 1951 film *A Place in the Sun* (starring Elizabeth Taylor and Montgomery Clift) with color footage shot by Stevens himself of Ravensbrueck's concentration camp (section 1a). Godard's montage interrogates the relationship between Hollywood and the Holocaust, fiction and the newsreel. The image selected from *A Place in the Sun*, an adaptation of Theodore Dreiser's novel *An American Tragedy*, is of a radiant Elizabeth Taylor. The iconic proximity of happiness and murder creates in this case a sublime, irresolvable self-contradiction that through visualization brings to light the impossibility of mediation between the two images. As Alan Wright suggests, the very process of editing in *Histoire(s)*, as it aspires to the impossible and sublime, unveils the traumatic kernel of the Real. According to an aesthetic and ethical economy formulated respectively by Lacan and Žižek, we ought to consider the Real as the impossible and the sublime as the failure of representation to reach the Thing.[75] In this case, then, Godard deconstructs the technique of montage by means of "*correspondance*," stripping the idea of any residual consoling or compensatory function.

At a time when the commodity culture of postmodernity has enforced a reencounter with the decorative or picturesquely beautiful through the pervasiveness of spectacularized visual culture, Godard's career represents an attempt to resist the twilight of the sublime. If his effort is one of the most significant, this is because it is applied to cinema. The director tackles the most important issue of postmodernity, the colonization of reality and culture by popular spectacle. Godard's films read increasingly like philosophical and critical essays because of his determination to fight against the complacency of our contemporary visual culture and its definition of the postmodern as the epoch of unrelenting spectacle. His appropriation of Baudelaire's poetics marks his effort to delimit a new postmodern critical space in which film might work as a form of thought.

Godard Between Proust and Benjamin

If memory is the broad, manifest theme of *Histoire(s)*, Godard seems in particular to want to show how the cinema alters our very conception of memory, transforming it from the faculty of willed recall into a ghostly element of involuntary reminiscences. On this score, he demonstrates to what extent the film medium possesses a Proustian aspect, insofar as movies return to haunt us according to the logic of the involuntary. Indeed, he argues cogently that our memory of film consists of the emotional shape of certain images, not their phenomenological content. Godard's meditation on the temporality of cinema is poignantly articulated in the film *Nouvelle vague* in the mouth of the character Lennox: "It is not enough to have remembrances, it is necessary to forget them when they are numerous, and it is necessary to have the patience to await their return."[76] In *Histoire(s)*, Godard is less interested in recuperating the mannerist phenomenology of Proustian involuntary memory than in exploring its more problematic allegorical operation as a form of shock, the horizon in which the involuntary coincides with the highly traumatic sphere of the intermittencies of the heart. Indeed, the experience of *la mémoire involontaire* that is the novel's philosophical nucleus functions as a superimposition or "beating" of two images, a process that in its psychological, temporal, and visual aspects ultimately achieves the effect of cinematic montage.[77]

As we shall see, what makes Godard's *Histoire(s) du cinéma* such a suggestive adaptation of the *Recherche* is in large part the film's successful assimilation and refinement of a Benjaminian view of Proust's novel.[78] That Benjamin in his major essay on Proust focuses on the central role of the image within the *Recherche* is no accident. He observes that Proust treats the relation of resemblance between two things according to the code of the dream world, through the intervention of a third element: "the image."[79] Rather than providing a smooth synthetic integrity, the image jars the reader of Proust through its "beatings of wings" and "small shocks."[80] "The beating of wings" aptly typifies the Proustian mise-en-scène of superimposition, a poetic that corresponds as well to the crucial notion of *les intermittences du coeur*.[81] For Benjamin the novel's central concept of involuntary memory elaborates the trope of life as a cinematic spectacle, which, as Benjamin points out, is comparable in effect to the rapid screening of an emotionally charged or significant image. In a handwritten text found among the critic's paperwork after his death and entitled, "Of a Brief Speech on Proust on the Occasion of My Fortieth Birthday," he explicitly compares *la mémoire involontaire* to a movie trailer or preview of our death:

Concerning involuntary memory . . . one might say that a tiny image, a photo of ourselves, is appended to our deepest moments exactly as on certain packs of cigarettes. And that "whole life" that, as we often hear, passes before the dying or before those people who are in danger of dying, is composed precisely of such tiny images. They present a rapid streaming like in those notebooks, the precursors of cinematographs, in which, when we were children, we could admire a boxer, a swimmer, or tennis player at his art.[82]

Godard's *Histoire(s)* aspire to be in their construction and spirit the latter-day equivalent of those notebooks, humble but sublime, described by Benjamin.

The Proustian inspiration of Godard's work is evident not only in the reliance on superimposition and intermittency, but also in the overarching hermeneutic strategy of his project. This position dovetails neatly with a Deleuzian view. According to the French philosopher, not only should we be convinced that, had he lived longer, Proust would have written in cinematic terms, but we ought to regard him in some sense as the proper originator of the sophisticated concept of the time-image: "But the direct time-image always gives us access to that Proustian dimension where people and things occupy a place in time which is incommensurable with the one they have in space. Proust indeed speaks in terms of cinema, time mounting its magic lantern on bodies and making the shots coexist in depth."[83] Godard enlarges on Deleuze's intuition to compose a history of cinema that instead of adopting a conventionally chronological approach enacts the rhythm of the time-image. *Histoire(s) du cinéma* thus pertinently reframes the question of the relationship between Proust's novel and cinematic memory.

In the *Recherche*, however, motion pictures do not receive a flattering representation. We find only five references to the "*cinématographique*," of which four occur in *Time Regained*, and all reaffirm the superiority of literary or metaphoric representation over the cinematic.[84] In such passages, Proust shows little awareness that the impact of film resides not in the ability of the camera to capture realistic images, but in the potential of montage to incorporate time.

On the other hand, Proust firmly defines the novel as a whole as the "optical instrument" [*instrument optique*] with which the writer furnishes the reader to refine his or her perception of the world.[85] If we surmise that the model for this optical instrument is film, we do so not simply because, ever since his childhood in Combray, the narrator has been beguiled by the mysterious "*lanterne magique*" that projects the endlessly mesmerizing story of Golo and Geneviève de Brabante.[86] In fact, even at the level of its linguistic microeconomics, the *Recherche* relies on an inherently cinematic device. The novel's well-known predilection for metaphorical expression is not manifested through the mere choice of the appropriate, poetic image; the *Recherche* rather develops a sort of mise-en-scène of metaphor through an insistence on the technique of superimposition. That is to say, the *Recherche* aims to capture in writing how consciousness sustains moments of optical equivocation, how the mind blends together one image with another, a practice compounded by photographic technology. The cinematic logic propounded by involuntary memory in the famous tripping scene in the Guermantes courtyard defamiliarizes the very itinerary of recollection from the slow motion unwinding of the epiphany through its culminating freeze-frame of the narrator to the ultimate superimposition of two images—one of Venice, the other of the Guermantes courtyard—that have no organic connection to one another.[87]

Histoire(s) du cinéma should be regarded as an exploration of the autobiographical value of the time-image, an effort advanced in a Proustian mood to distill from the fractured remnants of the past a "pure history." If Godard's *Histoire(s)* shares with Proust's *Recherche* a similar inspiration, we should also note that it runs a similar risk of appealing to a regressive or at least nostalgic mentality. Because film (as opposed to television or video) represents for Godard a sort of romanticized infancy of art, his enterprise in *Histoire(s) du cinéma* may be regarded, like Proust's in *A la recherche du temps perdu*, as an attempt to regain the lost innocence of childhood (1b:238).

In *Histoire(s) du cinéma*, Godard intends to superimpose his personal experience on the collective, public face of cinema. *Histoire(s)* is an autobiographical enterprise in spirit because the material traces of film are also reflections of Godard's own personal life story.[88] As he himself phrases it, "Without cinema I would not have any history" [*Sans cinéma je n'aurais pas d'histoire*] (2a:39). Proclaiming the visual language of film as the mother tongue of the twentieth century, Godard refuses to provide an ostensibly objective, chronological overview of the medium. To the question of historical origin he responds instead by taking the invention of motion pictures as the revolutionary new beginning of a certain way of looking at the world, the emergence of cinema in this sense standing for the birth of a peculiarly modern consciousness of estrangement. We thus find three historical levels "superimposed" on one another in the *Histoire(s)*: the personal, the communal, and the cinematic. The titles of the first two segments—"Toutes les histoires" and "Une histoire seule"—imply the constantly viable possibility in *Histoire(s) du cinéma* of a gestalt switch between two ways of thinking about the medium: in terms of its social currency as spectacle or in terms of its psychical value as allegory.

According to Godard, cinema is best defined not in terms of ontological presence à la Bazin, but rather in terms of metaphorical and historical representation.[89] And like Proust, Godard affirms a poetics of shock or paradox by cultivating visual superimposition in order to sustain epistemological instabilities, by performing a "*battéments*" of images, a deployment of signs that we might describe in Benjaminian accents as a "beating of wings."[90] At stake in this agitated beating of images is the "*fatale beauté*" of film, its uniquely sublime quality. As Godard declares elsewhere in *Histoire(s)*, "*seul le cinéma*" mobilizes itself with such unnerving ostentation. To better highlight the metaphorical function of film, Godard, like Proust, actively experiments with the condensation and displacement of images, confronting us with a visual archive of the century that exemplifies the paradox of superimposition: "That which is above all at the base, it's always two, always presenting from the start two images instead of one; it's what I define as the image, this image made of two, that is to say the third image."[91] As a strategy of visualization, superimposition corresponds to a complicated and enigmatic philosophy of history within whose terms the past manifests itself as a palimpsest that is always in the process of being revised. Godard, the narrator, orients our cinematic excursion through the labyrinth of history by means of a sardonic, frequently melancholic commentary that propounds a poetics of quotation.

By way of an allegorical recapitulation of the project of the *Recherche*, Godard aspires to recapture his ideal of the "*film perdu*," once a certain type of cinema has run its course:

We can say, in general, that a certain idea of cinema, not Lumière's but that which was perhaps pursued by Feuillade and continued by Delluc, Vigo, and from which I do not consider myself to be far, this idea of cinema is over, as the Fontainebleau school is over, as Italian painting is over. . . . One can say that a certain cinema has now been achieved. As Hegel put it, an epoch is finished. Afterward it is different. One feels sad because childhood has been lost.[92]

Just like literature in the *Recherche*, cinema in *Histoire(s)* is not "sheltered from time" [*à l'abri du temps*], but simply "the shelter of time" [*l'abri du temps*] (4b:299). This is another way of saying that Godard's *Histoire(s)* does not embrace the machinery of archival history. To the order of the archive, Godard opposes the aura of involuntary memory.

Indeed, Godard's intuitive, dreamlike layering of images resembles involuntary memory more than it does organized montage. As if to drive the point home, we are repeatedly shown during the four-hour course of the *Histoire(s)* a self-referential scene of the director gazing with somewhat lax attention at the film as it passes by on his editing table. Although we might regard such an image as a way of thematizing the hermeneutical problematic of the film, that problematic is framed by Godard not in analytic terms, as Bergala has remarked, but in emotional terms, in terms of distress and consolation: "We should most of all refrain from thinking, *before the authority of the completed work*, that Godard has always been sure about which *shots* he was looking for, and that he knew in which films and in which place in those films to find them. The most troubling shots are those regained when they were inaccessible to the convocation of his voluntary memory."[93]

In the choice of images that constitute the *Histoire(s)*, we should recognize not so much Godard's logical ordering of experience as his spontaneous election to an intensified state of consciousness by his memories of forgotten films. The obsessive return of certain images suggests that Godard has been chosen by his memories insofar as he allows them to resurface.[94] We might say that Godard unveils the Proustian unconsciousness of cinema to the extent that he reveals even montage in its ostensible identity as a visual technology to obey the intermittent rhythms of the subjective. A sly illustration of this point may be found in section 3b, where, after an eruption of fragments from Rossellini's *Paisà* and Cocteau's *La belle et la bête*, we abruptly encounter the legend, "Hardly Working," which ironically raises the question of the psychic labor behind the editing.[95] Although, on the one hand, montage may be work, its result resembles the effortless arbitrariness of the intermittencies. It is on this ground that Aumont rightly considers Godard to be Proust's "brother."[96]

In section 2b of the *Histoire(s)*, which is entitled "Fatale beauté," references to the *Recherche* are made openly and at some length. Godard emphatically repeats the name of Marcel's vanished and mysterious love, Albertine. On the screen the phrase "le temps perdu" flashes several times. This evocation of Proust's enigmatic female protagonist occurs, not accidentally, during a meditation on the nature of cinema, which Godard equates with its function neither as art nor as technique, but as *mystery*: "I said: not an art, nor a technique, but a mystery (voice of Godard). Time found. Only cinema. All alone. Mystery" [Je disais: pas un art, ni un technique, mais un mystère (voix de Godard). Le temps trouvé. Seul le cinema. Tout seul. Mystère] (2b:154–55). Yet his very insistence on the value of film as the embodiment of regained time may also be read as an admission of the medium's untimely status or condition. If the *Recherche* is written at the dawn of cinema, the *Histoire(s)* awakens to its sunset, a distance that Godard captures by ironically rewriting Proust's famous first sentence, "For a long time I used to go to bed early" [*Longtemps, je me suis couché de bonne heure*], as "For a long time I used to wake up unhappily" [*Longtemps je me suis reveillé de malheur*]. The punning conversion of "*bonne heure*" (which itself echoes "*bonheur*") to "*malheur*" or unhappiness brings to light at once the proximate, but also mutated, condition of Godard's present relative to Proust's past. The director's mise-en-scène must dispense with elegiac niceties, and his own search for lost cinema will be conducted, according to Aumont, as the potential final chapter in the history of art.[97] Indeed, immediately after airing his revision of Proust's *incipit,* Godard indulges in a bit of wordplay on the phrase "*le temps retrouvé*" by typographically highlighting the "*trou,*" the hole or empty space, at the heart of the adjective "*retrouvé.*"

In fact, Godard's effort is not to construct a systematic catalog of film memories that provide immediate access to history, but to retrieve a few fragmentary touchstones that, like Proust's involuntary memories, redeem the past by means of indication or suggestion. Paradoxically, these touchstones can be recovered only through a process of forgetting. It is precisely in the readiness of consciousness to brave the threat of erasure that he locates the possibility of recollection as an aesthetic act: "Whoever wishes to remember must trust to oblivion, to that risk which is absolute oblivion, and to the beautiful accident that might then become the remembrance" [Qui veut se souvenir doit se confier à l'oubli à ce risque qu'est l'oubli absolu et à ce beau hasard que devient alors le souvenir] (4a:128–29). Whereas the visual composition of *Histoire(s) du cinéma* demonstrates that the movies may provide the material analogue par excellence of memory, Godard's assertion implies that their evocative power rests on what Aumont defines as *amnésie.*[98] At the very moment when the cybernetic practice of the information archive or database seemingly replaces that of a living cultural memory, it is Godard's intention to save a select few auratic images and thus the essence of art cinema.[99]

Yet ultimately, Godard manages to escape or to overcome the solipsistic framework of the Proustian enterprise. How the Swiss director achieves this feat may become clearer if we recognize that he composes his *Histoire(s)* through the contamination of Proust's doctrine of involuntary memory with Benjamin's problematic of history. Godard and Benjamin's interpretations of Proust coincide insofar as both privilege an understanding of *la mémoire involontaire* in terms of an expressly visual dialectic of recollection and forgetfulness. However, Benjamin's work provides Godard not only with an aesthetics of reminiscence, but also with an ideal of the politically redemptive value of history. As the French director himself puts it, "the future blazes amid memories" [*l'avenir éclate parmi les souvenirs*] (3a:12). Godard's ambiguous description of the arrival of the future as a violent or shocking occurrence already hints at the political and cultural fatalism that will frame his unveiling of a Proustian history of cinema. Such an attitude represents an extension of Benjamin's melancholy position with regard to history, capitalism, and the epoch of the commodity.

One essay crucial to an understanding of *Histoire(s) du cinéma* is Benjamin's "Theses on the Philosophy of History." In *The Arcades Project*, Benjamin had defined history not as an objective science but as a form of subjective remembrance [*Eingedenken*].[100] On this score, it is in Benjamin's wake that we should position Godard's resistance to linear narrative and preference for constellations of images.[101] Given Benjamin's understanding of the image as the presentiment of an uncanny similarity between disparate things, we should not be surprised that in the "Theses on the Philosophy of History" Benjamin also identifies the image as the proper means of access to the historical past.

The "Theses" conceive of history as a stream of visual "monads" that by virtue of their perpetual recombination fleetingly suggest a larger pattern of correlation. At the center of this current of fragments we encounter the most elusive image of all: "The true image of the past flits by. The Past can be seized only as an image which flashes up at the instant when it can be recognized and is never seen again."[102] Benjamin's definition of history in the "Theses" never strays very far from the language with which he discusses memory in Proust. His insistence that history's authentic image vanishes at the moment it "flashes up" bears a strong resemblance to his exposition of *la mémoire involontaire* in "The Image of Proust": "When the past is reflected in the dewy fresh 'instant,' a painful shock of rejuvenation pulls it together. . . . But this very concentration, in which things that normally just fade and slumber consume themselves in a flash is called rejuvenation."[103] To stress the latency or dormancy of the material expended by involuntary memory seems particularly fitting when we consider the dreamlike suddenness with which the apparition of the narrator's dead grandmother in the novel is superimposed on the empty room where Marcel is about to take off his boots.[104]

Godard's affinity for the critic's view of history embraces not only a common imagistic method, however, but also a similar preoccupation with the end of time in its political and religious dimensions. Godard shares with the later Benjamin a belief, albeit ambivalent or "weak" in the philosophical sense, that history provides the messianic horizon of a possible resurrection of art as cinema.[105] Indeed, the image for Godard inherently carries a promise of the redemption of reality: "The image is first of all of the order of redemption, look here, that of reality" [*L'image est d'abord de*

l'ordre de la rédemption, attention, celle du réel] (3b:149). In the age of commodification nothing speaks to the contemporary *Zeitgeist* with more iconoclastic candor, nor offers greater hope of cultural salvation. We should not
forget that Christianity represents for Godard the ideal origin of cinema,
precisely because it constructs an allegorical iconology on the foundation
of a revolutionary historiography. It is hardly accidental that one of the epigrammatic refrains of the film, inspired by Saint Paul, avows that "the image will return at the time of resurrection" [*l'image viendra au temps de la
resurrection*] (4a:75).

     For Godard, as for Benjamin, the messianic horizon is linked to a
"moment of danger." Benjamin writes: "To articulate the past historically
does not mean to recognize it 'the way it really was' (Ranke); it means to
seize hold of a memory as it flashes up at a moment of danger. . . . In every
era the attempt must be made anew to wrest tradition away from a conformism that is about to overpower it."[106] There is no doubt that it is to the
mindless conformism of Hollywood and the totalizing domination of
mass-market consumerism that Godard opposes his *Histoire(s)*:

Yes, it is of our times that I am the fugitive enemy, yes, the totalitarianism of the
present as it is applied mechanically every day more oppressively at the planetary
level, this tyranny without a face that overwhelms everything for the exclusive
profit of the systematic organization of the unified time of the instant . . . because
I try in my works to show an ear that listens to time.[107]

If Godard and Benjamin share similar notions of memory and of history,
their respective approaches to cinema might seem at first sight very different. Certainly, Godard would reject the German critic's initial appraisal of
cinema. As is well known, Benjamin in his 1936 essay, "The Work of Art in
the Age of Mechanical Reproduction," links the emergence of cinema to
the destruction of the aura of the work of art. However, Benjamin also
labors to elucidate the politically liberating consequences of the discon-
nection of film from traditional culture.[108] Yet by the time of his 1939 article, "Some Motifs in Baudelaire," Benjamin proceeds to explore the question of aura in a different frame of mind, complicating his first "political"
definition with nostalgic overtones.

     In his accompanying textual commentary on *Histoire(s) du cinéma*,
Godard does not so much express nostalgia for the aura of lost cinema as
perform "nostalgia," ironizing the sentimental and consumerist impulses
behind the attitude by theatricalizing or spectacularizing them. We should

bear in mind here that he defines film neither as an art nor a science, but rather as a "mystery," a word that invites interpretation in terms of the auratic and the sublime.[109] According to Miriam Hansen, the auratic in Benjamin never coincides with the unveiling of a symbolic integrity, but on the contrary with a "catastrophic and dislocating impact."[110] The same is true of Godard's auratic cinema. In his eyes, film is mysterious because it performs an allegorical movement, an alternating dispersion and concentration of signification. *Histoire(s) du cinéma* aims to witness just that movement, in the process bringing to light the messianic possibility of a catastrophic change. Whereas for Benjamin history must attend to the experience of the vanquished, for Godard film must be given attention insofar as it has been vanquished by video, by digital technology, and more generally by what he defines as the "totalitarianism of the present" (4b:286). It is telling in this regard that the Swiss director assigns the title of section 1a, "Toutes les histoire(s)," to a compendium of notional, never-realized film projects. The title thus pays homage to the epitome of "vanquished" films: Orson Welles's *Don Quixote.*

In the most celebrated passage of the "Theses on the Philosophy of History," Benjamin imagined history as the allegorical subject of Klee's painting "Angelus Novus," a divine spectator who looks back on the past while being propelled into the future amid a hail of debris by a wind blowing from paradise.[111] Strikingly, Benjamin revives the metaphor at a pivotal juncture in "The Work of Art in the Age of Mechanical Reproduction" when he imagines the advent of film: "Then came the film and burst this prison-world asunder by the dynamite of the tenth of a second, so that now, in the midst of its far-flung ruins and debris, we calmly and adventurously go traveling."[112] The resemblance of the two passages suggests that at some level Benjamin associated cinema with the paradise from which the storm of the future originates. Godard quite consciously appropriates and redeploys this association. In the first, televised version of *Histoire(s) du cinéma,* at the end of section 1b, we thus encounter the image of Klee's angel dramatically (and perhaps a bit self-aggrandizingly) superimposed on that of Godard himself.[113] Behind Godard's enterprise stands a Benjaminian insistence on the critical recuperation of history, a retrieval of ephemeral images "flashing up" to demand analysis in the present because, as Benjamin puts it, "Every image of the past that is not recognized by the present as one of its own concerns threatens to disappear irretrievably."[114] Film offers the ideal reservoir of such images, a reservoir that offers the advantage of presenting historical events without adding causal explanations from outside the events themselves.

If the philosophical standpoint of Godard's *Histoire(s)* is the same as that of Benjamin's "Theses," its methodology is closer to that of *The Arcades Project*. Indeed, as an attempt to delineate the specific physiognomy of the twentieth century from its fragmentary cultural traces, through a collage of images and texts, *Histoire(s) du cinéma* reveals a genealogical relation to *The Arcades Project*. As has been well documented, Benjamin pursued until the end of his life the project of a history of the "minor" or marginal, a project applying the practices of historical materialism and articulated around the emblematic figures of the nineteenth century: arcades, whores, gamblers, gilded mirrors, mechanical dolls. The resulting epigrammatic sketches, organized into a kind of patchwork of quotations, contribute to what Benjamin defined as a "dialectic at a standstill," a sort of intransitive unveiling of the truth that avoids the illusion of linear narrative progress. But as in the case of the "Theses," the theory of collective memory developed in the *Arcades* also owes its inspiration to the Proustian notion of involuntary memory, of which it represents a sort of "objective," material aspect.[115] Godard's *Histoire(s) du cinéma* identifies the twentieth-century analogue of the arcade in the movie theater. Like the arcade, film is able to provide a centrifugal mode of access to meaning and history.

Not only do Benjamin and Godard espouse in common a poetics of montage or quotation, they share a determination to escape the strictures of conventional historicism in order to unveil the allegorical figures that arise from the ruins of history. Even Godard's written commentary on *Histoire(s)* mimics the visual procedures of montage, linking as it does citations or pastiches of a variety of authors—philosophers, film critics, songwriters, poets, and directors—who are listed at the end of each volume, but not individually attributed. Film clearly represents for Godard a sort of private or personal historical arcade, a spectacular space that provides us with an "involuntary memory" of the century. In this light, Benjamin and Godard may be seen to share much the same project; both aim to perform a materialist critique of culture by means of Proustian acts of remembrance, to expose the hidden costs of production by means of a poetic recovery of the past. Such a critique, far from enforcing an objectively verifiable or scientific picture of events, provides access to history via the digressive, subjective paths of allegory. Godard underlines this emphasis when he writes, "Why simplify when one can complicate?" [*Pourquoi faire simple quand on peut faire compliqué?*] (2a:78). If history becomes legible for Benjamin by alternation between the mystical perspective of the "Theses" and the materialist approach of the *Arcades*, we find in Godard the possibility of bringing the two modes into convergence through the language of cinema, a language that according to Godard expresses the "equality and fraternity between the real and fiction" [*égalité et fraternité entre le réel et la fiction*] (3b:126–27).

What Are Directors for in a Destitute Time?

In each of the first two episodes of *Histoire(s) du cinéma*, an evocative text is read in voice-over: "Night has fallen, another world rises, hard, cynical, illiterate, amnesiac, turning aimlessly, spread out and flattened, as if perspective, the vanishing point, had been suppressed. The strangest thing is that the living dead of this world are made in the image of the preceding world: their reflections, their sensations are from before." It could be argued that this statement details the negative aspect of postmodernity, its inability as a culture to be anything more than a traumatic repetition. However, coinciding with the disconsolate pessimism that is in fact the most anachronistic side of *Histoire(s)*, an original *pars construens* also may be found.

Godard's visual essay refrains from carrying out the equivalent of a successful, Freudian work of mourning for the movies, thus avoiding the mechanical, harrowing, "bit by bit" process of withdrawal from the moving image. In section 3b, his epigrammatic characterization of montage as "hardly working" hints that what is at stake is not the orderly strategy of overcoming loss devised by Freud, but the recitation of a litany of film memories, a performance that the director ultimately presents in quasi-Heideggerian terms.

We may think of *Histoire(s)* as Godard's cinematic convalescence because of his overt evocation of the Heideggerian figure for the mourning of metaphysics. If Heidegger in his later writings aims to take leave of metaphysics and what he defines as "the age of the world picture," Godard wishes to take leave of the notion of movies as a mere spectacle, of the camera as will to power.[116] For Heidegger, the only feasible philosophical operation is to acknowledge the "convalescence" or "overcoming" [*Verwindung*] of metaphysics. Using the concept of *Verwindung* to replace the Hegelian notion of a dialectical *Aufhebung*, Heidegger stresses the necessity not of "suppressing" metaphysics, but of accepting it. It is not so much that the metaphysical tradition has to be forgotten, but rather to be mourned, to be looked at with pietas and devotion in an attitude of commemoration that Heidegger, following Hölderlin, captures with the German word *Andenken* [remembrance].[117] In section 1b of *Histoire(s)*, Godard quotes one of the most suggestive passages of Heidegger's essay on the seminal role of art, "What Are Poets For?": "The default of God forebodes something even grimmer, however. Not only have the gods and the god fled, but the divine radiance has become extinguished in the world history. The time of the world's night is the destitute time because it becomes ever more destitute. It has already grown so destitute, it can no longer discern the default of God as a default."[118]

Godard's recuperation of religion and aesthetics in the 1980s and 1990s marks the attempt to abandon the strong political inspiration that characterized his Maoist phase to settle instead for what could be defined, borrowing Vattimo's term, as the "weak thought" of film. The concept of weak thought designates, according to the Italian philosopher, the post-metaphysical space of a convalescent philosophy.[119] A similar intention might be attributed to *Histoire(s) du cinéma*, a film in which we are not confronted with the aesthetic lightness of our fragmented memories of motion pictures, but with their messianic "weakness," a litotes first used by Benjamin to designate a horizon of possible redemption: "Like every generation that preceded us, we have been endowed with a weak Messianic power, a power to which the past has a claim."[120] In this sense, the weakness of critical postmodernity would imply a renunciation of any dialectic of overcoming, any search for transcendental conditions in favor of a conception of history as a form of remembrance. The difference between lightness and weakness corresponds to the distinction between a populist and a critical postmodernity. We might observe the significance of Godard's attitude in *Histoire(s)* by recalling how, in the 1960s, his appropriation of mass culture and his "Americanism" converged to produce an idiosyncratic style that Wollen has labeled "lifestyle modernism," a combination of a keen interest in a journalistic and sociological mode of exploration with an attraction to the quotidian rhythms of life.[121] During this period, Wollen suggests, Godard recognized and, to an extent, reflected the availability of art for reappropriation by consumerism.[122] Before his self-conscious effort of political engagement starting after 1968, Godard's films revolved in endless fascination around the ambient logic of popular culture. His "lifestyle modernism" coincides with an early, uncritical version of postmodernism.

However, in the 1980s and 1990s and particularly in *Histoire(s)*, his movies adopt new artistic strategies and achieve an altogether different effect. The pastichelike quality of his work, coupled with his responsiveness to Benjamin's methodological and ethical inspiration, redeems Godard from potential accusations of a naive attempt to "recreate" modernism. The objective is to take leave of modernity without making grandiose claims to the pathos of the new or indulging a cliché nostalgia. At the same time, the director tries through acts of poetic imagination to explode postmodernity from within, liberating the energy too often restrained by the mannerist game of style. An example of his critically engaged postmodernism, of his revisionist attitude toward modernist paradigms, comes to light if we compare Blanchot's tragic rendering of the Orpheus myth to Godard's later variation on the same theme. Blanchot's Orpheus twice sacrifices Eurydice by virtue of an overwhelming artistic inspiration that compels him to look back: "Writing begins with the gaze of Orpheus" [*Écrire commence avec le regard d'Orphée*].[123] According to Blanchot's definition, writing depends on an act of nostalgic abandon to the power of the origin and the ethics of sacrifice.

For Godard instead, by virtue of its nonchalance of retrospection, film makes it possible to rewrite the myth of Orpheus in a less catastrophic key: "Cinema authorizes Orpheus to turn back without killing Eurydice" [*Le Cinéma autorise Orphée de se retourner sans faire mourir Eurydice*] (2a:96–97). Cinema rephrases and reinvigorates the Orphic metaphor by supplying contemporary culture with the analogon of an absolute visual memory. As Godard reimagines the narrative, Orpheus is safe and so is Eurydice; from this perspective, Orpheus, liberated from tragic necessity, embodies a postmodern mythology in which the presence of the past is safely guaranteed by the celluloid medium.

However, if film's historicity refurbishes the myth of Orpheus in a compelling way, *Histoire(s) du cinéma* at the same time bears witness to the approaching terminus of such historical lucidity, to the disappearance of film's Orphic potential. *Histoire(s)* ends on a freeze-frame of a rose superimposed over a still image of Godard himself. Over this literally arresting vision, the voice-over intones, "If a man crossing paradise in a dream received a flower as proof of his transit and, on awakening, found the flower in his hands, what else would he say but I was this man" [*si un homme traversait le paradis en songe qu'il reçût une fleur comme preuve de son passage et qu'à son réveil il trovât cette fleur dans ses mains que dire alors j'étais cet homme*] (4b:306–11). The passage resonates sharply with the inaugural quote of *Histoire(s)*, which, as we have discussed, derives from the dream recounted in Freud's case history: "Father, don't you see I am burning." In both cases, cinema establishes the space of an encounter with the Real, a confrontation that advances beyond nostalgia to open a new space of thinking and redemption. Godard's wager at the end of the twentieth century is that the aesthetic might exude a political meaning insofar as cinema is proposed as the performance of remembrance, not the glorification of simulacra. *Histoire(s) du cinéma* undertakes to inaugurate a temporality in which the alternative between single and multiple stories, identity and contradiction is suppressed in favor of a narrative in which "*toutes les histoires*" and "*une histoire seule*" coexist and mirror each other. If what Godard defines as the projective nature of cinema entails the abandonment of any power of synthesis within the symbolic order, the very heterogeneity of the film medium makes it an apt expression of contemporary culture. Finally, Godard leaves us with a work eliciting not only aesthetic delight, but with a sense of purpose: that of reinterpreting tradition, of reinvigorating the canon of great film—not for a narrow-minded attachment to what is canonical, but as a renewal of attention to the challenges of the past and the hopes of the future. Although to some degree Godard may risk unduly privileging the genealogy of high art, his *Histoire(s)* raises the possibility of a critical response to the anguish of loss, and in so doing, he suggests a vision of ethical and political resistance to the banality of consumer culture.

Notes

1. Although a certain sort of skepticism toward history conceived as a series of objective events or, as in the idealist philosophical tradition, as the gradual unveiling of the truth might be welcome, I find regrettable the apparent indifference of much contemporary culture to history conceived as an ethical task or project.

2. By the term, one might wish to denote, as Andreas Huyssen does, the movement in art and architecture that has usurped the place of a debilitated modernism; or as Fredric Jameson does, the cultural logic of "late capitalism"; or as Jean-François Lyotard does, a revived philosophy of the avant-garde that shows a degree of continuity with modernism, i.e., "postmodernism not as a modernism at its end, but in a nascent state." See Lyotard's *Postmodern Explained*, trans. Don Barry, Bernadette Maher, Julian Pefanis, Virginia Spate, and Morgan Thomas (Minneapolis: University of Minnesota Press, 1992), 13. To the wide range of modernisms identified by readers correspond at least as many shades of postmodernism—from the affirmative and historically self-conscious to the jaded and consumerist. Although the designation is notoriously equivocal, I wish to retain the concept here as a call to the ongoing interpretation of a certain epistemological shift or turn that can no longer be denied. The Italian philosopher Gianni Vattimo has summed up this change in reference to two lines of Hölderlin often cited by Heidegger: "Full of merit, yet poetically, dwells/Man on this earth" [voll verdienst, doch dichterisch, wohnt/Der Mensch auf dieser Erde]. Vattimo writes: "These lines from Hölderlin define the condition of man in the moment of transition to the postmodern: the doch, the 'yet,' is what signals the turn. One can think of modernity, then, as defined by the idea of a dwelling voll verdienst, of a life 'full of merit'—which is to say, full of activity. . . . The doch, then, altogether beyond Hölderlin's intentions and perhaps those of Heidegger too, could mean the turn, the change in direction which brings us to the postmodern condition." See Vattimo's "The End of Modernity, the End of the Project," in *Rethinking Architecture*, ed. Neil Leach (New York: Routledge, 1997), 148.

3. Philippe Ariès, *The Hour of Our Death*, trans. Helen Weaver (Oxford: Oxford University Press, 1991).

4. Ibid., 575.

5. Ibid., 595.

6. Guy Debord, *Comments on the Society of the Spectacle*, trans. Malcolm Imrie (London: Verso, 1998).

7. Sigmund Freud, *The Standard Edition of the Complete Psychological Works*, 24 vols., trans., ed. James Strachey (London: Hogarth Press, 1953–74), 14:306.

8. "Il n'est guère de deuil sans la question: que dirait-il? qu'aurait-il dit? sans le regret ou le remords de n'avoir pas suffisamment pu dialoguer, entendre ce que l'autre avait à dire" [There is certainly no mourning without the question, what would he say, what would he have said, without the regret or remorse of not being able to hold a sufficient dialogue, to understand what the other had to say]. Jean Laplanche, *La révolution copernicienne inachevée* (Paris: Aubier, 1992), 379. The English translation is mine.

9. For an acute reflection on the different meanings of the word *beyond* in Nietzsche and Freud, see Todd Dufresne, *Tales from the Freudian Crypt* (Stanford: Stanford University Press, 2000), 85–86.

10. Jacques Derrida, *The Post Card: From Socrates to Freud and Beyond*, trans. Alan Bass (Chicago: University of Chicago Press, 1987), 353.

11. Sigmund Freud, "Trauer und Melancholie," in *Studienausgabe Band III* (Frankfurt am Main: Fisher, 1982), 198–99.

12. Jacques Lacan, *Séminaire IV: La rélation d'objet* (Paris: Éditions du Seuil, 1994), 15.

13. Jacques Lacan, *Séminaire XI: Les quatres concepts fondamentaux de la psychanalyse* (Paris: Éditions du Seuil, 1973), 246–47. An English translation has been published as *Seminar XI: The Four Fundamental Concepts of Psychoanalysis*, ed. Jacques-Alain Miller, trans. Alan Sheridan (New York: Norton, 1998), 274–75.

14. As Derrida has put it in a recent text on the *états d'âme* [states of soul] of psychoanalysis, the future of the discipline might reside in openly exploring and addressing the question of the very mourning and grief from which it suffers at the moment. Rather than celebrating or bemoaning the decline of psychoanalysis, he proposes a mourning and reassessment of its legacy that could lead to new mappings both of psychology and of culture. Jacques Derrida, *États d'âme de la psychanalyse* (Paris: Galilée, 2000), 27.

15. See in this regard Kristeva's *Black Sun*, trans. Leon Roudiez (New York: Columbia University Press, 1989), *La révolte intime* (Paris: Fayard, 1997), and *The Sense and Non-Sense of Revolt: The Powers and Limits of Psychoanalysis*, trans. Jeanine Herman (New York: Columbia University Press, 2000). At the same time, her response to Lacan and handling of mourning often threaten to limit her to a weakly nostalgic aestheticism that fetishizes psychoanalysis as an object of regret.

16. Jacques Derrida, *Specters of Marx: The State of the Debt, the Work of Mourning, and the New International*, trans. Peggy Kamuf (New York: Routledge, 1994).

17. Jean-Luc Godard, *Jean-Luc Godard par Jean-Luc Godard, tome 2: 1984–1998*, ed. Alain Bergala (Paris: Cahiers du Cinéma, 1998), 430.

18. For more on the opposition between the Greek and Latin conceptions of the pictorial, see Serge Tisseron, *Le mystère de la chambre claire* (Paris: Flammarion, 1996), 53.

19. Derrida rightly points out that there is no metalanguage for the work of mourning: "This is also why one should not be able to say anything about the work of mourning, anything about this subject, since it cannot become a theme, only another experience of mourning that comes to work over the one who intends to speak." Jacques Derrida, *The Work of Mourning*, ed. Pascale-Anne Brault and Michael Naas (Chicago: University of Chicago Press, 2001), 143.

20. In his essay on Goethe's *The Elective Affinities*, Benjamin characterizes the work of the critic as an "alchemical" mourning ritual: "If, to use a simile, one views the growing work as a burning funereal pyre, than the commentator stands before it as a chemist, the critic as an alchemist. Whereas, for the former, wood and ash remain the sole objects of his analysis, for the latter only the flame itself preserves an enigma: that of what is alive. Thus, the critic inquires into the truth, whose living flame continues to burn over the heavy logs of what is past and the light ashes of what has been experienced." Moreover, Benjamin famously links the obsolescence of storytelling to the impossibility of the transmission of wisdom at the moment of death, a moment increasingly removed from the perceptual and symbolic world of meaning. Cf. Walter Benjamin, "Goethe's Elective Affinities," in *Walter Benjamin: Selected Writings I, 1913–1926*, ed. Marcus Bullock and Michael W. Jennings (Cambridge: Harvard Belknap, 1999), 296, and "The Storyteller," in *Illuminations*, ed. Hannah Arendt, trans. Harry Zohn (New York: Schocken Books: 1969), 94.

21. Margaret Cohen has addressed the issue of Benjamin's production of a cultural phantasmagoria in the *Passagenwerk*. See her *Profane Illuminations: Walter Benjamin and the Paris of Surreal Revolutions* (Berkeley: University of California Press, 1993).

22. Of course, both Heidegger and Derrida rework the philosophical scenario introduced by Nietzsche. If Nietzsche calls our attention to the death of God and hence the loss of our belief in metaphysical values, he does so as a mourner. Accordingly, he discusses in *Thus Spoke Zarathustra* the possibility of a convalescence [*Genesung*] of the mind, a notion that bears a certain affinity to that of mourning. Friedrich Nietzsche, *Werke*, vol. 2, ed. Karl Schlecta (Munich: Hanser, 1973), 461–67.

23. Martin Heidegger, "The End of Philosophy and the Task of Thinking," in *Basic Writings*, ed. David Farrell Krell (New York: Harper and Row, 1979), 369.

24. Jacques Derrida, *Margins of Philosophy*, trans. Alan Bass (Chicago: University of Chicago Press, 1986), 27.

25. See Gilles Deleuze and Felix Guattari, *Kafka: Toward a Minor Literature*, trans. Dana Polan (Minneapolis: University of Minnesota Press, 1975).

CHAPTER I

1. A valuable summation of the characteristics of high modernism may be found in Tyrus Miller's *Late Modernism: Politics, Fiction, and the Arts Between the Wars* (Berkeley: University of California Press, 1999), 86.

2. Julia Kristeva, *The Sense and Non-Sense of Revolt: The Powers and Limits of Psychoanalysis*, trans. Jeanine Herman (New York: Columbia University Press, 2000), 16.

3. For a convincing analysis of the "temporal balance" of psychoanalysis and of the retrospective orientation of Freudian theory, see Malcolm Bowie's *Psychoanalysis and the Future of Theory* (Oxford: Blackwell, 1993), 1–54.

4. For further consideration of this problematic, see note 2 in the Introduction.

5. Ibid., 26.

6. Fredric Jameson, *The Cultural Turn* (London: Verso, 1998), 51–54.

7. Ibid., 51.

8. Jacques Lacan, *Écrits: A Selection*, trans. Alan Sheridan (New York: Norton 1977), 104. For the French, see Jacques Lacan, *Écrits* (Paris: Éditions du Seuil, 1966), 319. Hereafter, I will cite from Sheridan's selected translations whenever possible, giving, however, page numbers in the text from both the English and French editions, differentiated by the abbreviations E and F. In cases where Sheridan has not translated material from Lacan's writings, I will give my own translation in the body of the chapter and place the French original in a endnote with a page reference to the Seuil edition.

9. Philippe Ariès, *The Hour of Our Death*, trans. Helen Weaver (Oxford: Oxford University Press, 1991), 575.

10. This argument is elaborated throughout Ariès's book. Derrida recognizes in Ariès's anthropological history of death strict semantic and "onto-phenomenological" limits: "The historian knows, thinks he knows, or grants himself the unquestioned knowledge of what death is, of what being-dead means; consequently he grants to himself all the criteriology that will allow him to identify, recognize, select, or delimit the objects of his inquiry or the thematic field of his anthropological historical knowledge. The question of the meaning of death and of the world 'death,' the question 'What is death in general?' or 'What is the experience of death?' and the question of knowing if death 'is'—and what death 'is'—all remain radically absent as questions." Jacques Derrida, *Aporias*, trans. Thomas Dutoit (Stanford: Stanford University Press, 1993), 25.

11. In March 1915, six months after the outbreak of World War I, two essays were published: "The Disillusionment of the War" and "Our Attitude Toward Death." By the end of the year, Freud revised the same theme in "On Transience" while simultaneously completing *Mourning and Melancholia*, which was not published until 1917.

12. Jean Laplanche, *La révolution copernicienne inachevée* (Paris: Aubier, 1992), 363.

13. For an acute reading of the humanist background of the Freudian essay, see Juliana Schiesari, *The Gendering of Melancholia* (Ithaca: Cornell University Press, 1992), 5–8, 53–62.

14. Ariès, *Hour*, 581.

15. It is crucial in understanding the essay to note that Freud systematically disregards the intersubjective dimension of the mourning process in *Mourning and Melancholia*, underscoring the solipsism of the grieving subject. He never considers funeral rites or the kind of anthropological concerns regarding consecration of the dead previously discussed in *Totem and Taboo*. Unlike Freud, Abraham stresses in his essay the anthropology and ethnology of mourning and focuses on ritual behavior such as cannibalism. See "Esquisse d'une histoire du développement de la libido." On Freud's solipsistic depiction of mourning, see Jean Allouch, *L'érotique du deuil: au temps de la mort sèche* (Paris: E.P.E.L., 1997), 124.

16. One of the most interesting reinterpretations of the Freudian scenario of mourning has been proposed by Jean Laplanche, who redescribes the elaborate temporal protocol of the *Trauerarbeit* in the linguistic terms of a process of "detranslation–retranslation" [*detraduction–retraduction*]. Analysis in Laplanche's theory may help a patient to achieve less symptomatic and repressive "translations" of his psychic representations. It is clear to Laplanche that in this sense, analytic therapy models itself after the spontaneous sorrow work of mourning that structures human life by enabling the dissolution and eventual reconstruction of libidinal attachments. Laplanche, *Révolution*, 317–35.

17. Bersani points out that whereas other modernities have regarded their break with the past as relative, after the twentieth century, a partial or qualified historical discontinuity becomes inconceivable. Leo Bersani, *The Culture of Redemption* (Cambridge: Harvard University Press, 1990), 47–48.

18. Sigmund Freud, *The Standard Edition of the Complete Psychological Works*, 24 vols., trans., ed. James Strachey (London: Hogarth Press, 1953–74), 2:162. All further references to Freud's works, unless otherwise noted, are from this edition and will be given in the text by volume and page number.

19. "Ich glaube, daß es nichts Gezwungenes enthalten wird, sie in flogenden Art darzustellen: Die Realitätsprüfung hat gezeigt, daß das geliebte Objekt nicht mehr besteht, und erläßt nun die Aufforderung, alle Libido aus ihren Verknüpfungen mit diesem Objekt abzuziehen. . . . Das Normale ist, daß der Respekt vor der Realität den Sieg behält. Doch kann ihr Auftrag nicht sofort erfüllt werden. Er wird nun im einzelnen unter großem Aufwande von Zeit . . . durchgeführt. . . . Jede einzelne der Erinnerungen and Erwartungen, in denen die Libido an das Objekt geknüpft war, wird eingestellt, überbesetzt and un ihr die Lösung der Libido vollzogen." Sigmund Freud, *Gesammelte Werke*, vol. 10 (London: Imago, 1949), 430. I think it is hardly coincidental that Benjamin employs the very same word, *Lösung*, when referring to the decline of the auratic work of art: "Die Reproduktiontechnik, so lässt sich allgemein formulieren, löst das Reproduzierte aus dem Bereiche der Tradition ab" [The technique of reproduction detaches the reproduced object from the domain of tradition]. Walter Benjamin,

"Das Kunstwerk im Zeitalter seiner technischen Reproduzierbarkeit," in *Gesammelte Schriften*, 1.2, ed. Rolf Tiedemann and Hermann Schweppenhäuser (Frankfurt am Main: Suhrkamp, 1974), 438; "The Work of Art in the Age of Mechanical Reproduction," in *Illuminations*, ed. Hannah Arendt, trans. Harry Zohn (New York: Schocken Books, 1969), 221.

20. Kaja Silverman has observed that Freud presents the lost object as the heterogeneous collation of memories to which the process of mourning cannot have simultaneous access, an amassing of material that can only be recovered through an extraordinary expense of effort and time. Silverman, *World Spectators* (Stanford: Stanford University Press, 2000), 41.

21. Dominick LaCapra incisively describes the process as a sort of homeopathic ritualization of the repetition compulsion turned against the death drive. See LaCapra's "Reflections on Trauma, Absence, and Loss," in *Whose Freud?*, ed. Peter Brooks and Alex Woloch (New Haven: Yale University Press, 2000), 189.

22. It is possible to imagine that the Freudian idea of work might be inscribed within the early institutional tradition of treating madness by enforcing the ideal of labor as a moral imperative. Michel Foucault, *Madness and Civilization* (New York: Vintage, 1988), 246–48.

23. For the latter, see *The Interpretation of Dreams* (5:509–10).

24. Even after the introduction of the death instinct in 1925, mourning and reality-testing for Freud remain intrinsically related. In the essay "Negation," where Freud regards reality-testing as critical to the formulation of the judgment of existence (which affirms or denies that a certain representation has a correlate in reality), he makes clear that effective reality-testing presupposes a state of mourning, for the contrast between subjective and objective does not at first appear evident but takes shape only by virtue of the psyche's ability to revive an object, after it has been lost to perception, by reproducing it as an image, without the effective presence of the external object: "Thus the first and immediate aim of the process of testing reality is not to discover an object in real perception to correspond to what is imagined, but to rediscover such an object, to convince oneself that is still there . . . it is evident that an essential precondition for the institution of the function of testing reality is that objects shall have been lost which have formerly afforded real satisfaction" (19:235–36).

25. LaCapra, "Reflections," 179, 183.

26. See Compagnon's *Five Paradoxes of Modernity*, trans. Franklin Philip (New York: Columbia University Press, 1994).

27. As I make clear in the second section of this chapter, I disagree with LaCapra that the outcome of Lacan's fascination with absence might best be characterized as melancholia. I think the term *tragicomedy* would be more appropriate. Readers who embrace the hermeneutic approach of trauma studies generally ignore the more playful and skeptical aspects of Lacanian thought, preferring to focus only on tragic pathos.

28. The English title, "On Transience," translates the German "*Vergänglich-*

keit," a word found in common, everyday usage, although given Freud's fondness for Goethe, it is possible that the title was meant to suggest an echo of *Faust*: "Alles Vergängliche ist nur ein Gleichnis" [What is transient is only a metaphor]. The events of World War I occasion the essay in the sense that it was written for inclusion in *Das Land Goethes*, a 1916 volume of patriotic and memorial essays; among the contributors were Hugo von Hoffmansthal, Arthur Schnitzler, Richard Strauss, and Albert Einstein.

29. The essay ought to be read against the background of the cultural battle between historicism and modernism, a battle that grew particularly acrimonious in Austria, and toward which Freud took a resolute stance. Carl Schorske, *Thinking with History* (Princeton: Princeton University Press, 1998), 191–219.

30. Pierre Fedida, *L'absence* (Paris: Gallimard, 1978), 77–78.

31. It has been suggested that these two "characters" were Lou Salomé and Rainer Maria Rilke, whom Freud had met in Munich in September of 1913 at the fourth Congress of the IPA. See note b in Sigmund Freud, *Oeuvres complètes*, trans. Jean Laplanche and François Robert (Paris: Presses Universitaires de France, 1988), 321; and Donald Prater, *A Ringing Glass: The Life of Rainer Maria Rilke* (Oxford: Clarendon Press, 1986), 233. We learn from Prater that "in Munich, [Rilke] arrived just in time to attend some of the session of the Congress with Lou, and she was active in introducing him to prominent participants, including Freud, with whom they spent an evening."

32. What strikes Freud as an "incontestable" line of thought seems not to have occurred to his friends (or not to have convinced them, at any rate). Consequently, their enjoyment of beauty is doomed from the start. "The idea that all this beauty was transient," Freud suggests, "was giving these two sensitive minds a foretaste of mourning over its decease" (14:305). What takes place in their minds Freud characterizes as an emotional "revolt" against mourning.

33. Kristeva perceives the crux of Freud's essay as "the riddle of beauty," rather than the riddle of mourning. Julia Kristeva, *Black Sun*, trans. Leon Roudiez (New York: Columbia University Press, 1989), 98.

34. "Il n'est guère de deuil sans la question: que dirait-il? qu'aurait-il dit? sans le regret ou le remords de n'avoir pas suffisamment pu dialoguer, entendre ce que l'autre avait à dire." Laplanche, *Révolution*, 379. The translation is mine.

35. Malcolm Bowie, *Lacan* (Cambridge: Harvard University Press, 1991), 9.

36. Ibid., 10.

37. Ernest L. Freud, ed., *Letters of Sigmund Freud*, trans. Tanya and James Stern (New York: Basic Books, 1960), 386.

38. For an insightful commentary on the role played by melancholia in the formation of the ego, see Judith Butler, *The Psychic Life of Power* (Stanford: Stanford University Press, 1997), 132–39.

39. However, as both Jacques Derrida and Kaja Silverman have pointed out, we encounter different types of repetitions in *Beyond the Pleasure Principle*, from compulsion to a kind of obsessive effort of mastery (as exemplified by the

Fort-Da game) and even to therapy itself, a form of benign linguistic repetition that diminishes the pathogenic impact of our memories. See the second chapter of Silverman's *Male Subjectivity at the Margins* (New York: Routledge, 1992); and Derrida's "Freud's Legacy," in *The Post Card: From Socrates to Freud and Beyond*, trans. Alan Bass (Chicago: University of Chicago Press, 1987), 292–337.

40. Cf. Samuel Weber, *The Legend of Freud* (Minneapolis: University of Minnesota Press, 1982). Weber argues persuasively that in the more speculative late phase of his career, Freud operates according to theoretical premises that make the attempt to refute his system by appeal to empirical criteria increasingly dubious. I think this coincides with a certain abandonment of an epistemological point of view, in particular in "Beyond the Pleasure Principle."

41. Derrida's interest in psychoanalysis often has overlapped with his fascination with mourning. This is particularly evident in his contribution to the volume *Cryptonymie* by Nicolas Abraham and Maria Torok for which he wrote the preface, "Fors." Abraham and Torok have enriched significantly the phenomenological spectrum of mourning and melancholia through their insistence on the distinction between introjection (successful mourning) and incorporation (pathological grieving) and by proposing the notion of a "psychic crypt." Such a space, they suggest, is generated by an impossible mourning in which the Other is kept inside the self unconsciously, as though buried alive. See Jacques Derrida, "Fors," in Nicolas Abraham and Maria Torok, *Cryptonymie: Le verbier de l'homme aux loups* (Paris: Aubier-Flammarion, 1976), 9–73.

42. Derrida, *Post Card*, 327.

43. Ibid., 340, 335.

44. Ibid., 327.

45. Ibid., 335.

46. Nicolas Abraham and Maria Torok, *L'écorce et le noyau* (Paris: Aubier-Flammarion, 1978), 233–39.

47. The risk of Derrida's position, LaCapra has observed, is that whereas deconstructive practice generally might be said to facilitate the working-through or effective mourning of the loss of "full presence," such an approach, when applied to historically particular losses, betokens a dangerous fascination with, and complacency toward, the "melancholic assimilation of metaphysical and historical frames of reference." "Reflections," 191.

48. Derrida, *Post Card*, 377.

49. On this point, see Jean Laplanche, *Entre séduction et inspiration: l'homme* (Paris: Presses Universitaires de France, 1999), 251.

50. Jacques Derrida and Bernard Stiegler, *Échographies* (Paris: Galilée-INA, 1996), 129. Derrida points out that against all initial expectation, modern technology has increased the hold of a ghostly imaginary, a fascination clearly recognized by psychoanalysis and by film.

51. Derrida, *États d'âme de la psychanalyse* (Paris: Galilée, 2000), 54–69. For Judith Butler, for example, psychoanalysis must mourn traditional ideas of family

and kinship that have become obsolete and even invidious, when they are assumed to provide a universal foundation of culture. "If psychoanalysis, in its theory and practice, retains heterosexual norms of kinship as the basis of its theorization," writes Butler, "if it accepts these norms as coextensive with cultural intelligibility, then it, too, becomes the instrument by which melancholia is produced at a cultural level." Judith Butler, "Quandaries of the Incest Taboo," in *Whose Freud?*, 46.

52. Lyotard, *Postmodern Explained*, 15–16.

53. LaCapra, "Reflections," 184.

54. Jacques Lacan, *The Seminar of Jacques Lacan, Book II: The Ego in Freud's Theory and in the Technique of Psychoanalysis, 1954–55*, ed. Jacques-Alain Millet, trans. Sylvana Tomaselli (New York: Norton, 1991), 326. For the French, see *Le séminaire de Jacques Lacan, livre II: Le moi dans la théorie de Freud et dans la technique de la psychanalyse 1954–1955* (Paris: Éditions du Seuil, 1978), 375.

55. Henry Sussman has asserted that Lacan marks the transition of psychoanalysis from modernism to postmodernism. Henry Sussman, "Psychoanalysis Modern and Postmodern," in *Psychoanalysis and . . .* , ed. Richard Feldstein and Henry Sussman (New York: Routledge, 1990), 129–50.

56. Silverman, *World*, 63.

57. Ibid., 63–64.

58. Samuel Weber, *Return to Freud* (Cambridge: Cambridge University Press, 1990), 10, 101. Weber points out that especially in his earlier texts, Lacan "returns" to the very Freudian idea of the theatricality of the unconscious, converting even pedagogy into theatricality through his persistent recurrence to a performative, apostrophic rhetoric. Indeed, it seems to me that Lacan generally evinces a much stagier, self-regarding approach to writing than Freud, demonstrating that not only does theatricality (associated with the Symbolic) constitute a core topic of the French theorist's thinking, but also the basis of the therapeutic practices he advocates. For Lacan (but not for Freud), the analyst can be considered as merely a listener or spectator, eliciting the patient's "theatrical" performance by means of his or her presence. On this question, see also Silverman, *World*, 68.

59. In "Function and Field of Speech and Language in Psychoanalysis," Lacan is also clearly under the spell of Heidegger's *Being and Time*, which names the future past as the temporal orientation of "Being toward death."

60. Weber, *Return*, 9.

61. Lyotard, *Postmodern Explained*, 15.

62. Bowie, *Lacan*, 9–10.

63. Derrida, *Post Card*, 292, 405.

64. Bowie thinks that in this endeavor, only Proust compares with Lacan: "In twentieth-century France, he is comparable only to Proust in the copiousness, wit, and disabused intelligence with which he restages as text the tragicomedy of desiring human speech." Bowie, *Lacan*, 200.

65. Jacques Lacan, *The Seminar of Jacques Lacan, Book VII: The Ethics of Psychoanalysis, 1959–1960*, ed. Jacques-Alain Miller, trans. Dennis Porter (New

York: Norton, 1992), 252. The French reads: "Vous êtes donc délivrés de tout souci-même si vous ne sentez rien, le Choeur aura senti à votre place." Jacques Lacan, *Le séminaire de Jacques Lacan, livre VII: L'éthique de la psychanalyse 1959–1960* (Paris: Éditions du Seuil, 1986), 295.

66. Slavoj Žižek, *The Sublime Object of Ideology* (London: Verso, 1989), 35.

67. Ibid., 35.

68. Slavoj Žižek, *Looking Awry* (Cambridge: MIT Press, 1997), 142–43.

69. Weber, *Return*, 160.

70. On this point, see Žižek, *Looking*, 146.

71. Jacques Lacan, *Book VII*, 118. French: "L'objet est de sa nature un objet retrouvé. Qu'il ait été perdu, en est la conséquence-mais après-coup." Lacan, *Séminaire VII*, 143.

72. Regarding the periodization of Lacan's thought, I take as my jumping-off point Žižek's three-phase partition of the intellectual production of the French psychoanalyst. Žižek perceives three different stages in the development of Lacan's understanding of the relation between the death drive and the symbolic order. In order to discuss the evolution of the status of the object, I am interested in retaining the last two. Žižek, *Sublime*, 131–32.

73. "In analysis the object is a point of imaginary fixation which gives satisfaction to the drive." Lacan, *Book VII*, 113. French: "Dans l'analyse, l'objet est un point de fixation imaginaire donnant, sous quelque registre que ce soit, satisfaction à une pulsion." Lacan, *Séminaire VII*, 135.

74. Lacan, *Écrits*, E 141–42, F 431–32.

75. Weber, making reference to the unauthorized version of Lacan's *Séminaire X* on anxiety, reminds us that Lacan compares the *objet a* to the frame of a window, citing the case of the *Wolfman* or the curtain of a theater. Weber, *Return*, 161.

76. "The lesson of modernism is that structure, the intersubjective machine, works as well if the Thing is lacking, if the machine revolves around an emptiness; the postmodernist reversal shows the thing itself as the incarnated, materialized emptiness." Žižek, *Looking*, 145.

77. Ibid., 156.

78. On the question of the negativity of desire, see Patrick Guyomard's extremely lucid exposition in *Le désir d'éthique* (Paris: Aubier, 1998), 67–76.

79. "Derrida repeatedly reproaches Lacan for the paradoxical gesture of reducing lack through its affirmation of itself. Lack is localized in a point of exception which guarantees the consistency of all the other elements, by the mere fact that it is determined as 'symbolic castration,' by the mere fact that the phallus is defined as its signifier." Žižek, *Sublime*, 154.

80. Bowie, *Lacan*, 202.

81. Julia Kristeva, *La révolte intime* (Paris: Fayard, 1997), 226.

82. Jacques Derrida, *Specters of Marx: The State of Debt, the Work of Mourning, and the New International*, trans. Peggy Kamuf (New York: Routledge, 1994), 21.

83. Bruce Fink has observed that what is truly original in Lacan's seminar is how certain crucial moments of the play are shown to evince or to enact symbolic castration, hence to sustain the same mechanism. Bruce Fink, "Reading Hamlet with Lacan," in *Lacan, Politics, Aesthetics*, ed. Willy Apollon and Richard Feldstein (Albany: State University of New York Press, 1996), 182. In his article, Fink does an excellent job of making explicit Lacan's interpretive logic, even if his reasons for disagreeing with Lacan's conclusion—that in the end Hamlet is able to act, thus completing the process of his *Bildung*—are traditionally Freudian and less convincing.

84. In *Séminaire VI*, the French analyst reformulates the Freudian interpretation of dreams in order to place emphasis not on the moment of the fulfillment of the wish-dream, but on that of its frustration—the moment that is the origin of desire. I will make reference for the most part to James Hulbert's translation of the third section of Lacan's seminar on *Hamlet*, which Hulbert titles "Desire and Interpretation of Desire in *Hamlet*," published in *Literature and Psychoanalysis*, ed. Shoshana Felman (Baltimore: Johns Hopkins, 1989). The original *séminaire*, published under the title "*Hamlet*, par Lacan," appeared in three installments in the journal *Ornicar?* during the early 1980s. Section 1 appeared in issue 24 (1981), 7–31; section 2 in issue 25 (1982), 13–26; and section 3 in issue 26–27 (1983), 7–44. When I revert to the French version of section 3, this is due to an omission in Hulbert's translation. English translations of sections 1 and 2 are my own; references to the French texts will be flagged by the journal title and given by section and page number.

85. As Alenka Zupančič points out, the tragedy does not illustrate the graph, it is the graph. Alenka Zupančič, *Ethics of the Real* (London: Verso, 2000) 171.

86. Julia Reinhard Lupton and Kenneth Reinhard, *After Oedipus: Shakespeare in Psychoanalysis* (Ithaca: Cornell University Press, 1993), 1.

87. If Freud identifies with Hamlet, it is allegorically, through the complicated mediation of the figure of the mourning Shakespeare. In *The Interpretation of Dreams*, Freud observes that, according to Georg Brandes, *Hamlet* was written shortly after the death of Shakespeare's father (4:265–66), thus establishing a parallel between the play and *The Interpretation of Dreams* itself, which, as Freud confesses, was written to work through his own father's death (4:xxvl).

88. With regard to this point, Lacan never tires of identifying in Hamlet's knowledge of his father's murder not a reason to act, but its opposite. His paralyzing consciousness of the crime is compounded by the Ghost's disclosure of having been "cut off even in the blossoms of my sin." That Hamlet, unlike Oedipus, knows he must revenge an earlier wrong inhibits rather than increases his determination. For Lacan, knowing and procrastination are intimately related, because knowledge implies awareness of the subject's submission to the signifying order and consequent lack of freedom to reach "independent" conclusions, thereby unveiling the absence of any firm ground on which the truth may be established. Lacan, *Ornicar?*, 1:16.

89. "C'est à cet abord si juste, si équilibré, à ce premier jet si clair de la perception de Freud, qu'il nous faudra référer par la suite tout ce qui s'imposera à nous comme excursion et broderies." Lacan, *Ornicar?*, 1:10.

90. On the relationship between modernity and the awareness of decadence, see Matei Calinescu, *Five Faces of Modernity* (Durham: Duke University Press, 1987), 157.

91. "Est-ce que nous pouvons nous contenter de la remarque de Freud que *Hamlet*, fabulation moderne, met en scène de gens qui par rapport à la structure des anciens, seraient en quelque sort de pauvre dégénérés? Nous sommes là dans le style du dix-neuvième siècle. . . . Et nous ne saurons jamais, encore que soit probable, si Freud à cette époque connaissait Nietzsche. Cette référence aux modernes doit-elle nous suffire? Pourqois les modernes seraient-ils plus névroses que les anciens? C'est certainement une pétition de principe. Essayons d'aller plus loin." Lacan, *Ornicar?*, 1:12.

92. Since Baudelaire's example, an explicit link between modernity and decadence had been established, a connection so resonant as to make the triumph of nerves over blood appear to define the very physiognomy of modernity. On modernity and decadence, see Charles Baudelaire, *Oeuvres Complètes* (Paris: Pléiade, 1975), 1525; and Émile Zola, *Mes haines* (Paris: Charpentier-Fasquelle, 1913), 57–58.

93. Žižek points out that Lacan persists in equating the experience of analysis with the production of truth value, even when such production is structured in the manner of a fiction. Žižek, *Sublime*, 154.

94. Felman, *Literature*, 19–20. "C'est en cela que le drame d'Hamlet a la résonance même, métaphysique, de la question du héros moderne. Depuis les temps antiques, quelque chose en effet a changé dans le rapport du héros à son destin. Je vous l'ai dit, ce qui distingue Hamlet d'Oedipe, c'est que lui, Hamlet, sait. Ce trait explique par example la folie d'Hamlet. Il y a dans la tragédie antique, des héros qui sont fous, mais à ma connaissance il n'y en a pas . . . qui fasse le fou. Or, Hamlet fait le fou." Lacan, *Ornicar?*, 3:15.

95. Felman, *Literature*, 33.

96. Lacan, *Book VII*, 251. "Pourquoi au seuil des temps modernes, Hamlet ferait-il le témoignage d'une spéciale débilité de l'homme à venir au regard de l'action? Je ne suis pas si noir, et rien ne nous oblige à l'être, sinon un cliché de la décadence, dans lequel Freud lui-même tombe, quand il compare les attitudes diverses d'Hamlet et d'Oedipe au regard du désir." Lacan, *Séminaire VII*, 293.

97. Derrida, *Specters*, 21.

98. Lacan, *Écrits*, E 47, F 255.

99. In *Séminaire II* on the Freudian notion of the ego, Lacan identifies that domain of consciousness "beyond" Oedipus, which Sophocles delineated in *Oedipus at Colonus*, as the most crucial for psychoanalysis: "If the tragedy *Oedipus Rex* is an exemplary work, analysts should also be acquainted with this beyond of the drama realised in the tragedy of *Oedipus at Colonus*." Lacan, *Book II*, 210. "Si la tragédie d'*Oedipe roi* est une oeuvre exemplaire, les analystes doivent connaître

aussi cet au-delà du drame que realisé la tragédie d'*Oedipe à Colone.*" Lacan, *Séminaire II*, 245. The conclusion of the Oedipus cycle is particularly meaningful for Lacan because it confronts us with a protagonist who has acknowledged and assumed responsibility for his desire and who thus bridges the distance, as Felman points out, between myth and history. Felman regards Colonus as the truly Lacanian psychic space insofar as it represents a place of exile in which it nonetheless becomes possible for the exiled subject to accept his own past. Shoshana Felman, "Beyond Oedipus: The Specimen Story of Psychoanalysis," in *Jacques Lacan and the Adventure of Insight* (Cambridge: Harvard University Press, 1987), 147. It is an open question, however, whether the nostalgic, modernist interpretation of Lacan's position that Felman favors is the most accurate illustration of the French analyst's stance: he was not only expelled from the International Psychoanalytic Association, but dissolved his own school, *l'École Freudienne*, in 1980. In this sense, I wish to argue that in his theory the most significant topos is not Colonus but Elsinore, the "beyond of the beyond," a place of supreme awareness in which *Oedipus Rex* is overcome not by any ethical integration or synthesis, but by being "cited" with a certain irony. If it is possible to look on Colonus as that space in which Oedipus at last can enter historical existence by recognizing his destiny, it is more difficult to assign such a definitive function to Elsinore, the haunted locale of Hamlet's consciousness beyond Colonus. According to Felman, analysis teaches us that there is no getting beyond the Oedipal myth, although the very plot of the Sophoclean drama performatively advances us past the shock of the foundational *peripeteia.* However, Lacan's interpretation of *Hamlet* demonstrates that the price exacted by the inevitable confrontation with the myth is indeed a certain erasure of historical depth because what follows after Colonus is the territory of knowingness. What is at stake in the French analyst's interpretation of the tragedy, then, is nothing less than the establishment of a postmodern rhetoric of "the beyond." See Felman's acute comparison of Freud and Lacan's respective interpretations of the Oedipus myth in *Adventure*, 98–159.

100. Derrida, *Specters*, 22–23.

101. As Žižek points out, Hamlet is inhibited not by his own desire, but by his mother's desire, the fulfillment of which is read in terms of a "filthy" enjoyment. Žižek, *Sublime*, 120–21.

102. Lupton and Reinhard, *After Oedipus*, 58.

103. Lacan, *Ornicar?*, 1:25, 28. A lucid account of the Lacanian reading of *Hamlet* in terms of the graph of desire, "Che Vuoi?", can be found in Žižek, *Sublime*, 120.

104. Felman, *Literature*, 47. "Peut-être pouvons nous éclairer le déclin de l'Oedipe comme deuil du phallus à partir de ce qui nous a été donné dans l'oeuvre freudienne concernant le mécanisme de deuil. Il y à une synthèse à faire." Lacan, *Ornicar?*, 3:37.

105. See Ferenczi's letter of March 24, 1924, cited in an editorial note (19:171).

106. Felman, *Literature*, 46. Lacan, *Ornicar?*, 3:37.

107. Felman, *Literature*, 47. "Là comme partout, il a sa place à part." Lacan, *Ornicar?*, 3:37.

108. Felman, *Literature*, 48. Lacan, *Ornicar?*, 3:38.

109. Lacan, *Ornicar?*, 3:23.

110. Felman, *Literature*, 39. "D'un bout à l'autre d'*Hamlet* on ne parle que de deuil." Lacan, *Ornicar?*, 3:32.

111. Felman, *Literature*, 37. "Qu'est-ce que c'est l'incorporation de l'objet perdu? En quoi consiste le travail du deuil? On reste dans une vague qui explique l'arrêt de toute spéculation dans la voie pourtant ouverte par Freud dans *Deuil et Mélancolie*. La question n'a pas été convenablement articulée." Lacan, *Ornicar?*, 3:29.

112. Felman, *Literature*, 38. "Ce signifiant trouve là sa place. Et en même temps il ne peut la trouver, puisque il ne peut s'articuler au niveau de l'Autre." Lacan, *Ornicar?*, 3:30.

113. Felman, *Literature*, 38. "Le travail de deuil s'accomplit au niveau du logos—je dis *logos* pour ne pas dire *groupe* or *communauté*, bien que le groupe et la communauté en tant que culturellement organisé en soient le supports. Le travail du deuil est d'abord a satisfaction donnée à ce qui se produit de désordre en raison de l'insuffisance des éléments signifiants à faire face au trou créé dans l'existence. Car c'est le système signifiant dans son ensemble qui est mise en cause par le moindre deuil." Lacan, *Ornicar?*, 3:30–31.

114. Lacan, *Écrits*, E 287, F 691.

115. In the rest of the essay, Lacan seems to distinguish the functions of castration, of frustration, and of privation, where the first articulates loss at the symbolic level, the second at the imaginary, and the third at the Real. Lacan, *Ornicar?*, 3:38–39.

116. "Ce qu'il a apporté en sacrifice, en holocauste à la fonction du signifiant manquant." Lacan, *Ornicar?*, 3:40.

117. "Let me tell you that it isn't simply the defense of the sacred rights of the dead and of the family, nor is it all that we have been told about Antigone's saintliness. Antigone is borne along by a passion." Lacan, *Book VII*, 254. ["Je vous le dirai, ce n'est pas simplement la défense des droits sacrés du mort et de la famille, ni non plus tout ce qu'on a voulu nous représenter d'une sainteté d'Antigone. Antigone est portée par une passion." Lacan, *Séminaire VII*, 297.]

118. Lacan, *Book VII*, 270–87, and *Séminaire VII*, 315–33.

119. Žižek, *Sublime*, 135.

120. Ibid., 136.

121. "Yet she pushes to the limit the realization of something that might be called the pure and simple desire of death as such. She incarnates that desire." Lacan, *Book VII*, 282. ["Mais Antigone mène jusqu'à la limite l'accomplissement de ce que l'on peut appeler le désir pur, le pur et simple désir de mort comme tel. Ce désir, elle l'incarne." Lacan, *Séminaire VII*, 329.]

122. Lacan, *Book VII*, 218–30, and *Séminaire VII*, 257–70.

123. Lacan, *Book VII*, 217, and *Séminaire VII*, 256.

124. Lacan, *Book VII*, 299, and *Séminaire VII*, 346.

125. In support of this hypothesis, I wish to point out Lacan's insistence in *Séminaire VII* on Antigone's "éclat" [splendor] and beauty, a radiance that Lacoue-Labarthe rightly suggests should be interpreted as a manifestation of the sublime mode. "Le Beau, dit Lacan. Je dirais plutôt le sublime, qui n'est pas moins aveuglant" [The Beautiful, says Lacan. I would rather say the sublime, which is not less blinding]. Philippe Lacoue-Labarthe, "De l'éthique: à propos d'Antigone," in *Lacan avec les philosophes* (Paris: Albin Michel, 1991), 35.

126. Lacan in fact goes so far in *Seminar XI* as to theorize the very possibility of an "undead" object-libido, of a life without place in the symbolic order, through the notion of "the lamella," the domain of inhumanity. Jacques Lacan, *Seminar XI: The Four Fundamental Concepts of Psychoanalysis*, ed. Jacques-Alain Miller, trans. Alan Sheridan (New York: Norton, 1998), 197–98. For the French, see Jacques Lacan, *Le séminaire de Jacques Lacan, livre XI: Les quatres concepts fondamentaux de la psychanalyse* (Paris: Éditions du Seuil, 1973), 179–80. Of course, there are different versions of the end of the analysis, according to the different language games played by Lacan. However, the underlying condition of the different hypotheses seems to be the destitution of the subject and his or her realization of the possibility of symbolic death. For a comprehensive approach to the question of the end of analysis in Lacan's three fundamental articulations (the Crossing of Fantasy, the Identification with the Symptom, and the Destitution of the Subject) see Anne Durand, "The End of Analysis (I) and (II)," in *Reading Seminar XI*, ed. Richard Fedstein, Bruce Fink, and Maire Jaanus (Albany: SUNY, 1995), 243–59.

127. Lacan, *Book VII*, 304. "Au terme de l'analyse didactique, le sujet doit atteindre et connaître le champ et le niveau de l'expérience du désarroi absolu." Lacan, *Séminaire VII*, 351.

128. Žižek, *Looking*, 141.

129. As Žižek points out, popular wisdom about Lacan holds that in his theory only the subject is divided, when in fact Lacan's most radical contribution has been to recognize that the symbolic order itself is structured around a fundamental impossibility. Žižek, *Sublime*, 122.

130. See Bowie, *Lacan*, 172

131. Žižek has rightly recognized in Lacan's theory, "the most radical contemporary version of the Enlightenment." Žižek, *Sublime*, 7.

132. See note 123 above.

133. Consequently, what Richard Halpern has defined as the "mournful machinery" of Lacan's seminars, his insistent display of the entire array of psychoanalytic signifiers, cannot be considered, as Halpern claims, his expression of an unsatisfied impulse to mourn Freud. Richard Halpern, *Shakespeare Among the Moderns* (Ithaca: Cornell University Press, 1997), 267–68.

134. In this sense, Lacanian analysis would fully reflect the tendency of so-

ciety at large. LaCapra, for example, recognizes that it is not so easy to promote mourning rituals in a society which has become increasingly indifferent to their therapeutic effect: "The possibility of even limited working through may seem foreclosed in modern societies precisely because of the relative dearth of effective rites of passage, including rituals or, more generally, effective social processes such as mourning." LaCapra, "Reflections," 194.

135. Ibid., 194.

136. Žižek, *Sublime*, 2.

137. Jean-François Lyotard, "Introduction," in *The Postmodern Condition: A Report on Knowledge*, trans. Geoff Bennington and Brian Massumi (Minneapolis: Minnesota University Press, 1991), xxiv.

138. Ibid., 41, 81. The similarity between Lacan's and Lyotard's work ought to be limited to the question of postmodernity. Indeed, Lyotard's own rereading of Freudian theory in terms of a "libidinal economy" entails a criticism of Lacan's "dialectical unconscious" and his attempt to "put the mind where there are pulsions." Jean-François Lyotard, *Libidinal Economy*, trans. Iain Hamilton Grant (Bloomington: Indiana University Press, 1993), 127.

139. "The emphasis can be placed on the powerlessness of the faculty of presentation, on the nostalgia for presence felt by the human subject, on the obscure and futile will which inhabits him in spite of everything. The emphasis can be placed, rather, on the power of the faculty to conceive, on its 'inhumanity.'" Lyotard, *Postmodern Condition*, 79.

140. "La psychanalyse a un poids dans l'histoire. S'il y a des choses qui appartiennent à l'histoire, ce sont des choses de l'ordre de la psychanalyse." Jacques Lacan, "Conférences et entretiens dans les universités nord-américaines," in *Scilicet 6/7* (Paris: Éditions du Seuil, 1975), 20.

141. Weber, *Return*, 15.

142. According to Elisabeth Roudinesco, Lacan's attitude toward history was exceptionally ambivalent; on the one hand, he refused to historicize Freud, while on the other, he was eager to leave to posterity a conspicuous trace of his own teaching. Elisabeth Roudinesco, *Généalogies* (Paris: Fayard, 1994), 102.

143. Lacan, *Ornicar?*, 3:39.

144. Pierre Ginésy, "Trahir Lacan," in *Depuis Lacan*, ed. Patrick Guyomard and René Major (Paris: Aubier, 2000), 55–56.

145. In *Séminaire VII*, Lacan affirms a correspondence between the macrocosm of philosophy and the microcosm of psychoanalysis. In this sense, psychoanalysis for Lacan at least implicitly promises an epochal disclosure within the horizon of the history of Being: "It is because the movement of desire is in the process of crossing the line of a kind of unveiling that the advent of the Freudian notion of the death drive is meaningful for us." Lacan, *Book VII*, 236. ["C'est parce que le mouvement du désir est en train de passer la ligne d'une sorte de dévoilement, que l'avènement de la notion freudienne de la pulsion de mort a son sens pour nous." Lacan, *Séminaire VII*, 277.]

146. On the implications of Lacan's "logical" approach to history, see Stephen Melville's "Depuis Lacan," in *Lacan avec les philosophes* (Paris: Albin Michel, 1999), 394.

147. Bowie, *Lacan*, 161–62.

148. Lacan, *Ornicar?*, 2:32.

149. See note 118 above.

150. Felman, *Literature*, 50–51. "Nous nous émouvions à l'époque de savoir pourqoi, apres tout, on n'assassinait pas Hitler. . . . N'est-ce pas quelque chose qui nous permet de rejoindre ce dont nous sommes en train de parler?" Lacan, *Ornicar?*, 3:42.

151. Jacques Lacan, *Book XI*, 275. "Je tiens qu'aucun sens de l'histoire, fondé sur les prémisses hégéliano-marxistes, n'est capable de rendre compte de cette résurgence, par quoi il s'avère que l'offrande à des dieux obscurs d'un objet de sacrifice est quelque chose à quoi peu de sujets peuvent ne pas succomber, dans une monstrueuse capture." Lacan, *Séminaire XI*, 246–47.

152. Guyomard, *Désir*, 183.

153. It is interesting to remember that *Séminare XI* was published in 1964, one year after the publication of Arendt's account of the trial of Eichmann.

154. LaCapra, "Reflections," 178–204.

155. Ibid., 187. LaCapra's criticism, though quite lucid, applies to Lacan more than to Freud. We have seen that although for Freud the passage from nature to culture is indeed regulated through the Oedipus complex, which functions as the equivalent of a structural trauma, he insists on historicizing the notion by proposing a narrative of decadence in which absence becomes loss. By contrast, Lacan refuses to consider even the Holocaust as an historical event, preferring to treat it as a metaphor for the trauma that structures every psychic life.

156. Žižek, *Looking*, 145

157. Slavoj Žižek, *The Ticklish Subject* (London: Verso, 1999), 161.

158. Ibid., 308–9.

159. For further consideration of Lacan's view of the Holocaust, see Žižek, *Sublime*, 50.

160. LaCapra, "Reflections," 199.

161. Jacques Derrida, *Dissemination*, trans. Barbara Johnson (Chicago: University of Chicago Press, 1981), 110.

162. "Tout retour à Freud qui donne matière à un enseignement digne de ce nom, ne se produira que par la voie, par où la vérité la plus cachée se manifeste dans les révolutions de la culture. . . . Elle s'appelle: un style." Lacan, *Écrits*, F 458. Sheridan omits this essay, "La psychanalyse et son enseignement," from his selection; the English translation is mine.

163. Bowie, *Lacan*, 196.

164. Patrick Guyomard gives voice to this criticism in his examination of Lacan's treatment of *Antigone*. Guyomard, *La jouissance du tragique* (Paris: Aubier, 1992), 115.

165. Jacques Lacan, *Television*, trans. Denis Hollier, Rosalind Krauss, and Annette Michelson (New York: Norton, 1990), 41. For the French, see *Télévision* (Paris: Seuil, 1974), 65.

166. Lacan, *Television*, 22. The French reads as follows: "La tristesse, par exemple, on la qualifie de dépression, à lui donner l'âme pour support, ou la tension psychologique du philosophe Pierre Janet. Mais ce n'est pas un état d'âme, c'est simplement une faute morale, comme s'exprimait Dante, voire Spinoza: un péché, ce qui veut dire une lâcheté morale, qui ne situe en dernier ressort que de la pensée, soit du devoir de bien dire ou de s'y retrouver dans l'inconscient, dans la structure." *Télévision*, 39.

167. In *The Order of Things*, Foucault maintains that among what once were called the human sciences, psychoanalysis and ethnology offer distinct advantages inasmuch as both disciplines approach the unconscious precisely through a direct confrontation with it. However, he also contends that by addressing death, desire, and law, psychoanalysis can never establish an adequate corpus of knowledge, because precisely those three topics delimit the conditions of possibility of all human knowledge. Far from resembling a general theory of human consciousness, then, psychoanalysis would simply designate by the terms "death," "desire," and "law" figures of finitude that enact the dissolution of the human. Foucault's assessment of psychoanalysis fits Lacan's theory much better than it does Freud's because what is clearer in the former's work is the importance of finitude and the a priori status of the major analytic categories. See Michel Foucault, *The Order of Things*, ed. R. D. Laing (New York: Vintage, 1970), 373–87.

168. Guyomard, *Jouissance*, 115.

169. Kristeva, *Black Sun*, 258–59.

170. See, for instance, *La révolte intime*, as cited in note 80 above.

171. "L'univers médiatique de l'image sans dehors et sans questions est l'univers d'une conscience en train de s'abolir parce qu'elle a oblitéré son néant" [The mass-media universe of the image with no exterior and with no questions is the universe of a conscience on the way to abolishing itself, because it has obliterated its nothingness]. Kristeva, *La révolte intime*, 217.

172. Kristeva, *Sense*, 15.

173. Ibid., 50.

174. Ibid., 29.

175. Kristeva stresses the fact the one possible translation of the Freudian notion of the *Zeitlos* is indeed "temps perdu." Kristeva, *La révolte intime*, 63.

176. "Je repete que j'emploi le mot 'revolte' au sens etymologique et proustien du terme: retour du sens à la pulsion et vice versa, pour révéler la mémoire et recommencer le sujet." Julia Kristeva, *L'avenir d'une révolte* (Paris: Calman Levy, 1998), 56. My translation.

177. Ibid., 56.

178. Judith Butler has pointed out the political importance of melancholia in the context of the Freudian theory of the constitution of the ego and in its po-

sition with regard to the social domain: "Survival is a matter of avowing the trace of loss that inaugurates one's own emergence. To make of melancholia a simple refusal to grieve its losses conjures up a subject who might already be something without its losses. . . . From the start, this ego is other than itself; what melancholia shows is that only by absorbing the other as oneself does one become something at all." Butler, *Power*, 195–96. However, it should be noted that Butler is also wary of any implication that psychoanalysis might "sacralize" mourning by transforming it into a sort of interminable yet reassuring ritual. She sets out instead to contravene the idealization of mourning by reinterpreting grief as the cultural expression of aggression toward what is lost. *Power*, 162–63.

179. Judith Butler, "Quandaries," 46.

180. Derrida, *États d'âme*, 29.

181. Ibid., 69.

182. "Si la psychanalyse n'est pas morte, personne ne peut en douter, elle est mortelle, et elle le sait. . . . En tout cas, elle semble porter un deuil dont elle ne sait pas si c'est ou non le sien. Quelle est la doléance, autrement dit la douleur et le grief, la souffrance et le deuil, dont la psychanalyse, après un siècle d'existence, trouve à se plaindre? . . . De quoi les psychanlystes du monde entier acceptent-ils ou refusent-ils de faire leur deuil, d'avouer leur travail de deuil, leur *grief* mais aussi leur *grievance*, leur grief, leur revendication, leur réclamation, leur demande?" Derrida, *États d'âme*, 27. The translation is mine.

CHAPTER 2

1. Antoine Compagnon, note in Marcel Proust, *A la recherche du temps perdu*, gen. ed. Jean-Yves Tadié, 4 vols. (Paris: Gallimard, 1988) 3:1226–27. English citations in what follows are from *Remembrance of Things Past*, trans. C. K. Scott Moncrieff and Terence Kilmartin, 3 vols. (New York: Vintage Random, 1982). Throughout this book, I will refer to Proust's novel in English as *In Search of Lost Time*, which more accurately renders the French title and avoids Moncrieff's gesture of Shakespearean quotation in his rendering. For short quotations, I will cite the Moncrieff-Kilmartin translation by volume and page number in the text of my argument, followed in each case by the French in parentheses with volume and page reference to the corresponding passage in Tadié's French edition, which I will flag with the label JYT. For lengthier quotes, I will cite only the English in the text and place the French in endnotes.

2. Richard Rorty, *Contingency, Irony, and Solidarity* (New York: Cambridge University Press, 1989), 96–121.

3. Ibid, 97.

4. Ibid, 103.

5. Malcom Bowie, *Freud, Proust, and Lacan: Theory as Fiction* (Cambridge: Cambridge University Press, 1987), 96–97.

6. Gilles Deleuze, *Proust and Signs*, trans. Richard Howard (New York: Braziller, 1972), 51–65.

7. Ibid., 54.

8. Ibid., 135.

9. Anne Henry, *La tentation de Marcel Proust* (Paris: Presses Universitaires du France, 2000), 147.

10. Antoine Compagnon, *Five Paradoxes of Modernity*, trans. Franklin Philip (New York: Columbia University Press, 1994), 107.

11. Max Pensky, *Melancholy Dialectics* (Amherst: University of Massachusetts Press, 1993), 175.

12. We might also wish to recall the sense attributed to the term by Lévi-Strauss when he distinguishes between hot societies that have internalized historicity and "cold" ones that seem timeless. Claude Lévi-Strauss, *Structural Anthropology*, trans. Claire Jacobson and Brooke Grundfest Schoepf (New York: Basic Books, 1963).

13. Leo Bersani, *The Culture of Redemption* (Cambridge: Harvard University Press, 1990), 11.

14. On this score, my opinion differs sharply from Michael Sprinker's assessment of the place of history in Proust's opus. See Michael Sprinker, *History and Ideology in Proust* (Cambridge: Cambridge University Press, 1994).

15. The question of ideology has been revised by Žižek in terms of its imaginary function, of ideology's reflection of our phantasmatic relationship to power. Slavoj Žižek, *The Sublime Object of Ideology* (London: Verso, 1989).

16. Henry, *Tentation*, 73.

17. Roland Barthes, *Camera Lucida*, trans. Richard Howard (New York: Noonday Press, 1991), 98. I also evoke "the publicity of the private" in discussing the role of photography in the episode of Mlle. Vinteuil's mourning of her father; see note 38 below.

18. Film history is littered with attempted screenplays of the *Recherche* by writers as various as Harold Pinter in collaboration with Joseph Losey and Suso Cecchi D'Amico with Visconti, but a smaller number of realized productions (though the number is slowly increasing). Those who brought their adaptations to the screen often have delivered disappointing results, as was the case with Völker Schlöndorff's tepidly received *Swann in Love* (1983). The list of rationalizations for the generally unhappy fate of such productions includes the impossibility of filming the whole work, Proust's own dislike of motion pictures, and the inherent inadequacies of cinematic adaptations of literature. However, it seems to me that what is most feared in a possible adaptation is the unveiling of the very theatricality and artificiality of Proust's notion of involuntary memory.

19. Gilles Deleuze, *Cinema II: The Time-Image*, trans. Hugh Tomlinson and Robert Galeta (Minneapolis: University of Minnesota Press, 1989), 39.

20. For instance, see Pascal Ifry's "*Le temps retrouvé* de Raoul Ruiz ou le temps perdu au cinémam," *Bulletin Marcel Proust* 50 (2000): 66–179. See also Stéphane Bouquet's "Tous en scène," *Cahiers du cinéma* 535 (September 23, 1999).

21. Bouquet, "Tous en scène," 44. The translation is mine.

22. Ruiz's remarks are reported in Stéphane Bouquet, "Dans le laboratoire de *La recherche*: Entretien avec Raoul Ruiz," *Cahiers du Cinema* 535 (September 23, 1999): 48.

23. "Je restais, quitte à faire rire la foule innombrable des wattmen, à tituber comme j'avais fait tout à l'heure, un pied sur le pavé plus élevé, l'autre pied sur le pavé plus bas. Chaque fois que je refaisais rien que matériellement ce même pas, il me restait inutile; mais si je réussissais, oubliant la matinée Guermantes, à retrouver ce que j'avais senti en posant ainsi mes pieds, de nouveau la vision éblouissante et indistincte me frôlait comme si elle m'avait dit: 'Saisis-moi au passage si tu en as la force, et tâche à résoudre l'enigme de bonheur que je te propose'" (JYT 4:445–46).

24. Compagnon has acutely observed that postmodernism, or at least its critical version, is not so much incompatible with Baudelaire's modernity as with the avant-garde; see his *Five Paradoxes*, 131. He suggests furthermore that what postmodernism opposes is the deification of the new and of the future espoused by the avant-garde, not Baudelaire's more balanced view, which perceives modernity not only as a matter of transience, but also as one of tradition and timelessness.

25. If the first view of Proust as the quintessential poet of nostalgia has become the more popular one, giving rise to the odd phenomenon of Proustian kitsch, which manifests itself in the fascination with madeleines and childhood memorabilia such as magic lanterns, it is a picture that has prevailed in part because of the willingness of readers to ignore sections of the novel that are much more ambivalent about memory. One way of measuring how successful Proust's response to the modernist problematic of memory has been is to assess the reception of that paradigm in fully postmodern times. Not only has the French novelist become a philosophical hero for Richard Rorty, who equates the best sides of Derrida's writing (as distinct from Heidegger's) with what he defines as the Proustian ability to avoid nostalgia, but Proust has even been turned into the subject of a best-selling self-help book, Alain de Botton's *How Proust Can Change Your Life* (New York: Pantheon Books, 1997). Rorty, "From Ironist Theory to Private Allusions: Derrida," in *Contingency*, 136–37.

26. Antoine Compagnon, *Proust Between Two Centuries*, trans. Richard E. Goodkin (New York: Columbia University Press, 1992).

27. Compagnon, *Five Paradoxes*, 128.

28. There is, however, an inherent contradiction between the allegorical and auratic functions of the artwork. Whereas the first figure demands the formulation of a meaning all too voluntarily imposed, the auratic inheres in the "involuntary" production of sense. In the *Recherche*, the function of involuntary memory with its auratic halo is to veil ideologically what Benjamin defines as the "one most vital mystery of [the author's] class: the economic aspect." See "The Image of Proust," in *Illuminations*, ed. Hannah Arendt, trans. Harry Zohn (New York: Schocken, 1969), 210. One of the functions of the veil, as Benjamin points out is in *The Arcades Project*, is to preserve a certain distance, to keep intact a degree of "auratic

saturation": "Allegory recognizes many enigmas but it knows no mystery. An enigma is a fragment that together with another, matching fragment, makes up a whole. Mystery, on the other hand, was invoked from time immemorial in the image of the veil, which is an old accomplice of distance . . . epochs which tend toward allegorical expression will have experienced a crisis of aura." Benjamin, *The Arcades Project*, trans. Howard Eiland and Kevin McLaughlin (Cambridge: Harvard Belknap, 1999), 365.

29. Bersani, *Culture*, 11.

30. "Mais dès que je les [meubles] retrouvai dans la maison où ces femmes se servaient d'eux, toutes les vertus qu'on respirait dans la chambre de ma tante à Combray, m'apparurent, suppliciées par le contact cruel auquel je les avais livrées sans défense! J'aurait fait violer une morte que je n'aurais pas souffert davantage" (JYT 1:568).

31. Brassaï, *Proust sous l'emprise de la photographie* (Paris: Gallimard, 1997), 92.

32. According to Mieke Bal's analysis, the narrator's description of the scene establishes a close-up perspective achieved through a zoomlike emphasis that finally results in the effect of a well-framed photograph. Mieke Bal, *The Mottled Screen: Reading Proust Visually*, trans. Anna-Louise Milne (Stanford: Stanford University Press, 1997), 216.

33. "Quand je dis nous voir, je veux dire nous voir lire, c'est assommant, quelque chose insignifiante qu'on fasse, de penser que des yeux vous voient" (JYT 1:159).

34. "Quand même on nous verrait ce n'en est que meilleur" (JYT 1:159).

35. "Oh! ce portait de mon père qui nous regarde, je ne sais pas qui a pu le mettre là, j'ai pourtant dit vingt fois que ce n'était pas sa place" (JYT 1:160).

36. Barthes, *Camera*, 92.

37. Ibid., 98.

38. Proust allegorically demonstrates through the desecration of M. Vinteuil's picture the obsolescence of the cult value attached to the image. So directly exposed or unveiled by technology, the referent already seems on its way to desecration. Benjamin's discussion in "The Work of Art in the Age of Mechanical Reproduction" of the erosion of the cult value of the image in favor of its exhibition value is germane to this issue: "It is no accident that the portrait was the focal point of early photography. The cult of remembrance of loved ones, absent or dead, offers a last refuge for the cult value of the picture. For the last time the aura emanates from the early photographs in the fleeting expression of a human face." Benjamin, *Illuminations*, 226.

39. "Comme elle n'en aurait pas le culte, elle ne trouverait pas un plaisir sacrilège à les profaner" (JYT 1:162).

40. That the narrator identifies with Mlle. Vinteuil (and her friend) is never in doubt; he displays an extraordinary capacity for empathy and psychological divination when speaking of their characters. He informs us, for example, that Mlle. Vinteuil's friend was ultimately tormented by the thought of M. Vinteuil's

death and that Mlle. Vinteuil herself was not able to take pleasure in her sadistic acts: "This idea that it was merely a pretence of wickedness spoiled her pleasure. But if this idea recurred to her later on, since it had spoiled her pleasure so it must have diminished her grief. 'It wasn't me,' she must have told herself, 'I was out of mind. I can still pray for my forgiveness.' Only it is possible that this idea, which had certainly occurred to her in her pleasure, may not have occurred to her in her grief. I would have liked to be able to put it into her mind. I am sure that I would have done her good and that I could have reestablished between her and the memory of her father a more comforting relationship" (3:264). The narrator formulates an extremely complicated psychological hypothesis to explain Mlle. Vinteuil's behavior, pretending to know her motivations without the benefit of real social intimacy with her.

41. "Elle avait dégagé, de papiers plus illisibles que des papyrus ponctués d'écriture cunéiforme, la formule éternellement vraie, à jamais féconde, de cette joie inconnue, l'espérance mystique de l'ange écarlate du matin" (JYT 3:766–67).

42. Benjamin, "Moscow Diary," ed. Gary Smith, trans. Richard Sieburth, as excerpted in *October* 35 (winter 1985): 94–95.

43. In the essay "*A propos du style de Flaubert,*" Proust confides that his original impulse was to entitle the entire opus "*Les intermittences du coeur.*" See *Contre Sainte-Beuve* (Paris: Gallimard, 1971), 599.

44. Samuel Beckett, *Proust* (New York: Grove, 1957), 25.

45. Deleuze, *Proust and Signs*, 63. We should note that the dreamlike quality of Proust's narrative is strongly reminiscent of Nerval's *Sylvie* and *Aurelia*, which Proust comes close to admitting when he proposes rechristening Nerval's entire corpus with his own favored title, "Les intermittences du coeur." Proust, *Contre Sainte-Beuve*, 599.

46. See Compagnon's note in 3:1226–27 of the Gallimard edition under Tadié's general editorship.

47. Ibid., 1225.

48. "Ne voit-on pas, dans la chambre même où ils ont perdu un enfant, des époux bientôt de nouveau entrelacés donner un frère au petit mort?" (JYT 3:179).

49. "Je venais d'apercevoir dans ma mémoire, penché sur ma fatigue, le visage tendre, préoccupé et déçu de ma grand'mère, telle qu'elle avait été ce premier soir d'arrivée; le visage de ma grand'mère non pas de celle que je m'étais étonné et reproché de si peu regretter et qui n'avait d'elle que le nom, maid de ma grand'mère véritable dont, pour la première fois depuis les Champs-Élysées où elle avait eu son attaque, je retrouvais dans un souvenir involontaire et complet la réalité vivante" (JYT 3:153).

50. "Peu à peu voici que je me souvenais de toutes les occasions que j'avais saisies, en lui laissant voir, en lui exagérent au besoin mes souffrances, de lui faire une peine que je m'imaginais ensuite effacée par mes baisers" (JYT 3:155).

51. In this sense, Proust's idea of memory differs radically from Heidegger's celebration of *Andenken* [remembrance], a poetic way of mourning the past that

the philosopher discusses in relationship to Hölderlin's poetry. At issue in the eponymous poem by Hölderlin is the possibility of an intersection between personal mourning and mythical past. Heidegger was far more concerned with the mythical Greek past evoked by the German poet than with any sense of personal pathos. In Proust, there is no possibility of *Andenken* in the sense imagined by Heidegger. The way to memory in the *Recherche* is not only individualistic and idiosyncratic, but also indifferent to the collective dimension of history and myth.

52. "Tu peux être tranquille. Sa garde est une personne ordonnée. On envoie de temps en temps une toute petite somme pour qu'on puisse lui acheter le peu qui lui est nécessaire. Elle demande quelquefois ce que tu es devenu. On lui a même dit que tu allais faire un livre. Elle a paru contente. Elle a essuyé une larme" (JYT 3:158).

53. "Cette impression douleureuse et actuellement incompréhensible, je savais, non certes pas si j'en dégagerais un peu de vérité un jour, mais que si ce peu de vérité je pouvais jamais l'extraire, ce ne pourrait être que d'elle" (JYT 3:156).

54. Bersani, *Culture*, 10.

55. Anne Henry indeed has remarked that "Les intermittences du coeur" is perhaps the most significant chapter of the *Recherche*, precisely because there we find the narrator still deprived of the redemptive ideology of art that he will spell out only in *Le temps retrouvé*: "Aussi la véritable naissance du livre ne se trouve-t-elle point dans l'intermittence du passé mais dans les quelques pages qui évoquent le mystère de cette souffrance, qui tentent, à défaut de le pénétrer, de le circonscrire: angoisse enfantine devant la nuit que seul peut apaiser un geste rituel, déchirure de l'intermittence du coeur" [So the real birth of the text is not to be found in the intermittence of the past, but in the few pages that evoke the mystery of this suffering, trying, in the impossibility of penetrating it, to circumscribe it: infantile anguish in the face of the night that only a ritual gesture can assuage, laceration of the intermittency of the heart]. See Henry, *Tentation*, 224. The translation is mine.

56. "J'avais beau croire que la vérité suprême de la vie est dans l'art, j'avais beau, d'autre part, n'être pas plus capable de l'effort de souvenir qu'il m'eût fallu pour aimer encore Albertine que pour pleurer encore ma grand-mère, je me demandais si tout de même une oeuvre d'art dont elles ne seraient pas conscient serait pour elles, pour le destin de ces pauvres mortes, un accomplissement . . . un livre est un grand cimitière où sur la plupart des tombes on ne peut plus lire le noms effacés" (JYT 4:481–82).

57. On the similarity between involuntary memory and trauma, see Richard Terdiman, *Present Past* (Ithaca: Cornell University Press, 1993), 200.

58. "Tous les jours suivants ma mère descendit s'asseoir sur la plage, pour faire exactement ce que sa mère avait fait, et elle lisait ses deux livres préférés, les *Mémoires* de Mme de Beausergent et les *Lettres* de Mme de Sévigné" (JYT 3:167).

59. On this score, we should recall that Proust was a virtuoso of verbal mimicry and pastiche, of which we find hilarious evidence in the last section of the

novel, where he slyly burlesques the manner of the Goncourt Journal. Indeed, the novelist's penchant for pastiche runs deeper than the isolated diversion in the *Recherche* or the celebrated rewritings of "l'affaire Lemoine" in the manner of other authors such as Balzac and Flaubert. See Marcel Proust, "Affaire Lemoine," in *Pastiches et melanges* (Paris: Gallimard, 1992), 13–62. Whether he is assuming the sober tone of a moralist or the decadent pose of a libertine, Proust's writing most often inclines in the direction not of the elegiac, but of a beguilingly parodic irreverence.

60. "Dès que je la vis entrer, dans son manteau de crêpe, je m'aperçus—ce qui m'avait échappé à Paris—que ce n'était plus ma mère que j'avais sous les yeux mais ma grand-mère. Comme dans les familles royales et ducales, à la mort du chef le fils prend son titre et de duc d'Orléans, de prince de Tarente ou de prince des Laumes, devient roi de France, duc de la Trémoïlle, duc de Guermantes, ainsi souvent, par un avènement d'un autre ordre et de plus profonde origine, le mort saisit le vif qui devient son successeur ressemblant, le continuateur de sa vie interrompue" (JYT 3:166).

61. The episode of the grandmother's portrait, we should remember, revolves around the narrator's irritation at his grandmother's apparently narcissistic desire to be photographed by Saint-Loup and subsequent guilt on learning after her death that she wished to leave this image as a last memento to her grandson. That the drama of this episode, like that of Mlle. Vinteuil's spitting on her father's picture, derives from actual incidents in Proust's life is significant. At Evian, a few days before her death in 1905 as the result of an apoplectic attack, Mme. Proust asked Mme. Catusse to take her picture. In a letter addressed to Mme. Catusse several years later, Proust wrote: "Elle voulait et ne voulait pas être photographié, par desir de me laisser une dernière image et par peur qu'elle fût trop triste" [She did and didn't want to be photographed, out of desire to leave me a last image and fear that it would be too sad]. Proust, letter of November 1, 1910, *Correspondance*, ed. Philip Kolb, 21 vols. (Paris: Plon, 1970), 10:215. My translation.

62. "Elle ne me connaît plus . . . c'était une étrangère. Cette étrangère, j'étais en train d'en regarder la photographie par Saint-Loup" (JYT 3:172).

63. "Je tenais mes yeux fixés . . . sur la photographie que Saint-Loup avait faite, quand tout d'un coup, je pensai de nouveau: 'C'est grand-mère, je suis son petit-fils,' comme un amnésique retrouve son nom, comme un malade change de personnalité" (JYT 3:172).

64. "Quelques jours plus tard la photographie qu'avait faite Saint-Loup m'était douce à regarder. . . . Mais en regard de l'idée que je me faisais de son état si grave, si douloureux ce jour-là, la photographie, profitant encore des ruses qu'avait eues ma grandmère et qui réussissaient à me tromper même depuis qu'elles m'avaient été dévoilées, me la montrait si élégante, si insouciante, sous le chapeau qui cachait un peu de son visage, que je la voyais moins malheureuse et mieux portante que je ne l'avait imaginé. Et pourtant, ses joues ayant à son insu une expression à elles, quelque chose de plombé, de hagard, comme le regard d'une bête qui se sentirait déjà choisie et désignée, ma grand-mère avait un air de

condamnée à mort, un air involontairement sombre, inconsciemment tragique qui m'échappait mais qui empêchait maman de regarder jamais cette photographie qui lui parissait moins une photographie de sa mère que de la maladie de celle-ci, d'une insulte que cette maladie faisait au visage brutalement souffleté de grand-mère" (JYT 3:176).

65. Barthes, *Camera*, 56.

66. On other occasions, Proust's narrator voices distaste for the static nature of the medium, treating the photograph as the antithesis of the writer's aim to capture existence as transformation or process: "Our fault is to present things as they are, words as they are written, people in the inflexible notion that photography and psychology give us of them" (3:462; JYT 4:153). Photography, like psychology, strikes the narrator as repellent on account of its critical dullness, its lack of subtlety or sophistication. During the process of mourning, however, the photograph proves curiously comforting and reparative.

67. "En réalité il y a bien loin des chagrins véritables comme était celui de maman—qui vous ôtent littéralement la vie pour bien longtemps, quelquefois pour toujours, dès qu'on a perdu l'être qu'on aime—à ces autres chagrins, passagers malgré tout comme devait être le mien, qui s'en vont vite comme ils sont venus tard, qu'on ne connaît que longtemps après l'événement parce qu'on a eu besoin pour les ressentir de le 'comprendre'; chagrins comme tant de gens en éprouvent, et dont celui qui était actuellement ma torture ne se différenciait que par cette modalité du souvenir involontaire" (JYT 3:165).

68. Martha Nussbaum, *Love's Knowledge* (Oxford: Oxford University Press, 1990), 261–79.

69. It is useful to recall that in his early manifesto, *Contre Saint-Beuve*, Proust criticized Balzac for his rude depiction of cold-hearted climbers such as Vandenesse or Rastignac, whose romances (e.g., the love affair with Mme. de Mortsauf) are utterly forgotten and are reported with neither any hint of remorse nor any sense that remembrance might have marked the later lives of the seducers. Adopting Proust's own youthful vocabulary, we might recognize in the narrator of the *Recherche* a sort of "bleak adventurer" for whom, as for Balzac's protagonists, romantic sentiment and even the anguish of loss are reduced finally to no more than a ghostly "play of refracted light." The difficulty with such a line of reasoning is that whereas the callousness of Balzac's heroes finds a ready motivation in greed and social ambition, it is harder to justify Proust's narrator's total forgetfulness within a novel ostensibly devoted to the problematics of memory. Proust, *Contre Sainte-Beuve*, trans. Sylvia Townsend Warner (New York: Carroll and Graf, 1984), 160.

70. "C'est le malheur des êtres de n'être pour nous que des planches de collections fort usable dans notre pensée. Justement à cause de cela on fonde sur eux des projets qui ont l'ardeur de la pensée; mais la pensée se fatigue, le souvenir se détruit: le jour viendrait où je donnerait volentiers à la première venue la chambre d'Albertine, comme j'avais sans aucun chagrin donné à Albertine la bille d'agate ou d'autres présents de Gilberte" (JYT 4:138).

71. "Si ces curiosités étaient si vivaces, c'est que l'être ne meurt pas tout de suite pour nous, il reste baigné d'une espèce d'aura de vie qui n'a rien d'une immortalité véritable mais qui fait qu'il continue à occuper nos pensées de la même manière que quand il vivait" (JYT 4:92).

72. "Sans doute ce moi gardait encore quelque contact avec l'ancien comme un ami, indifférent à un deuil, en parle pourtant aux personnes présentes avec la tristesse convenable" (JYT 4:175).

73. The point is further dramatized in the *La prisonnière* during the famous episode in which the narrator, confronted by the sight of his own article in *The Figaro*, for several long minutes fails to recognize it as his own (3:579–80; JYT 4:148).

74. Henry, *Tentation*, 81.

75. Charles Taylor, *Sources of the Self* (Cambridge: Harvard University Press, 1989), 456.

76. "Au bout du même temps où un malade atteint de cancer sera mort, il est bien rare qu'un veuf, un père inconsolable ne soient pas guéris" (JYT 4:223).

77. "Albertine n'avait été pour moi qu'un faisceau de pensées, elle avait survécu à sa mort materielle tant que ces pensée vivaient en moi; en revanche maintenant que ces pensées étaient mortes, Albertine ne ressuscitait nullement pour moi avec son corps" (JYT 4:220).

78. If Benjamin's work is relevant to postmodernity, however, it is so less because he was interested in popular culture, than because he consistently puts forward a form of criticism in which social and political considerations inform and shape his aesthetic judgments. For an acute assessment of Benjamin's postmodernity, see Scott Lash, *Sociology of Postmodernism* (New York: Routledge, 1990), 153–71.

79. On Benjamin's original interpretation of the work of art, see Gianni Vattimo, *The Transparent Society*, trans. David Webb (Baltimore: Johns Hopkins University Press, 1992), 57–58.

80. Benjamin, *Illuminations*, 156.

81. Ibid., 194.

82. Ibid., 188.

83. Ibid., 192–94. Rainer Rochlitz argues that Benjamin's "sacrifice of the aura," in Baudelaire represents the prelude to Adorno's aesthetics of negativity as set forth in his *Aesthetic Theory*. Rochlitz, *The Disenchantment of Art*, trans. Jane Marie Todd (New York: Guilford Press, 1996), 165–66.

84. Theodor Adorno, *Aesthetic Theory*, trans. Robert Hullot-Kentor (Minneapolis: University of Minnesota Press, 1997), 79.

85. Vattimo, *Transparent Society*, 57–58.

86. "Mon cher, vous connaissez ma terreur des chevaux et des voitures. Tout à l'heure, comme je traversais le boulevard, en grande hâte, et que je sautillais dans la boue, à travers ce chaos mouvant où la mort arrive au galop de tous les côtés à la fois, mon auréole, dans un mouvement brusque, à glissé de ma tête dans la fange du macadam. Je n'ai pas eu le courage de la ramasser. J'ai jugé moins désagréable de perdre mes insignes que de me faire rompre les os. Et puis, me suis-

je dit, à quelque chose malheur est bon. Je puis maintenant me promener incognito, faire des actions basses, et me livrer à la crapule, comme les simples mortels." Charles Baudelaire, *"Perte d'auréole,"* in *Le spleen de Paris*, ed. David Scott and Barbara Wright (Paris: Flammarion, 1987), 172.

87. Indeed, the very figure of tripping over cobblestones in the street as a metaphor for the accidental progress of poetic writing may be traced directly back to Baudelaire's "Le soleil," where the poet depicts himself "trébuchant sur le mots comme sur les pavés" [stumbling over words like cobblestones]. Charles Baudelaire, *Les Fleurs du Mal*, trans. Richard Howard (Boston: David R. Godine, 1983), 88, 266.

88. "J'étais entré dans la cour de l'hôtel de Guermantes, et dans ma distraction je n'avais pas vu une voiture qui s'avançait; au cri du wattman je n'eus que le temps de me ranger vivement de côté, et je reculai assez pour buter malgré moi contre les pavés assez mal équarris derrière lesquels était une remise" (JYT 4:445). The genealogy of the image may be traced back to Rousseau. See *Les reveries du promeneur solitaire*, ed. Henry Roddier (Paris: Garnier, 1960), 16.

89. Benjamin, *Illuminations*, 192–94.

90. Ibid., 194.

91. Benjamin, *Arcades*, 335.

92. Benjamin, *Illuminations*, 188.

93. See Walter Benjamin and Franz Hessel, trans., *Herzog in von Guermantes* (Munich: Piper, 1930).

94. "Oui, si le souvenir, grâce à l'oubli, n'a pu contracter aucun lien, jeter aucan chaînon entre lui et la minute présente, s'il est resté à sa place, à sa date, s'il a gardé ses distances, son isolement dans le creux d'une vallée, ou à la pointe d'un sommet, il nous fait tout à coup respirer un air nouveau, précisément parce que c'est un air qu'on a respiré autrefois, cet air plus pur que les poètes ont vainement essayé de faire régner dans le Paradis et qui ne pourrait donner cette sensation profonde de renouvellement que s'il avait été respiré déjà, car les vrais paradis sont les paradis qu'on a perdu" (JYT 4:449).

95. "The deterioration of experience manifests itself in Proust in the complete realization of his ultimate intention. There is nothing more ingenious or more loyal than the way in which he nonchalantly and constantly strives to tell the reader: Redemption is my private show." Benjamin, *Illuminations*, 200 n. 15.

96. Ibid., 222–23. As I have noted in the text, the cited English translation unfortunately fails to capture Benjamin's Proustian emphasis on breathing [*atmen*] in the final clause: "Es empfiehlt sich, den oben für geschichtliche Gegenstände vorgeschlagenen Begriff der Aura an dem Begriff einer Aura von natürlichen Gegenständen zu illustrieren. Diese letztere definieren wir als einmalige Erscheinung einer Ferne, so nah sie sein mag. An einem Sommernachmittag ruhend einem Gebirgszug am Horizont oder einem Zweig folgen, der seinen Schatten auf den Ruhenden wirft—das heißt die Aura dieser Berge, dieses Zweiges atmen." *Gesammelte Schriften*, 1.2:479.

97. We should recall as well that in "Little History of Photography" (1931), Benjamin defines aura using precisely the same formulation: "What is aura, actually? A strange weave of space and time: the unique appearance or semblance of distance, no matter how close it might be. While at rest on a summer's noon, to trace a range of mountains on the horizon, or a branch that throws its shadow on the observer, until the moment or the hour become part of their appearance—this is what it means to breath the aura of those mountains, that branch." Benjamin, "Little History of Photography," in *Selected Writings Volume 2: 1927–1934*, ed. Michael W. Jennings, Howard Eiland, and Gary Smith, trans. Rodney Livingston et al. (Cambridge: Harvard Belknap, 1999), 518–19. A comment by Adorno puts in perspective the extent to which Benjamin felt himself to be under Proust's spell: "Walter Benjamin once told me that he did not want to read one more word of Proust that he had to translate, because otherwise he would fall into addictive dependency that would impede him in his own production, which was certainly original enough." Adorno, *Notes to Literature*, vol. 2, trans. Sherry Weber Nicholsen (New York: Columbia University Press, 1992), 313.

98. Robert Kahn, *Images-Passages: Marcel Proust et Walter Benjamin* (Paris: Éditions Kimé, 1998), 96. The translation is mine.

99. Benjamin, *Gesammelte Schriften*, ed. Rolf Tiedemann and Hermann Schweppenhäuser (Frankfurt am Main: Suhrkamp, 1989), 7.2:679.

100. Benjamin, *Arcades*, 560–61.

101. "Car l'analyse de Proust et la sienne se rejoignent en ce point fondamental: ces nouvelles techniques font apparaître l'aura au moment même où elles la condamnent." Kahn, *Images-Passages*, 97. (The English rendering is my work.)

102. Benjamin recognizes in Proust's work a truth that the German critic is not able to articulate in his own—that is to say, as Weber incisively has pointed out, that aura may be renewed precisely by those media supposedly responsible for its "decline." See Samuel Weber, "Mass Mediauras; or Art, Aura and Media in the Work of Walter Benjamin," in *Walter Benjamin: Theoretical Questions*, ed. David S. Ferris (Stanford: Stanford University Press, 1996), 27–49.

103. Adorno, letter of March 18, 1936, *Walter Benjamin, Theodor Adorno: The Complete Correspondence 1928–1940*, ed. Henry Lonitz, trans. Nicholas Walker (Cambridge: Harvard, 1999), 127–34.

104. Bejamin, *Illuminations*, 157.

105. Ibid., 157.

106. In "Some Motifs," Benjamin establishes an opposition between a conservative memory and a destructive souvenir in keeping with Reik's development of a Freudian institution in "Der Überraschte Psychologe" (1935). *Illuminations*, 160.

107. Benjamin's decision to resituate involuntary memory and trauma within the context of a history of civilization is hardly orthodox from a psychoanalytic perspective because it entails his rereading the notions of involuntary and voluntary memory in terms of *Erfahrung* and *Erlebnis* and then associating the former with trauma. As Leo Bersani observes, however, when Freud discusses the in-

compatibility of consciousness and memory traces, he is strictly referring to the mental apparatus and not to a vague notion of experience. Bersani, *Culture*, 51.

108. Benjamin, *Illuminations*, 160–61.

109. Benjamin develops the notion of a "dialectic at a standstill" in *Arcades*: "Dialectic at a Standstill—this is the quintessence of the method" (section P, 4), 865. The concept, which according to Tiedemann is doomed to remain "inconsistent" and "iridescent," was proposed by Benjamin to capture the configuration of the Now and the Then. See Rolf Tiedemann, "Dialectic at a Standstill," in Benjamin, *Arcades*, 942. However, it is possible to imagine tracing the genealogy of the German critic's concept back to Proust. It would in fact be derived from the image of the narrator at the most crucial moment of the *Recherche*, frozen at a "standstill" on the uneven pavement, suspended between the present and the past (3:899; JYT 4:445).

110. In "Paris, Capital of the Nineteenth Century," Benjamin had defined as "wishful fantasies" the cultural images in which the new is intermingled with the old in order to transfigure the contradictions of the social system of production. Benjamin, *Reflections*, ed. Peter Demetz (New York: Schocken Boks, 1978), 148.

111. Benjamin, *Illuminations*, 188.

112. The German reads as follows: "'Einige, die Geheimnisse lieben, schmeichen sich, daß den Dingen etwas von den Blicken bleibt, welche jemals auf ihnen ruhten.' (Doch wohl das Vermögen, sie zu erwidern.) 'Sie sind der Meinung, daß Monumente und Bilder nur unter dem zarten Schleier sich darstellen, den Liebe und Andacht so vieler Bewunderer im Laufe der Jahrhunderte um sie gewoben haben. Diese Chimäre,' so schließt Proust ausweichend, 'würde Wahrheit werden, wenn sie sie auf die einzige Realität beziehen würden, welche für das Individuum vorhanden ist, nämlich auf dessen eigene Gefühlswelt.'" *Gesammelte Schriften*, 1.2:647. The Moncrieff-Kilmartin translation of the same passage misses the contrafactual conditionality of the original's last sentence, which Benjamin does a better job of capturing: "Certain people, whose minds are prone to mystery, like to believe that objects retain something of the eyes which have looked at them, that old buildings and pictures appear to us not as they originally were but beneath a perceptible veil woven for them over centuries by the love and contemplation of millions of admirers. This fantasy, if you transpose it into the domain of what is for each one of us the sole reality, the domain of his own sensibility, becomes the truth" [Certains esprits qui aiment le mystère veulent croire que les objets conservent quelque chose des yeux qui les regardèrent, que les monuments et les tableaux ne nous apparaissent que sous le voile sensible que leur ont tissé l'amour et la contemplation d tant d'adorateurs, pendant des siécles. Cette chimère deviendrait vraie s'ils la transposaient dans le domaine de la seule réalité pour chacun, dans le domaine de sa propre sensibilité] (3:920; JYT 4:463).

113. Benjamin, *Illuminations*, 188; *Gesammelte Schriften*, 1.2:647.

114. Benjamin, *Illuminations*, 157.

115. "Une oeuvre où il y a des théories est comme un objet sur lequel on laisse la marque de prix" (JYT 4:461).

116. Adorno, in a letter dated March 18, 1936, exposes the relation between the two procedures when he expresses disapproval of the idea of liquidation as a *concept marchand* or, to use his own term, an "inverse taboo." Benjamin-Adorno, *Correspondence*, 130.

117. Benjamin, *Illuminations*, 188.

118. Weber discusses Benjamin's first simplistic assessment of the auratic in "The Work of Art" and shows how Benjamin's definition in "Some Motifs" of aura as the projection of the reciprocated glance implies the idea that technological media might actually be responsible for a reproduction of the auratic. Weber, "Mass Mediauras," 27–49.

119. Benjamin, *Illuminations*, 159.

120. Ibid., 200.

121. Ibid., 159.

122. Ibid., 159.

123. Ibid., 194.

124. Benjamin, *Arcades*, 329–31.

125. Through the notion of *correspondance*, Baudelaire instead had managed to find a *trait-d'union* between the individual subject and the collective, between personal reminiscence and "prehistorical data" that by Proust's time has been irretrievably lost. Moreover, as Benjamin puts it, "The important thing is that *correspondances* record a concept of experience which includes ritual elements. . . . The *correspondances* are the data of remembrance—not historical data but data of prehistory. What makes festive days great and significant is the encounter with an earlier life." *Illuminations*, 181–82.

126. Benjamin makes this point with reference to Baudelaire's lines from "Le goût de néant" [Craving for Oblivion]: "Et le Temps m'engloutit minute par minute/Comme la neige immense un corps pris de roideur" [Moment by moment, Time envelops me/Like a stiffening body buried in snow]. Baudelaire, *Fleurs*, 78, 255. The German critic comments, "In the spleen, time becomes palpable; the minutes cover a man like snowflakes. This time is outside history, as is that of *mémoire involontaire*. But in the spleen the perception of time is supernaturally keen; every second finds consciousness ready to intercept its shock." Benjamin, *Illuminations*, 184.

127. "Chez Baudelaire enfin, ces réminiscences, plus nombreuses encore, sont évidemment moins fortuites et par conséquent, à mon avis, décisives. C'est le poéte lui-même qui, avec plus de choix et de paresse, recherche volontairement, dans l'odeur d'une femme par exemple, de sa chevelure et de son sein, les analogies inspiratrices" (JYT 4:498).

128. Benjamin, *Illuminations*, 183.

129. Benjamin's nonchalance in reading the passage is all the more puzzling if we recall that in the essay "The Paris of the Second Empire in Baudelaire" (1938), he even comes to describe Baudelaire's conflation of past and present as a "great achievement of the will." Walter Benjamin, "The Paris of the Second Empire in

Baudelaire," in *Charles Baudelaire: A Lyric Poet in the Era of High Capitalism,* trans. Harry Zohn (London: NLB, 1973), 94.

130. Gilles Deleuze, "Antilogos, or the Literary Machine," in *Proust and Signs,* 101. (This is a chapter added to the English edition.)

131. Ibid., 102.

132. Benjamin, *Illuminations,* 181.

133. See Benjamin, *Arcades* (J31a, 3), 285. The quotation reappears in a more extended form in (J39, 3), 299. The translation differs in "The Paris of the Second Empire in Baudelaire": "Regarding the attire, the covering of the modern hero, . . . does it not have a beauty and charm of its own? . . . Is this not an attire that is needed by our epoch, suffering, and dressed up to its thin black narrow shoulders in the symbol of constant mourning? The black suit and the frock coat not only have their political beauty as an expression of general equality, but also their poetic beauty as an expression of the public mentality—an immense cortège of undertakers, political undertakers, amorous undertakers, bourgeois undertakers. We all observe some kind of funeral." As cited in Benjamin, *Baudelaire,* 77.

134. Benjamin, *Arcades* (J52, 1), 322.

135. Deleuze rightly observes that references to the law in Proust have nothing to do with guilt or moral problems, but with a world devoid of logos, in which emerges the need to control parts without a whole. Deleuze, *Proust and Signs,* 126.

136. Benjamin compares Baudelaire favorably to Bergson when it comes to his ability to retain genuine historical experience, because the former, unlike the latter, does not suppress the prospect of death. *Illuminations,* 185.

137. Benjamin, "Addendum" to *Baudelaire,* 106. Cf. Adorno, letter of March 18, 1936, where he mentions his hope that Benjamin will write a study of Mallarmé in which he might confute his own rigid interpretations of the autonomous work of art as set forth in the 1935 essay. Benjamin-Adorno, *Correspondence,* 128.

138. Benjamin, *Illuminations,* 210.

139. Marcel Proust, "Concerning Baudelaire," in *Against Sainte-Beuve and Other Essays,* trans. John Sturrock (London: Penguin, 1988), 290. The essay originally appeared in the form of a letter to the editor, Jacques Rivière, in the *Nouvelle Revue Française* in June 1921.

140. Ibid., 296.

141. Žižek, *Sublime,* 45. Benjamin, *Illuminations,* 157.

142. Fredric Jameson is one of the few critics to have emphasized Proust's objectivation of time and memory. "The eclipse of inner time (and its organ, the 'intimate' time sense)," writes Jameson, "means that we read our subjectivity off the things outside: Proust's old hotel rooms, like old retainers, respectfully reminded him every morning how old he was, and whether he was on vacation or 'at home,' and where—that is to say they told him his name and issued him an identity, like a visiting card on a silver salver. . . . Subjectivity is an objective matter, and it is enough to change the scenery and the setting, refurnish the rooms, or de-

stroy them in a aerial bombardment for a new subject, a new identity, miraculously to appear on the ruins of the old." Jameson, *The Cultural Turn* (London: Verso, 1998), 52.

143. Proust vehemently criticizes the idea that his conception of memory had been influenced by Bergson: "Mon oeuvre est dominée par la distinction entre la mémoire involontaire et la mémoire volontaire, distinction qui non seulement ne figure pas dans la philosophie de M. Bergson, mais est même contredite par elle." Proust, *Contre Sainte-Beuve*, 615.

144. Jameson recognizes he is establishing the ideological contours of the Proustian operation by contrasting Proust to Baudelaire. Jameson contends that Proust only superficially can seem more elegiac than the French poet because if Baudelaire finds a true objective correlative for his longings, namely Paris, Proust subjectivizes his experiences and pretends to mourn the self and the past rather than the houses and buildings of the city. Jameson does add in parentheses that Proust's language "knows better than its aesthetic ideology, by respecting the integrity of certain spaces." Jameson, *Cultural Turn*, 54.

145. Jameson, *The Geopolitical Aesthetic* (Bloomington: Indiana University Press, 1995), 163.

146. Ibid, 164.

CHAPTER 3

1. In his suspension between past and future, Pasolini may be thought to embody Dante's description in the tenth canto of *Inferno* of heretics as being able to see events past and to come while remaining utterly blind to the realities of the present.

2. Pier Paolo Pasolini, *Scritti Corsari* (Milan: Garzanti, 1990), 50.

3. Pier Paolo Pasolini, "Poeta delle Ceneri," *Nuovi Argomenti* 67–68 (July–December 1980): 3–29.

4. Pasolini describes the birth of his cinematic vocation in conjunction with his attendance of Roberto Longhi's art history course in Bologna: "What was Roberto Longhi doing in that small and isolated classroom on Zamboni street? Art history? His course was a memorable one on 'Facts About Masolino and Masaccio.' . . . On the screen were projected some pictures. The complete image or detailed fragments of the works executed at the same time and at the same place by Masolino and Masaccio. Cinema was 'acting' there even as a mere projections of photographs." Pier Paolo Pasolini, "Roberto Longhi, da Cimabue a Morandi," in *Descrizione di descrizioni* (Turin: Einaudi, 1979), 251–52.

5. The word *contamination* is used by Pasolini himself: "Il segno sotto cui lavoro è sempre la contaminazione" [the sign under which I always work is that of contamination]. "Una visione del mondo epico-religioso, colloquio con Pasolini," *Bianco e Nero* 25, no. 6 (June 1964): 32. Giuseppe Zigaina has insisted on the def-

inition of "total contamination," arguing that the contamination in the artist's work is not only literary but extends to the poet's life and even his "spectacular" death. As is well known, Pasolini was murdered in 1975 by a boy he had picked up, a sort of artistic mise-en-scène of the transition from life to death. Giuseppe Zigaina, *Hostia* (Venice: Marsilio, 1995), 18 ff.

6. Pasolini considered Saint Paul to be the great exemplar of the capacity to contaminate the *trasumanar* and *organizzar*, a conceptual oxymoron that provides the title for a late collection of poems. Pier Paolo Pasolini, *Il sogno del centauro*, ed. Jacques Duflot (Rome: Editori Riuniti, 1983), 1970.

7. Although David Ward agrees with me in recognizing in Pasolini's work an anticipation of postmodernism, he feels Pasolini exposes not only the strengths but also the limits of the postmodern. David Ward, *A Poetics of Resistance: Narrative and the Writings of Pier Paolo Pasolini* (London: Associated University Presses, 1995), 203.

8. Carla Benedetti, *Pasolini contro Calvino: per una letteratura impura* (Turin: Bollati Boringheri, 1998), 154, 180.

9. Alberto Marchesini, *Citazioni pittoriche nel cinema di Pasolini: de Accattone al Decamerone* (Florence: Nuova Italia, 1994), 9.

10. Pier Paolo Pasolini, "Terza Intervista," in *Con Pier Paolo Pasolini* (Rome: Bulzoni, 1977), 52.

11. Jacques Derrida, *Specters of Marx: The State of Debt, the Work of Mourning, and the New International*, trans. Peggy Kamuf (New York: Routledge, 1994).

12. Ibid., 14.

13. Ibid., 176.

14. Judith Butler, *The Psychic Life of Power* (Stanford: Stanford University Press, 1997), 132.

15. Andrea Zanzotto, "Pedagogy," in *The Poetic of Heresy*, ed. Beverly Allen (Saratoga: Anna Libri, 1984), 41.

16. Pier Paolo Pasolini, "L'Articolo delle Lucciole," in *Scritti Corsari*, 129. My translation.

17. Pier Paolo Pasolini, *Poesie a Casarsa*, as reprinted in *Bestemmia*, 2 vols., ed. Graziella Chiarcossi and Walter Siti (Milan: Garzanti, 1993), 2:1191–221.

18. The great Italian critic Gianfranco Contini immediately recognized Pasolini's achievement in *Poesie a Casarsa*, praising the author on philological and stylistic grounds for his originality in achieving a deliberate plurilinguism. Gianfranco Contini, *Letteratura dell'Italia unita* (Florence: Sansoni, 1972), 1025–26.

19. Pier Paolo Pasolini, *Passione e ideologia* (Milan: Garzanti, 1994), 472.

20. Massimo Cacciari, "Pasolini provenzale?", *Micromega* 4 (October–November 1995): 197.

21. In fact, as Keala Jane Jewell observes, "Pasolini revived sepulchral verse and lament to recast the funeral elegy into a discourse on political sorrow and hence to banish a purified, monumentalized elegy." Keala Jane Jewell, *The Poieisis of History: Experimenting with Genre in Postwar Italy* (Ithaca: Cornell University Press, 1992), 5.

22. For an acute reading of Pasolini's poetry and its historical meaning, see Jewell, *Poieisis.*

23. Eugenio Montale, *Collected Poems,* ed. and trans. Jonathan Galassi (New York: Farrar, Strauss, Giroux, 1998), 110, 222.

24. For Pasolini's production in Friulan dialect, see *La meglio gioventù* (1941–53), the volume that *Poesie a Casarsa* (1941–43) belongs to, in *Bestemmia,* 1:13–141.

25. See the prefix to Pascoli's *Poemetti,* where he states: "The memory is poetry and poetry does not exist without memory." Giovanni Pascoli, *Poesie* (Milan: Garzanti, 1981), 187.

26. Rinaldo Rinaldi, *Pier Paolo Pasolini* (Milan: Mursia, 1982), 24.

27. See note 19 above.

28. Pasolini, "Il canto popolare," in *Bestemmia,* 1:188. The translation is mine.

29. Ibid., 1:185.

30. For the English rendering of "The Tears of the Excavator" and other poems, as availability permits, I will quote the selection of translations entitled *Pier Paolo Pasolini: Poems,* ed. and trans. Norman MacFee and Luciano Martinengo (New York: Noonday Press, 1996), 53. For the Italian, see *Bestemmia,* 1:263. Hereafter, I will refer to these two editions for all citations of Pasolini's poetry, giving page numbers in the body of the chapter and distinguishing between the two editions by the abbreviations P and B. (For particularly long quotations, I will place the Italian in an endnote.) The only exception to this rule will be the poem "Poeta delle Ceneri," which has been published only in Italian in the journal *Nuovi Argumenti* (see note 3 above).

31. Philippe Sollers, "Pasolini, Sade, Saint Matthieu," in *Pasolini,* ed. Maria Antonietta Macciocchi (Paris: Grasset, 1992), 110.

32. On the ambiguities and contradictions in Pasolini's interpretation of the figure and work of Gramsci, see Zygmunt Baranski, "Pier Paolo Pasolini: Culture, Croce, Gramsci," in *Culture and Conflict in Postwar Italy* (New York: St. Martin's Press, 1990), 139–59.

33. Gramsci's *Prison Notebooks* were published by the Turin publisher Einaudi in five volumes of selections between 1948 and 1951. The sequence of publication was as follows: *Il materialismo storico e la filosofia di Benedetto Croce* (1948), *Gli intelletuali e l'organizzazione della cultura* (1949), *Il Risorgimento* (1949), *Note sul Machiavelli, sulla politica e sulla Stato moderno* (1949), and *Passatto e presente* (1951).

34. Benedetti, *Pasolini contro Calvino,* 150.

35. Jewell, *Poiesis,* 36.

36. "Ma come io possiedo la storia,/essa mi possiede; ne sono illuminato:/ ma a che serve la luce?" (B 1:228–29).

37. "Lì tu stai, bandito e con dura eleganza/non cattolica, elencato tra estranei/morti: Le ceneri di Gramsci" (B 1:225–26).

38. Derrida, *Specters,* 3–7.

39. "Lo scandalo del contraddirmi dell'essere/con te e contro di te; con te nel cuore,/in luce, contro di te nelle buie viscere" (B 1:227).

40. "Eppure senza il tuo rigore, sussisto/perché non scelgo. Vivo nel non volere/del tramontato dopoguerra: amando/il mondo che odio—nella sua miseria/sprezzante e perso—per un oscuro scandalo/della coscienza" (B 1:227).

41. "E se mi accade/di amare il mondo non è che per violento/e ingenuo amore sensuale così come, confuso adolescente, un tempo/l'odiai, se in esso mi feriva il male/borghese di me borghese" (B 1:227).

42. The cult of the dead is one of the most important themes in modernist Italian poetry and is celebrated in the verses of numerous authors from Pascoli to Montale, ultimately facilitating an implicit cultural identification of poetry with individual memory. Nonetheless, we can ascribe an "involuntary" political meaning to the cult of the dead in Italian poetry, if we bear in mind Pier Vincenzo Mengaldo's proposition that the sepulchral always ought to be read in opposition to capitalism insofar as the cult of the dead upholds the preservation and introjection of the practices of an older, eradicated civility. See Mengaldo's "Introduzione," in *Poeti Italiani del Novecento* (Milan: Mondadori, 1978), xxi.

43. Jahan Ramazani, *Poetry of Mourning* (Chicago: University of Chicago Press, 1994), 8.

44. See Ugo Foscolo, "Sepolcri," in *Sepolcri, odi, sonetti*, ed. Donatella Martinelli (Milan: Mondadori, 1987).

45. The notorious pronouncement, "To write poetry after Auschwitz is barbaric," first appears in 1949 in "Kulturkritik und Gesellschaft," which is then reprinted in 1951 in *Prismen*. See Theodor Adorno, *Prisms*, trans. Samuel and Sherry Weber (Cambridge: MIT Press, 1981), 34.

46. Taking as his point of departure Celan's poetry, Derrida (along with Levinas) has elaborated a "philosophy of traces" that likens memory to a process of incineration, the outcome of which are the spent signifier of the ash and an elemental, ephemeral reminder, *"une restance du reste,"* that cannot simply be conflated with the sign. Jacques Derrida, *Schibboleth* (Paris: Galilée, 1986), 62–77; and *Cinders*, trans. Ned Lukacher (Lincoln: University of Nebraska Press, 1991).

47. Pasolini, "Poeta delle ceneri," 3–29. Unfortunately, this poem has been anthologized in neither the standard Italian edition of Pasolini's poetry nor in the MacAfee selection of English translations. See notes 3 and 30 above.

48. The translation is my own.

49. W. H. Auden, "In Memory of W. B. Yeats," in *Selected Poems* (New York: Vintage, 1989), 82.

50. Ibid., 83.

51. Rinaldi, *Pasolini*, 94.

52. Derrida, *Specters*, 28.

53. Benedetti, *Pasolini contro Calvino*, 168–69.

54. Pasolini's work as a screenwriter started with Soldati's *La donni del fiume* (1955), Fellini's *Le notti di Cabiria* (1957), Bolognini's *La notte brava* (1959).

55. In a 1970 interview with Duflot, Pasolini downplayed the drama of his move from literature to cinema, insisting it was merely a question of changing

techniques. Jean Duflot, *Entretiens avec Pier Paolo Pasolini* (Paris: Belfond, 1970), 16. In "Poeta delle Ceneri," however, he articulates complex political and aesthetical reasons behind his move. In the eyes of the conservative, tradition-bound, and classicist Italian literary establishment, however, to become a filmmaker at the time certainly represented a disreputable decision, one that undermined Pasolini's credibility and standing as a potential literary "mandarin." Viano reminds us how Calvino, Siciliano, and Moravia were all in various ways contemptuous of Pasolini's move to film. Maurizio Viano, *A Certain Realism* (Berkeley: University of California Press, 1993), 49.

56. John Orr, *Contemporary Cinema* (Edinburgh: Edinburgh University Press, 1988), 162. In another study, Orr categorizes Pasolini's cinema as neomodern, even as he admits that Pasolini's films seem to contradict most of the features supposedly characteristic of neomodern cinema. According to Orr, in fact, the motion picture by definition can never be categorized as "postmodern," because pastiche, self-conscious narrative, ludic or game principles, and polyvalence are traits that belong to the film medium since the innovation of cinematic language and technique that takes place between 1958 and 1978. Orr defines this period as neomodern in order to stress not only the return of high modernist concerns in the cinematic domain, but also the indebtedness of the period to earlier, Italian neorealism, which Orr argues is the origin of the neomodern. However, Orr also regards a fundamental characteristic of neomodern cinema to be its engagement in an interrogation of the life of the upper middle class, its highlighting of the frailty, weakness, and spiritual dissolution of the bourgeoisie. On this view, only Asian and Eastern European filmmakers concern themselves over the period of the 1960s and 1970s with the clash between modernity and tradition, myth and religion. John Orr, *Cinema and Modernity* (Cambridge: Polity Press, 1993), 2–5, 6–7. The fact is that if Orr's insistence on the ethos he calls the neomodern suits the style and scope of directors such as Godard or Antonioni who are intent on exposing the limits of humanism, it does not grasp the sense and meaning of Pasolini's oeuvre. Only in *Theorem* and *Salò* does the Friulian director deal with the bourgeoisie. Moreover, he presents the bourgeoisie as in fact preoccupied with religious tradition, exploring this concern at length not only in *The Gospel According to Saint Matthew* [*Il Vangelo secondo Matteo*] but also in such "mythological" films as *Edipus* and *Medea* and the so-called Trilogy of Life (*Decameron, Canterbury Tales,* and *The Arabian Nights*). See also Orr, *Contemporary Cinema,* 1–32.

57. Fredric Jameson, *Postmodernism, or, The Cultural Logic of Late Capitalism* (Durham: Duke University Press, 1991), 279–96.

58. Viano, *Realism,* x–xi.

59. Sam Rohdie, *The Passion of Pier Paolo Pasolini* (Bloomington: Indiana University Press, 1995), 183.

60. Pier Paolo Pasolini, *Pasolini on Pasolini: Interviews with Oswald Stack* (Bloomington: Indiana University Press, 1969), 153.

61. Orr, *Cinema and Modernity,* 50.

62. André Bazin, *What is Cinema?*, 2 vols., trans. Hugh Gray (Berkeley: University of California Press, 1967–71), 2:25.

63. Ibid., 2:28.

64. Ibid., 2:10.

65. Pasolini's definition of a cinema of poetry contradicts Bazin's more traditional belief in the intrinsic relationship between cinema and the novel, pinpointing the limits of a naive poetic of realism in cinema. See Bazin, *What is Cinema?*, 2:26.

66. Sigfried Kracauer, *Theory of Film* (Princeton: Princeton University Press, 1997), 300.

67. Miriam Hansen points out that Kracauer is fully aware of the photographic affinity with contingency, chance, transience, and ambivalence. Miriam Hansen, "Introduction," in Kracauer, *Theory of Film*, xxxi.

68. Kracauer in his theory of film (the composition of which dates back to the 1940s, but which was not published until the 1960s) linked the increasing importance of cinema as a medium to the possession of the contemporary intellectual landscape by the "ruins of ancient beliefs," the prevailing lack of "ideological shelter," and the widespread taste for abstraction enforced by scientific practices. Kracauer's depiction of the contemporary intellectual landscape might be said to anticipate postmodernity and its end of ideological consolation. For Kracauer, film represents the last chance to embrace reality, to think the concrete, to reveal, in the manner of Poe's purloined letter, what is under everybody's eyes. Kracauer, *Theory of Film*, 287–91, 299.

69. Jean Cocteau, quoted in Lino Miccichè, *Pasolini nella città del cinema* (Venice: Marsilio, 1999), 36.

70. Kracauer suggests that tragic conclusions are incompatible with the continuity of the flow of life that a realist cinema ought to represent. Kracauer, *Theory of Film*, 268–70. Lino Miccichè considers Pasolini's cinema to be completely defined by an ideology of death. Miccichè, *Pasolini nella città*, 40.

71. Pier Paolo Pasolini, *Heretical Empiricism*, trans. Ben Lawton and Louise K. Barnett (Bloomington: Indiana University Press, 1988), 221–22.

72. Ibid., 198, 205.

73. For an excellent reconstruction of the cultural context behind Pasolini's notion of a cinema of poetry, particularly with respect to the important role of the Russian formalists Boris Eikenbaum, Victor Shlovsky, and Mikhail Bakhtin, see Naomi Greene, *Cinema as Heresy* (Princeton: Princeton University Press, 1990), 111–19.

74. Pasolini, *Empiricism*, 175. The most puzzling theoretical point in Pasolini's essay is his assertion that a cinema of poetry always depicts the psychological and visual perspective of a neurotic, "sick" character. He formulates this hypothesis, it seems to me, not only in order to justify a delirious, hyperbolic style of cinematography, but also to uphold his first, "phylogenetic" interpretation of film as an instrument of regression to the irrational and the dreamlike.

75. In his Roman novels, for example, Pasolini adopts the local dialect for the dialogue of his proletarian characters, thus enforcing a dissymmetry between the authorial language of the narration and that "reported" by the narrative and attributed to its dramatis personae.

76. Metz criticized Pasolini's genealogy of a cinema of poetry, maintaining that the latter had existed in film history well before modernism. Pasolini's answer to Metz is evasive and unconvincing. Pasolini, *Empiricism*, 229.

77. Ibid., 182.

78. Ibid., 179.

79. Ibid., 182.

80. Ibid., 187–96.

81. In the essay, Pasolini tries to show the limits of Herczeg's positions and to expand the latter's narrow focus on literature to painting. First of all, however, Pasolini attacks Herczeg's claim that the use of the past perfect tense is infrequent in comparison to other tenses in instances of indirect discourse. Pasolini is adamant in pointing out that there are entire books written in free indirect discourse in which the past perfect inevitably plays a crucial role in the linguistic system. *Empiricism*, 80.

82. In the first part of his essay, Pasolini discusses the ideological uses of free indirect discourse, comparing Dante's language to Ariosto's and showing that the former has a clearer and more democratic consciousness of social categories. *Empiricism*, 79–84.

83. Ibid., 87.

84. Ibid., 87.

85. As Greene points out, Deleuze is more radical than Pasolini in settling for a post-Kantian poetics of cinema, one indifferent to the binarisms of linguistic and semiotics and in favor of an ontological interpretation of cinema. Greene, *Heresy*, 108.

86. Mitry as cited in Gilles Deleuze, *Cinema I: The Movement-Image*, trans. Hugh Tomlinson and Barbara Habberjam (Minneapolis: University of Minnesota Press, 1991), 106.

87. Ibid., 108.

88. Pasolini, *Empiricism*, 194.

89. Ibid., 185.

90. Ibid., 185.

91. Deleuze has related the question of free indirect discourse to Rimbaud's dictum, but for him, what is at stake is the simulation of a story or the story of a simulation, not the quasimystical intention implied by Pasolini's theory. Gilles Deleuze, *Cinema II: The Time-Image*, trans. Hugh Tomlinson and Robert Galeta (Minneapolis: University of Minnesota Press, 1989), 153.

92. Ibid., 236–37.

93. Ibid., 235. By the time he formulates his poetics of cinema, Pasolini will obsessively emphasize the question of dying. Of the new American film directors

and their faux naturalism, Pasolini says that "they do not die enough in their works." *Cinema II*, 242.

94. Walter Benjamin, *Illuminations*, ed. Hannah Arendt, trans. Harry Zohn (New York: Schocken Books, 1969), 94.

95. Pasolini, *Empiricism*, 251.

96. For the German critic, the art of storytelling was coming to an end because, among other reasons such as the ascendancy of journalism and new technologies of communication, the moment of death had disappeared from bourgeois culture, making it possible through sanitizing social arrangements to avoid the sight of dying. Benjamin, *Illuminations*, 93.

97. As Pasolini pointed out in an interview with Oswald Stack, he disagreed with structuralism and its abandonment of the very notion of value. See *Pasolini on Pasolini*, 152.

98. Pasolini, *Empiricism*, 285.

99. Many critics, among them Christopher Wagstaff and Sam Rohdie, have insisted on the Crocean influence on Pasolini's aesthetics. However, in my opinion, these critics do not pay enough attention to the dramatic and very contemporary "drive" of Crocean idealism in the context of Pasolini's work, a drive I have tried to describe as a poetics of spectrality. Christopher Wagstaff, "Reality into Poetry: Pasolini's Film Theory," and Sam Rohdie, "Neorealism and Pasolini: The Desire for Reality," in *Pasolini Old and New*, ed. Zygmunt Baranski (Dublin: Four Courts Press, 1999), 185–227 and 163–85.

100. Pasolini, *Empiricism*, 286.

101. Ibid., 287.

102. Ibid., 287.

103.   Io sono una forza del Passato.
        Solo nella tradizione è il mio amore.
        Vengo dai ruderi, dalle Chiese,
        dalle pale d'altare, dai borghi
        dimenticati sugli Appennini e sulle Prealpi,
        dove sono vissuti i fratelli. . . .
        E io, feto adulto, mi aggiro
        più moderno di gni moderno
        a cercare fratelli che non sono più.

Pier Paolo Pasolini, *Alì dagli occhi azzurri* (Milan: Garzanti, 1965), 473. The translation is mine.

104. The film first confronts the question of mourning by means of reference to Tolstoy's "The Death of Ivan Ilych," a novella considered crucial by Philippe Ariès in the contemporary history of death and mourning. Ariès sees Tolstoy's short story as one of the crucial expressions of modern embarrassment with respect to death and mourning, epitomized by the radical solitude of Ivan and by his friend Ivan Ivanovich's suppression of his grief for Ivan. In *Teorema*, shortly after the guest arrives and succeeds in seducing Emilia, Lucia, and Pietro, the father

Paolo is struck by an illness that the guest is able to cure by following Gerasim's method in Tostoy's novella (placing Ivan's feet on his own shoulders and thereby assuaging Ivan's pain). Leo Tolstoy, *"The Death of Ivan Ilych" and Other Stories,* trans. David Magarshack (New York: Penguin Signet, 1960), 93–102. Philippe Ariès, *The Hour of Our Death,* trans. Helen Weaver (New York: Knopf, 1981), 536–37.

105. "La vera morale di questi avvenimenti—-come il lettore vedrà alla fine dell'operetta—sarà ancora una volta, l'ambiguità: un'ambiguità non agnostica, no, ma nella misura in cui lo stile di queste pagine lo consenta, tragica." Pier Paolo Pasolini, *Romanzi e racconti,* ed. Walter Siti and Silvia De Laude (Milan: Mondadori, 1998), 2:1981. Not accidentally, Pasolini expressed his preference for the second part of *Theorem,* revealing that the nature of the story resides less in a fascination with the divine visitor than in a clear devotion to unresolved and puzzling questions of mourning. Pier Paolo Pasolini, *Invettiva e azzurro* (Rome: Nuova Cultura, 1992), 89. Pasolini expressed his preference for the second part in reply to an article by the critic Paolo Milano that was published in *L'Espresso* in 1968; see *Romanzi,* 1982.

106. Pier Paolo Pasolini, *Theorem,* trans. Stuart Hood (London: Quartet Books, 1992), 9; *Teorema* in *Romanzi,* 901. All further citations of the novel will refer to these two editions; particularly long quotations in Italian will be given in a footnote.

107. Deleuze, *Cinema II,* 173.

108. Ibid., 175–76.

109. Rohdie, *Passion,* 6.

110. Ibid., 3.

111. In analyzing Pasolini's celebration of loss, I take a position very different from Rohdie, who believes that Pasolini, notwithstanding all of his denials, is a modernist and much closer to Viano's hypothesis that the Friulian director, particularly in *Theorem,* offers a very postmodern form of theory. Rohdie, *Passion,* 36. Viano, *Realism,* 200.

112. "*Teorema* libro è nato, come su fondo oro, dipinto con la mano destra, mentre con la sinistra lavoravo ad affrescare una grande parete (il film omonimo). In tale natura anfibiologica, non so sinceramente dire quale sia prevalente: se quella letteraria o quella filmica." Pasolini, *Romanzi,* 1978. The English translation is mine.

113. "[Un] angolo visuale estremistico, forse un po' dolce . . . ma, in compenso, senza alternative." Pasolini, *Romanzi,* 1979.

114. For example, Anne Dufourmantelle regards the phenomenal development of the image and the media as the "after-effect" of a broken pact with language. Anne Dufourmantelle, "Invitation," in Anne Dufourmantelle and Jacques Derrida, *Of Hospitality,* trans. Rachel Bowlby (Stanford: Stanford University Press, 2000), 122.

115. Derrida considers absolute, unconditional hospitality, hospitality not circumscribed by law and duty, to be the result of a certain ability to "suspend" language. Derrida, *Hospitality,* 135.

116. The choice of names is telling in itself: Paolo, as we'll see, bears more than a resemblance to Saint Paul, and Odetta, like her Proustian namesake, gives expression to the most cliché and banal expressions of nostalgia, as when she compulsively looks at her album of photos and possessions from the past.

117. The film, unlike the text where the "Investigation into the Donation of the Factory" is positioned toward the end, opens with Kierkegaard's language of *Geschwätz*, the questions of the journalist being incommensurable with the radicality of Paolo's act.

118. Pasolini, *Theorem*, 71. "E queste varianti di roccia, pietre o sabbia, non erano altro per gli Ebrei che il segno della ripetizione, la possibilità di pecepire una monotonia che entava nelle ossa come la febbre della peste." Pasolini, *Romanzi*, 961.

119. Pasolini, *Theorem*, 3. "É una stagione imprecisata potrebbe essere primavera, o l'inizio dell'autunno—o tutte e due insieme, perché questa nostra storia ha una successione cronologica." Pasolini, *Romanzi*, 895.

120. Pasolini, *Theorem*, 71. "Il paesaggio del contrario della vita si ripeteva dunque non offuscato o interrotto da niente. Nasceva da se stesso, e finiva in se stesso: ma non rifiutava l'uomo, anzi lo accoglieva, inospitale ma non nemico, contrario alla sua natura, ma profondamente affine alla sua realtà." *Romanzi*, 961.

121. Discussing the condition of the blind, outcast Oedipus at the end of his life in the land of the Eumenides, Derrida writes: "It will not be long before Oedipus invokes the 'respite' promised by Phoebus from all his misfortunes, at the time when 'in a last country,' he would find himself offered 'shelter and hospitality' from the fearful goddesses. This foreign guest appears like a ghost." Derrida, *Hospitality*, 37.

122. Ibid., 16.

123. "The question of the foreigner concerns what happens at death and when the traveler is laid to rest in a foreign land. 'Displaced persons,' exiles, those who are deported, expelled, rootless, nomads, all share two sources of sighs, two nostalgias: their dead ones and their language." Derrida, *Hospitality*, 87.

124. This is why for Dufourmentelle the motif of the threshold and the step beyond the threshold, the repetition-compulsion informing the formation and transgression of boundaries, acquires such significance in Derrida's exploration of hospitality, as it does in Pasolini's.

125. Millicent Marcus rightly observes that the pattern of disintegration depicted by the film after the guest's departure follows a very specific ritual because each character's confession of his or her distress takes place exactly in the same location of his or her sexual encounter with the guest. Millicent Marcus, *Italian Film in the Light of Neorealism* (Princeton: Princeton University Press, 1986), 249–50.

126. Ibid., 253.

127. In a footnote to *Teorema*, Siti formulates the hypothesis that the painting described by Pasolini corresponds to Lewis's 1914 painting "New York." Pasolini, *Romanzi*, 1982.

128. Pasolini, *Theorem*, 35–36. "Il quadro . . . è fortemente colorato di colori puri: osservandolo meglio, é come un reticolato di contorni, che lasciano delle superfici libere, triangoli e rettangoli rottondeggianti . . . è su queste superfici libere che sono distesi quei colori puri: blu di prussia e rossi; puri ma estremamente discreti, quasi in sordina; quasi velati da una patina di vecchio." Pasolini, *Romanzi*, 926.

129. Pasolini, *Theorem*, 39. "I primi che si amano/sono i poeti e pittori delle generazione precedente/o dell'inizio del secolo." Pasolini, *Romanzi*, 930.

130. Pasolini, *Theorem*, 41. "Abbi pure nostalgia di loro quando hai sedici anni,/Ma comincia subito a sapere/ . . . Che i poeti e i pittori vecchi o morti,/ Malgrado l'aria eroica di cui tu li aureoli, ti sono inutili, non t'insegnano nulla." Pasolini, *Romanzi*, 932.

131. Pasolini, *Theorem*, 116; *Romanzi*, 1000.

132. Pasolini, *Theorem*, 116; *Romanzi*, 1000.

133. Pasolini, *Theorem*, 125–26. "Costruirsi un modo proprio, con cui non siano possibili confronti. Per cui non esistano precedenti misure di giudizio. Le misure devono essere sempre nuove come la tecnica. Nessuno deve capire che l'autore non vale nulla." Pasolini, *Romanzi*, 1009.

134. Pasolini, *Theorem*, 118. "Ma Emilia non si lascia per nulla convincere, come invece si lascerebbe convincere qualche vicino di casa in lutto." Pasolini, *Romanzi*, 1002.

135. Pasolini, "Propositi di leggerezza," in *Bestemmia*, 1:892–95.

136. Emilia's fate in the novel is to reach the outskirts of Milan and to allow herself to be buried by a crane-mounted steam shovel. The image surely derives from Pasolini's description of a similar mechanical shovel in the poem "The Tears of the Excavator," published in the volume *The Ashes of Gramsci*. The poem's famous opening, "Only loving, only knowing matter, not past love nor past knowledge" [Solo l'amare, solo il conoscere conta, non l'aver amato, non l'aver conosciuto] (P 24–53; B 1:243–58), makes clear Pasolini's antielegiac task. In *Teorema*, Emilia is the character praised by the guest for her ability to live in the present: "Tu vivi tutta nel presente" [You live entirely in the present]. Pasolini, *Romanzi*, 978.

137. Pasolini, *Theorem*, 160–61; *Romanzi*, 1041.

138. In this sense, her character's situation resembles the condition that Lacan ascribes to Antigone of being "between two deaths" in his *Séminaire VII*. See Jacques Lacan, *The Seminar of Jacques Lacan, Book VII: The Ethics of Psychoanalysis, 1959–1960*, ed. Jacques-Alain Miller, trans. Dennis Porter (New York: Norton, 1992), 243–56. For the French, see Jacques Lacan, *Le séminaire de Jacques Lacan, livre VII: L'éthique de la psychanalyse 1959–1960* (Paris: Éditions du Seuil, 1986), 315–33.

139. Pasolini, *Theorem*, 174; *Romanzi*, 1051.

140. Pasolini, *Theorem*, 66; *Romanzi*, 956.

141. Pasolini, *Theorem*, 175. "Triste risultato, se questo deserto io l'ho scelto come il luogo vero e reale della mia vita! Colui che cercava per le strade di Milano

è lo stesso che cerca ora per le strade del deserto? E vero il simbolo della realtà ha qualcosa che la realtà non ha: esso ne rappresenta ogni significato, eppure vi aggiunge—per la sua stessa natura rappresentativa—un significato nuovo." Pasolini, *Romanzi,* 1054.

142. Pasolini, *Theorem,* 177; *Romanzi,* 1055.

143. Pasolini, *Theorem,* 177. "Ad ogni modo questo è certo: che qualunque cosa questo mio urlo voglia significare, esso è destinato a durare oltre ogni possibile fine." Pasolini, *Romanzi,* 1055–56.

144. Derrida, *Hospitality,* III. Derrida is referring in this passage to Antigone's father's tomb.

145. On the importance of enigmatic allegory for the economy of postmodern art, see Charles Altieri, *Postmodernism Now* (University Park: Pennsylvania State University Press, 1998), 288.

146. Pasolini, *Theorem,* 175, and *Romanzi,* 1054; *Theorem,* 177, and *Romanzi,* 1056.

147. "La mistificazione è leggerezza/La sinceritá è pesante e volgare: con essa è la vita che vince" (B 1:892–93).

CHAPTER 4

1. Pier Paolo Pasolini, *Heretical Empiricism,* trans. Ben Lawton and Louise K. Barnett (Bloomington: Indiana University Press, 1988), 181.

2. See the interview "Une boucle bouclée," in *Jean-Luc Godard par Jean-Luc Godard, tome 2: 1984–1998,* ed. Alain Bergala (Paris: Cahiers du Cinéma, 1998), 24.

3. Stanley Cavell, *The World Viewed* (Cambridge: Harvard University Press, 1971), 15. Consider also his reading of Baudelaire's "The Painter of Modern Life" as "an anticipation of film," 43.

4. Ibid., 96–99.

5. Ibid., 96.

6. Jacques Aumont indeed classifies Godard as a renewed classicist. See Aumont, *Amnésies* (Paris: P.O.L., 1999), 143 n.

7. Gilles Deleuze, *Cinema II: The Time-Image,* trans. Hugh Tomlinson and Robert Galeta (Minneapolis: University of Minnesota Press, 1989), 184–88.

8. Gilles Deleuze, *Cinema I: The Movement-Image,* trans. Hugh Tomlinson and Barbara Habberjam (Minneapolis: University of Minnesota Press, 1991), 214.

9. Annette Michelson, "Foreword," in Jean-Luc Godard, *Godard on Godard,* ed. Tom Milne (New York: Da Capo Press, 1986), v. See also Colin Myles MacCabe, "Jean-Luc Godard: A Life in Seven Episodes (to Date)," in *Jean-Luc Godard: Son + Image 1974–1991,* ed. Raymond Bellour with Lea Bandy (New York: Museum of Modern Art, 1992), 17.

10. Fredric Jameson, *The Geopolitical Aesthetic* (Bloomington: Indiana University Press, 1995), 164.

11. Ibid., 162.

12. Although early segments of *Histoire(s)* were shown on European television in 1989 and 1990, the project was not completed until the world premiere of the full-length version in 1997. In what follows, I will refer to the film by the section numbers assigned by Godard. Textual citations from the accompanying art-book will be given by section and page number. Jean-Luc Godard, *Histoire(s) du cinéma*, 4 vols. (Paris: Gallimard, 1998).

13. Debord in fact suggests that the onset of the society of spectacle ought to be regarded as occurring in the 1920s. Guy Debord, *Comments on the Society of the Spectacle*, trans. Malcom Imrie (London: Verso, 1998), 3.

14. Ibid., 12.

15. Jameson indeed suggests that this might be the case apropos of Godard's 1982 film *Passion* and the video text that accompanies it, *Scénario du film Passion* (1982). Fredric Jameson, *Signatures of the Visible* (New York: Routledge, 1992), 233.

16. "Whether the Sublime, and its successor Theory, have the capacity hinted at by Kant, to restore the philosophical component of such postmodernity, and to crack open the commodification implicit in the Beautiful, is a question I have not even begun to explore; but it is a question and a problem which is, I hope, a little different from the alternative we have thought we were faced with until now: namely whether, if you prefer modernism, it is conceivable, let alone possible, to go back to the modern as such, after its dissolution into full postmodernity. And the new question is also a question about Theory itself, and whether it can exist and flourish without simply turning back into an older technical philosophy whose limits and obsolescence were already visible in the nineteenth century." Fredric Jameson, *The Cultural Turn* (London: Verso, 1998), 87.

17. Youssef Ishaghpour and Jean-Luc Godard, *Archéologie du cinéma et mémoire du siècle* (Tours: Farrago, 2000).

18. For an interesting excursus on the director's use of titles and subtitles in *Histoire(s)*, see Aumont, *Amnésies*, 67.

19. Jean-Luc Godard, *Introduction à une véritable histoire du cinéma* (Paris: Éditions Albatros, 1977).

20. Godard, *Godard, tome 2*, 446.

21. Ishaghpour and Godard, *Archéologie*, 112.

22. MacCabe, "Jean-Luc Godard," 16.

23. It is no accident that Quentin Tarantino, one of the most successful practitioners of postmodern cinema, has named his production company "Band of Outsiders," a film whose influence is everywhere present in his celebrated *Pulp Fiction* (1994).

24. Ishaghpour and Godard, *Archéologie*, 108.

25. Jill Forbes explains how *Pierrot le Fou* may be considered a postmodern film *avant la lettre*: "The fragmentary nature of these stories, the mixtures of genres, and the complexity of intertextual references all render Pierrot le Fou a postmodern film before postmodernism was invented." Jill Forbes "Pierrot le Fou and

Post New Wave French Cinema," in *Jean-Luc Godard's Pierrot le Fou*, ed. David Wills (Cambridge: Cambridge University Press, 2000), 122.

26. Jameson, *Signatures*, 75.

27. Ibid., 78.

28. Kaja Silverman and Harun Farocki, *Speaking About Godard* (New York: New York University Press, 1998), 53.

29. Jean-Luc Godard, "Le Mépris," in *Jean-Luc Godard par Jean-Luc Godard, tome 1: 1950–1984*, ed. Alain Bergala (Paris: Cahiers du Cinéma de l'Etoile, 1985), 249. Commenting on Godard's movie, Phillipe Sollers notes that the film's search concludes on the eponymous note of contempt, rather than on the satisfaction of "time regained." Philippe Sollers, "Il y a des fantômes plein l'écran," *Cahiers du cinéma* 513 (May 1997): 47.

30. Godard, *Godard, tome 2*, 380.

31. It is interesting on this score to recall Susan Sontag's comparison in 1980 of Syberberg's film about Hitler to Godard's then-latest works, her judgment of the Swiss director's movies of the period as wanting on account of their self-indulgence and nebulosity, their "diffident logorrhea." Susan Sontag, *Under the Sign of Saturn* (New York: Noonday Press, 1980), 164.

32. On the question of cinema as the last chapter of art history, a theme developed in a sustained fashion throughout *Histoire(s)*, see "Dialogue entre Jean-Luc Godard et Serge Daney," *Cahiers du cinéma* 513 (May 1997): 49–55.

33. Peter Wollen, "L'éternel retour," in Bellour, ed., *Son + Image*, 187.

34. Andrew Sarris expresses this opinion about Godard's film *Nouvelle Vague* (1990), complaining that the director seems to be caught in "a losing wager" because "the cinema did not end with *Breathless* and the world did not end with *Weekend*." As quoted in Jonathan Rosenbaum, "Eight Obstacles to the Appreciation of Godard in the United States," in Bellour, ed., *Son + Image*, 202.

35. Sollers, "Fantômes," 315.

36. Godard's view of modernism as a completed or terminated epoch is explored in Jonathan Rosenbaum's "Trailer for Godard's *Histoire(s) du cinéma*," *Vertigo* 7 (1997): 12–20.

37. Godard, *Godard, tome 2*, 430.

38. "Le plaisir morose du deuil (du 'rien n'est plus comme avant') est derrière. Le deuil, aujourd'hui pèse. Il achève de se faire. En un sens, chacun est sommé de savoir de quoi est fait son deuil à lui. Godard est le seul qui dise en quoi ce qui a été approché (et raté) par le cinéma est d'une importance indicible." Serge Daney, *L'exercise a été profitable, Monsieur* (Paris: P.O.L., 1993), 322. The English translation is mine.

39. Godard, *Godard, tome 2*, 242.

40. "Malgré tout au montage l'objet est vivant, tandis qu'au tournage il est mort. Il faut le resusciter. C'est de la sorcellerie." *Godard, tome 2*, 245.

41. Ibid., 24.

42. The Swiss director regards Foucault's attempt to reduce the history of madness to the space of a book to be misguided. *Godard, tome 2*, 161.

43. Ibid., 336.

44. Ibid., 428.

45. Sollers, "Fantômes," 44.

46. Godard, *Godard, tome 2*, 32–33.

47. Ibid., 16. (My translation.)

48. Ibid., 143.

49. Orr speaks of the yearning of a nostalgia that increasingly pervades the cinematic domain. John Orr, *Cinema and Modernity* (Cambridge: Polity Press, 1993), 13.

50. Jameson has expounded on the topic of the nostalgia film in a number of places. See *Cultural Turn*, 129, as well as useful analyses in *Signatures*, 137–40, and in *Postmodernism, or the Cultural Logic of Late Capitalism* (Durham: Duke University Press, 1991), 279–96. He identifies George Lucas's *American Graffiti* (1973) as the inaugural film of the new aesthetic discourse (*Postmodernism*, 19) and offers a detailed analysis of both the American genealogy of this discourse from Coppola's *Godfather* (1972) to Lynch's *Blue Velvet* (1986) as well as its European counterparts, from Godard's *Hail Mary* (1985) to Jarman's *Caravaggio* (1986).

51. Jameson, *Cultural Turn*, 133–34.

52. André Bazin, *What is Cinema?*, 2 vols., trans. Hugh Gray (Berkeley: University of California Press, 1967–71), 1:9–10.

53. Ibid., 10.

54. Ishaghpour offers a keen comparison of Bazin and Godard's interpretation of cinema's epiphanic nature. Ishaghpour and Godard, *Archéologie*, 106.

55. Godard, *Godard, tome 2*, 387.

56. "Je dirais à ma manière qu'à partir du moment où on volait à la vie sa propre image, où la représentation était un vol, il fallait bien 'porter le deuil.'" *Godard, tome 2*, 245.

57. Ibid., 245, 387.

58. Sollers, "Fantômes," 42.

59. Sigmund Freud, *The Standard Edition of the Complete Psychological Works*, 24 vols., trans., ed. James Strachey (London: Hogarth Press, 1953–74), 5:509–10.

60. See Jacques Lacan, "Tuché and Automaton," in *Seminar XI: The Four Fundamental Concepts of Psychoanalysis*, ed. Jacques-Alain Miller, trans. Alan Sheridan (New York: Norton, 1998), 57–58. Cathy Caruth offers an acute reading of the Freudian and Lacanian interpretations of the dream in *Unclaimed Experience: Trauma, Narrative, History* (Baltimore: Johns Hopkins University Press, 1996), 91–112.

61. "Parce qu'il faut porter le deuil mais en l'oubliant n'est-ce pas et Madame de Staël nous a dit comment elle écrit à Napoléon la gloire, Sire, est le deuil éclatant du bonheur."

62. For instance, after citing the first four stanzas of the poem's first section, he cuts to the eighth stanza and then cuts again to the final stanza of the third section.

63. Charles Baudelaire, #*Les Fleurs du Mal*, trans. Richard Howard (Boston: David R. Godine, 1983), 157, 335.

64. On the relationship between the nature of film and Baudelaire's notion of a "memory of the present," see Cavell, *World*, 23.

65. Charles Baudelaire, *"The Painter of Modern Life" and Other Essays*, trans. Jonathan Mayne (London: Phaidon Press, 1964), 14.

66. Antoine Compagnon, *Five Paradoxes of Modernity*, trans. Franklin Philip (New York: Columbia University Press, 1994), x.

67. On the importance of restoring the philosophical component of postmodernity, see Jameson, *Cultural Turn*, 87.

68. Although he discloses the identity of his model in the essay, Baudelaire is keen to maintain the fiction of the Platonic type of the modern artist: "The Reader and I will preserve the fiction that Monsieur G. does not exist." Baudelaire, *Painter*, 5.

69. Ibid., 16.

70. Ibid., 17.

71. Ibid., 7.

72. Ibid., 7.

73. Ibid., 8.

74. Ibid., 15.

75. Alan Wright, "Elizabeth Taylor at Auschwitz: JLG and the Real Object of Montage," in *The Cinema Alone: Essays on the Work of Jean-Luc Godard*, eds. Michael Temple and James S. Williams (Amsterdam: Amsterdam University Press, 2000), 54.

76. "Il ne suffit pas même d'avoir des souvenirs, il faut savoir les oublier quand ils sont nombreux, et il faut avoir la patience d'attendre qu'il reviennent." Alain Bergala, *Nul mieux que Godard* (Paris: Collections Essais Cahiers du Cinéma, 1999), 201. My translation.

77. In his essay on Proust, Benjamin insistently characterizes *la mémoire involontaire* as "visual images." See "The Image of Proust," *Illuminations*, ed. Hannah Arendt, trans. Harry Zohn (New York: Schocken Books, 1969), 214. For an interesting analysis of the *Recherche* as a "visual novel," see Mieke Bal, *Images littéraires* (Toulouse: PUM, 1997).

78. As will be evident to anyone who has read his recent interviews about *Histoire(s)*, Godard seems drawn to Benjamin as a source of constant intellectual reflection. One example of Benjamin's influence is Godard's frequent recurrence to the word "constellation"—with explicit reference to the German critic's precedent—in order to signify his intention to establish a resonance between present and past. Allusions to Benjamin are also preponderant, Youssef Ishaghpour observes, in a recent film by Godard and Anne Marie Miéville about the Museum of Modern Art in New York. Ishaghpour and Godard, *Archéologie*, 9–10, 17–19.

79. Benjamin, "Image," 204–5.

80. Ibid., 208. In fact, Proust himself defines moments of epiphany in

terms of their "actual shock" [*l'ébranlement effectif*] to his senses. See Proust, *Remembrance of Things Past*, trans. C. K. Scott Moncrieff and Terence Kilmartin, 3 vols. (New York: Vintage Random, 1982), 3:905. For the French, see *A la recherche du temps perdu*, gen. ed. Jean-Yves Tadié, 4 vols. (Paris: Gallimard, 1988), 4:451. As I do in the second chapter, I will refer hereafter to Proust's novel in English as *In Search of Lost Time*, citing Moncrieff-Kilmartin by volume and page number, followed by volume and page reference to Tadié's French edition, flagged with the abbreviation JYT.

81. Benjamin, "Image," 203.

82. Walter Benjamin, "Of a Brief Speech About Proust On the Occasion of My Fortieth Birthday," in *Gesammelte Schriften*, eds. Rolf Tiedemann and Hermann Schweppenhäuser (Frankfurt am Main: Suhrkamp, 1987), 2:1064. The English rendition is mine.

83. Deleuze, *Cinema II*, 39.

84. Étienne Brunet, *Le vocabulaire de Proust* (Paris: Slatkine-Champion, 1983), 2:264. Under the entry "cinema" and its variants, Brunet tallies one occurrence in *A l'ombre des jeunes filles en fleur* (the episode involving Odette and the riders) and four in *Le temps retrouvé*.

85. Proust, *Search*, 3:949 (JYT 4:490).

86. "Someone had indeed had the happy idea of giving me, to distract me on evenings when I seemed abnormally wretched, a magic lantern, which used to be set on top of my lamp while we waited for dinner-time to come; and, after the fashion of the master-builders and glass-painters of Gothic days, it substituted for the opaqueness of my walls an impalpable iridescence, supernatural phenomena of many colours, in which legends were depicted as on a shifting and transitory window. . . . And, indeed, I found plenty of charm in these bright projections, which seemed to emanate from a Merovingian past and shed around me the reflections of such ancient history. But I cannot express the discomfort I felt at this intrusion of mystery and beauty into a room which I had succeeded in filling with my own personality until I thought no more of it than of myself." Proust, *Search*, 1:9–11; JYT 1:9. In this passage, Proust seems to provide a possible link between the luminosity of stained glass and the projectedness of film, a spectral effect that he associates with the two terms "mystery" and "beauty." The former term, we should note, also supplies Godard's definition of cinema in *Histoire(s)*. One of the litanies in fact recurring throughout his film is the sentence "neither an art nor a technique, a mystery."

87. Proust, *Search*, 3:899; JYT 4:445.

88. Aumont contends that Godard's narrative, like Proust's, represents a superimposition of different "*je.*" Aumont, *Amnésies*, 212.

89. Ishaghpour and Godard, *Archéologie*, 67.

90. Cf. Aumont, *Amnésies*, 132 and Benjamin, "Image," 203.

91. "Ce qui est plutôt la base, c'est toujours deux, présenter toujours au départ deux images plutôt qu'une, c'est ce que j'appelle l'image, cette image faite de

deux, c'est-à-dire la troisième image." Ishaghpour and Godard, *Archéologie*, 27. My translation.

92. "On peut dire, en gros, qu'une certaine idée du cinéma qui n'était pas celle de Lumière, mais qui était peut-être un peu celle de Feuillade et qui a continué avec Delluc, Vigo, et dont je ne me sens pas loin, cette idée du cinéma est passée, comme l'école de Fontainebleau est passée, comme la peinture italienne est passée. . . . On peut dire qu'un certain cinéma est maintenant achevé. Comme disait Hegel, une époque est terminée. Après c'est différent. On se sent triste parce que l'enfance s'est perdue." Ishaghpour and Godard, *Archéologie*, 87.

93. "Il ne faudrait surtout pas s'imaginer, *devant l'oeuvre finie et l'autorité dont elle témoigne,* que Godard a toujours été sûr des *plans* qu'il cherchait, et qu'il savait dans quels films et à quel endroit de ces films les trouver. Le plans le plus troublants sont ceux qu'ils retrouve alors qu'ils n'étaient pas disponibles à la convocation de sa mémoire volontaire." Bergala, *Nul mieux,* 241.

94. For some useful remarks on the unconscious or preconscious quality of Godard's images, see Bergala, *Nul mieux,* 213–15.

95. Aumont, *Amnésies,* 17.

96. Ibid., 225.

97. Ibid., 149.

98. Thus the title of Aumont's book.

99. Bergala, *Nul mieux,* 216.

100. Walter Benjamin, *The Arcades Project,* trans. Howard Eiland and Kevin McLaughlin (Cambridge: Harvard Belknap, 1999), 471.

101. For a discussion of Benjamin's visual approach to history in relationship to photography, see Eduardo Cadava, *Words of Light* (Princeton: Princeton University Press, 1997).

102. Benjamin, "Theses," in *Illuminations,* 255.

103. Benjamin, "Image," 211. Cf. Robert Kahn, *Images-Passages: Marcel Proust et Walter Benjamin* (Paris: Éditions Kimé, 1998), 181.

104. Proust, *Search,* 2:783; JYT 3:153.

105. "The past carries with it a temporal index by which it is referred to redemption. . . . Like every generation that preceded us, we have been endowed with a weak Messianic power, a power to which the past has a claim." Benjamin, "Theses," 254.

106. Benjamin, "Theses," 255.

107. "Oui, c'est de notre temps que je suis l'ennemi fuyant, oui, le totalitarisme du présent tel qu'il s'applique mécaniquement chaque jour plus oppressant au niveau planétaire cette tyrannie sans visage qui les efface tous au profit exclusif de l'organisation systématique du temps unifié de l'instant . . . parce que je tente dans mes compositions de montrer une oréille qui écoute le temps" (4b:286, 289).

108. See Samuel Weber, "Mass Mediauras; or Art, Aura and Media in the Work of Walter Benjamin," in *Walter Benjamin: Theoretical Questions,* ed. David S. Ferris (Stanford: Stanford University Press, 1996), 27–49.

109. Benjamin in his first essay chastises Abel Gance and Severin Mars for their obstinacy in reading ritual elements in film. Benjamin, "The Work of Art in the Age of Mechanical Reproduction," *Illuminations*, 227.

110. Miriam Hansen, "Benjamin, Cinema, and Experience: The Blue Flower in the Land of Technology," *New German Critique* 40 (winter 1987): 211.

111. Benjamin, "Theses," 257–58.

112. Benjamin, "Work," 236.

113. Bergala, *Nul mieux*, 222.

114. Benjamin, "Theses," 255.

115. Kahn, *Images-Passages*, 194.

116. Martin Heidegger, "The Age of the World Picture," in *The Question Concerning Technology*, trans. William Lovitt (New York: Harper and Row, 1977), 115–54.

117. Martin Heidegger, *Vorträge und Aufsätze* (Tübingen: Neske, 1967), 63–118.

118. Martin Heidegger, *Poetry, Language, Thought* (New York: Harper and Row, 1971), 91. The passage is quoted by Godard in French (1b:245).

119. An excellent summation by Vattimo of his position may be found in "The End of Modernity, the End of the Project," in *Rethinking Architecture*, ed. Neil Leach (New York: Routledge, 1997), 148. I briefly give some of the background to this essay and cite from it in the introduction to this book, note 2.

120. Benjamin, "Theses," 254.

121. Wollen, "L'éternel," 192.

122. Ibid., 192.

123. Maurice Blanchot, *L'espace littéraire* (Paris: Gallimard, 1955), 232.

Index

In this index "f" after a number indicates a separate reference on the next page, and "ff" indicates separate references on the next two pages. A continuous discussion over two or more pages is indicated by a span of numbers. "Passim" is used for a cluster of references in close but not consecutive sequence.

Cultural Memory | *in the Present*

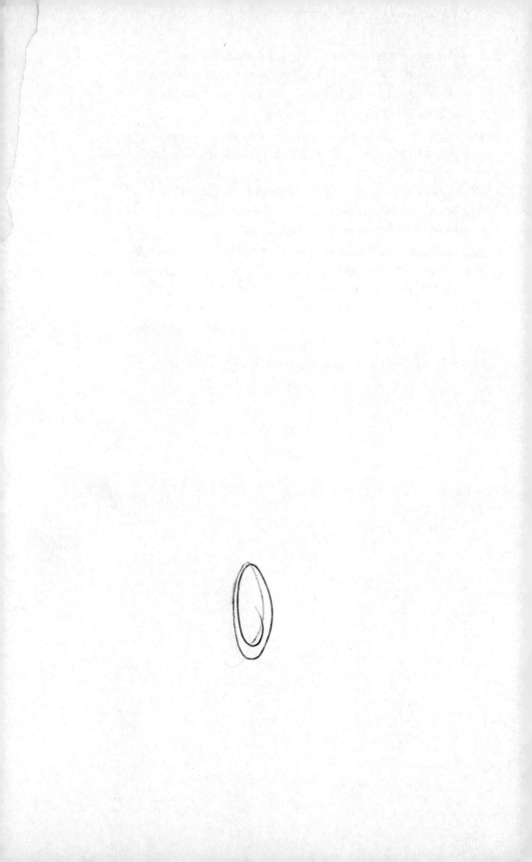